SHO IS... ...ONAL LIBRARY

MW00381037

WITH

Hidden Assets

An Adventure to Find Inner Resources

Mark Bryant

Copyright © 1998 by Mark Bryant

This book reflects the views and experiences of the author, and only the author. More information about the book and the topics it touches may be found on the Internet at **www.HiddenAssetsOnline.com**.

New Leaders Press (www.newleaders.com)
An imprint of Triune Communication
P.O. Box 301, Pleasanton, CA 94566-0030

Cover Design: Kathleen Savage and Victor Grey
Book Design and Production: Carol Hansen

All rights reserved. No part of this book may be reproduced or transmitted in any form or by any means, electronic or mechanical, including photocopying, recording, or by any information storage and retrieval system, without the written permission of Triune Communication, Inc., except in the case of brief quotations embodied in critical articles and reviews.

Publisher's Cataloging-in-Publication

Bryant, Mark, 1955-
      Hidden assets : an adventure to find inner resources / Mark Bryant. -- 1st ed.
      p. cm.
      Includes bibliographical references.
      ISBN: 1-886710-03-1

      1. Bryant, Mark, 1955- --Health. 2. Holistic medicine --Religious aspects--Christianity. 3. Sleep disorders--Patients--Biography. 4. Parapsychology--Religious aspects --Christianity. 5. Lucid dreams. I. Title.

BT732.B79 1998   261.8'321
                               QBI98-836

Printed in the United States of America
Distributed to the book trade by National Book Network
800-462-6420

This book is dedicated
to my loving wife, Vicki Bryant
and to our beloved children
Jonathan, Allison,
and Kristen

Table of Contents

Foreword

by John E. Renesch

Of all the books I've reviewed, excerpted, or edited as an executive editor over the years, I've never seen one like Mark Bryant's. Even among the many anthologies I've created, representing the writings of more than 300 authors on the subject of bringing more consciousness to business and more of the human spirit to people in business, I haven't seen anyone take on what Mark has in this work.

What's so unique? Mark, as a businessman and entrepreneur, embarks on a personal quest to learn and apply the practical and rewarding principles, values, and skills of the holistic/spiritual community, without abandoning his responsibilities. He ventures into an arena often avoided by business and religious people alike, particularly men.

Instead of seeing holistic practices as outside the traditional view, Mark looks at alternative approaches from an inquiring position, asking that which will allow him to be a better person— a better husband, father, and yes, even a better businessman. And he succeeds!

Hats off to Mark Bryant for having the openness to explore and bridge these communities. In so doing, he has pushed through to the next level of thought. Hats off to him for having the courage to put his adventure into words and write this book.

Anyone who is a business person, or who might know

someone who remains closed to the benefits from the holistic/ spiritual community because such an openness might be outside their religious beliefs or a concern to their material focus, should read this book. They will travel with Mark and his family and his business associates as he takes a two-year adventure into unknown and uncharted territory, exploring himself, his beliefs, and his assumptions to depths previously unexplored.

We all know people who have closed themselves off from valuable experiences and insights because of warnings delivered from the pulpit, or because of the pragmatic culture of the business world. To give them a copy of this book would be as meaningful a gift as I can imagine for these people if you care for them.

Bon voyage, dear reader, and may you and yours be inspired by Mark's story and learn from it.

John E. Renesch served as executive editor for New Leaders Press and editor/publisher of The New Leaders newsletter from 1990 to 1997. He has published more writings on the merging worlds of consciousness and business than any other person in the world.

Preface

As a successful entrepreneur, I've been trained to think in a logical, rational manner. My business experience, education and religious upbringing have all taught me to value the tangible and the material. Still, for some time there had been something stirring just below my consciousness. Suddenly, out of the blue, I developed a mysterious sleeping disorder and, before I knew it, I had embarked upon a most exciting personal adventure—an inquiry into the unseen aspects of my life. Through the exploration of the holistic/spiritual communities, I discovered priceless principles to obtain at all cost—"*hidden assets*" so to speak. Hence the name of this book.

Throughout my adventure, I continually grappled with the question, "*Is there a credible bridge between the physical and spiritual?*" The resulting answers are summarized and listed as "*Hidden Assets*" at the end of each chapter.

Hidden Assets are those practical and rewarding principles that increase our awareness of the skills, senses, and abilities we all possess but which lie dormant just beneath our consciousness. They are unseen resources that are useful when they are awakened.

I am writing this book as an example of how these *Hidden Assets* were awakened in myself. I am suggesting a simple thought process and easy-to-remember concepts that can be valuable for you. I've surrounded them with my own story to show how and why they have worked for me. This book can help you to be better equipped to discover this inner knowledge for yourself.

Holistic practitioners like to say that "thought creates reality."

My thoughts, taken from personal journals kept during the adventure, create the framework for the entire story. With this in mind, I have written the kind of book I would want to read when facing challenges. The information is practical and reliable and most of all based on what actually occurred. When requested, I have honored the desire of people for anonymity by changing their names in the book.

The book begins with my visit to a mysterious Russian healer and a discussion with her about my undiagnosed sleep disorder. The rest of the book is a chronology of my discoveries as I venture into alternative fields of thought, expression, and experience. The story unfolds into many fields of knowledge. I personally interviewed or met individually with over 150 people from the holistic/spiritual communities during this two-year adventure. Many of these sessions are recounted in the book.

Inquiring people throughout the world are transforming themselves by raising their level of consciousness. I hope this book will encourage you to undertake adventures of your own with just such a purpose in mind.

Mark Bryant
August 1998

Acknowledgments

I would like to thank my parents, Fred and Elizabeth Bryant, who have been my inspiration for everything I've accomplished.

There are several close friends who I'm honored to have worked with and who have contributed to this manuscript in extraordinary ways. My special thanks to: Mary Coleman, who was the first to urge me to write this book; Alexis McKenna, who added a conceptual framework to this creative project; and John Renesch, who skillfully improved the structure of my first draft. I am also forever indebted to Megan David, my developmental editor, whose wonderful insights helped to bring clarity to the entire work.

I wish to thank Mary Webb, Carol Hansen, Victor Grey, Kathleen Savage and Kristen Anundsen who worked behind the scenes to edit and proofread the manuscript, design the text, and give the cover its radiance.

I am sincerely grateful to my business partners who have supported me during the time it's taken to research and write this book.

With great respect I acknowledge all of those people from the holistic/spiritual communities who took time to meet with me and help me to understand how things work in their fields.

Finally, my deepest gratitude goes to my wife and family for being patient while I wrote this book along with providing encouragement each step of the way.

The voice of one crying in the wilderness,

Prepare the way of the Lord

make straight paths for him.

———◦○◦———

Mark 1:3

Chapter One

Falling Asleep to Wake Up

Seership

As I turn into "The Avenues," I leave Golden Gate Park behind me. The wide residential streets are empty at this time of the morning, and I park easily in front of the two-story San Francisco home.

"She's one of the top healers in Russia with the ability to see into the body, and she works side-by-side with Russian doctors," my friend had said when she gave me Valentina's phone number. Valentina Tolstoguzoua is here for a short time visiting with Russian relatives in San Francisco. Judging by my friend's experience with Valentina and subsequent recommendation, this should be quite an interesting meeting.

I get out of the car and walk past a large oak tree whose shade will surely be needed later today. It's going to be another hot summer day. I walk to the door and tap an antique door-knocker twice.

A tall, blonde woman greets me at the door with a smile and a warm handshake. Standing next to her is another woman who proves to be an interpreter.

"Valentina Tolstoguzoua welcomes you, Mark," says the interpreter. "She is glad you've come."

"Thank you," I reply and follow the two women into the modest living room. There is a strong musty smell that is often found in older homes near the Pacific Ocean. Oriental throw rugs cover the hardwood floors, while a number of religious icons hang on the walls. The front windows are opened slightly to let the breeze off the water come into the room. Valentina is the taller of the two women. With a long angular body, she looks as if she could have been an athlete on the Russian Olympic team. She is very graceful in her movements, almost like a ballerina.

"I'm Irena, and I will interpret for you as Valentina does not speak English fluently," the other woman explains. Irena is smaller than Valentina with short brown hair. She speaks clearly but with a strong accent.

"Would you like some coffee before we begin?"

"No, thank you," I reply. I begin to wonder whether the translation of my questions will be accurate.

"Good then. Do you have questions?"

"Yes," I respond, taking out the day planner that contains my agenda for the session. "First, I'm interested in knowing about Valentina's background." Valentina's eyes brighten at my interest in her.

"She has, of course, extensive training in homeopathy, massage, bioenergetics, anatomy, and other areas," Irena says. "Valentina is one of only ten healers from all of Russia selected to be studied by the faculty at the prestigious University at Moscow."

"I'm impressed!" I admit. "How are healers accepted in Russia as compared to the United States?"

I wait for Irena to translate my question into Russian for Valentina. Valentina responds and Irena reverses the process.

"Valentina says the Russian people are much more open to healers than Americans are," Irena says. "Healers existed in the Russian culture long before modern medicine appeared. The Russian people have kept the older traditions of a local healer with the advent of socialized medicine. There are still some difficulties for healers working in hospitals, but the minds of the Russian doctors are becoming more open."

"Really," I say.

"Valentina says that although the people of Russia accept these healing techniques, some people in the church are still opposed to her healing work in Russia. She feels it is very much the same in the United States."

I nod to Valentina to show her I understand what she is saying. She talks to Irena but keeps her eyes on me.

"Valentina's healing center in Moscow is right next to the hospital," Irena says. "That way she can work closely with the doctors."

"I see," I respond, hoping one day to visit Russia and some of the other Eastern Bloc countries now that the Berlin Wall has fallen and the cold war is over. When I was younger, my parents took us as far as West Germany, but during those days, it was difficult to travel into Eastern Europe.

"Russia does not have all the technical equipment you have here in America. Most villages and towns away from the large cities rely on a simpler, more old-fashioned way of practicing medicine," Irena says. "More dietary and herbal methods are employed." Valentina makes a motion with her hands and says something to Irena in Russian about me. I remember that when I set up the appointment, Irena said Valentina was training her in various healing techniques. This must be part of the training, as Valentina is obviously showing Irena something about my body.

"Valentina has a question for you," Irena says. "She can tell by the energy field around your body that you have not been well in the recent past. She feels it had something to do with sleep; as if you slept too long. She can see a faint trace of it still in your energy field."

I'm surprised that Valentina can sense something like this just by looking at me.

"Can you tell her about this?" Irena asks.

I speak directly to Valentina while Irena translates.

"It's a long story," I sigh, recalling that inescapable feeling of hopelessness that accompanied my sleep disorder. "But I'll try to be succinct. To put it simply, one morning about a year ago, I couldn't wake up. I mean I didn't wake up to go to work."

Irena smiles. "In Russia, you might say that a lot of people have that problem after staying out too late," she says, obviously making a little joke.

I laugh and then say, "But this was no joke. This had never happened to me before. I'm an entrepreneur in very physical industries: transportation, construction, physical distribution, and so forth. I'm an early to bed early to rise type of guy. At the time, I was working sixty to seventy hours a week managing several businesses at once." I pause to let Irena translate my comments to Valentina.

"At any rate, I continued to sleep through the afternoon even though my wife Vicki tried to wake me several times. She was concerned right away and thought I was ill because I'm usually out of the house by 5:30 every morning. But I didn't have a fever or anything. I finally did wake up before dinner, but then I went back to bed that night and slept for the next thirty-six hours."

"Hmm," Irena says, and Valentina also comments in Russian.

I notice that Valentina is very attentive. I look around at the various Russian art and family relics in the room as I'm speaking, though Valentina's eyes are always on me.

"It all happened out of the blue. You know, I have a house, a beautiful wife, two great kids, excellent health, and my career was going well. Anyway, to continue the story, I was finally able to go to work later that week. But then, a week later, the same thing happened. Then it happened again and again until I could hardly go a week without falling asleep for long periods. I started to panic a little and made an appointment with my doctor."

"What did your doctor say?" Irena asks as she translates my story to Valentina.

"He couldn't find anything wrong with me. After a battery of tests, he referred me to a specialist. She couldn't find anything either so she referred me to someone else and so on. I guess I went to six doctors in all and had numerous tests."

"Was there ever a diagnosis?" she asks, sensing my discouragement.

"No, and I even visited a psychologist I knew through business because a couple of doctors suggested that depression might be the cause of my sleeping so much. But he couldn't find anything unusual going on with me either. The psychologist believed that it was physiological in nature and suggested I see a doctor who specializes in sleep disorders. Unfortunately, this turned up no new information."

"This must have been difficult for you."

"Yes, it's like my life came to a screeching halt," I reply,

"Are you currently experiencing this sleep problem?" Irena asks.

"Not so much anymore," I admit. "For the first six months I took a sabbatical and stayed off work completely. But after that, I was able to return to work part time. After another six months, I was back at work full time. Occasionally, I still have a few days of sleepiness."

Valentina is looking at me, but it seems as if she is thinking about something else. She speaks to Irena in Russian, then turns her attention back to me as Irena translates. "Valentina says she senses something coming to you in your dreams."

"Yes, that's the flip side of this sleep experience. I started having some pretty vivid dreams and other unusual things happen to me."

"Valentina feels you are receiving guidance from—how do you say in your language, saints?— through your dreams."

Her comment surprises me but I try not to show it. I don't respond but look directly into Valentina's deep blue eyes.

"You know, *saints*—the people you see in stained glass windows?" Valentina interjects.

I nod my head to show I understand, but I'm not sure about this guidance thing. It sounds far-fetched and makes me a little nervous, but I continue to talk.

"I've had some other unusual things happen to me, too," I say, "like knowing when something was about to occur."

"Valentina can feel what you are describing. She says it is your psychic energy opening up. We all have this psychic energy to varying degrees; however, yours has been asleep—or how do you say it in English— dormant."

Again, I don't comment. It all sounds a little strange to me. My psychic energy was asleep and is being awakened after a sleep disorder? It sounds too coincidental—too unusual. Yet, I guess, psychic energy could account for some of the things that have been happening to me.

The two women converse in Russian and then Irena asks how I found out about Valentina. I tell them I was told about her by a person in the alternative health field who said that Valentina works with patients in Russia using a form of seership into the body. I add that I wanted to come see Valentina to check this out for myself.

"Good then. Valentina is going to look at your body," Irena says.

Valentina smiles and carefully looks over my body. "Valentina says she can feel that you have injured your lower back." Irena points to the place on herself. "When you move in this way," she demonstrates, "you experience pain."

"Yes, that's right," I confirm, sensing that Valentina can really feel the pain in me. "I injured my lower back playing organized football, and it does hurt when I make certain movements like that," I acknowledge, feeling a certain awe at her ability. She reminds me of the "empath" on one of the old Star Trek episodes— the woman who could feel what other people felt. I always thought of this as strictly science fiction, but Valentina is very practical and down to earth.

Valentina relaxes. "One exercise that will help you to alleviate some of the weakness in this area is to hang upside down from a bar for a few minutes each day," Irena instructs.

This sounds odd to me, but I make a note of it while she suggests additional exercises to strengthen this area.

"Valentina sees that you had ear damage as a child. Were you hospitalized for this?"

"Yes, I was," I respond.

Valentina spends the next five minutes describing what occurred, how it occurred and what was done to my ears. She moves from talking about my ears to other parts of my body. All the while she looks up and down at my body almost as if she is looking through me.

"She also sees that you've broken different bones in your body. There's been a hand, a rib, and your nose."

Valentina is right, yet I'm still not sure how she is doing this. What inner ability or faculty allows her to do this? For lack of a better description, it's like a body scan. She continues on for another ten minutes, identifying even more minute details about my body. She's not one hundred percent correct in all cases. A few things don't fit, but most of her comments are accurate.

"Valentina says your body is in reasonably good order. Are you ready for your healing session?" Irena asks.

"Yes," I answer as I follow the two women to an adjacent room in the house.

"I will assist Valentina. I'm a registered nurse here in the U.S.," Irena informs me before she asks me to remove my shirt and lower my pants to below my hips.

The women converse in Russian while I undress. I feel uncomfortable, half naked in front of them, particularly since I don't have a clue what they might be saying about my body. However, the fact that both women have been trained in anatomy helps me to feel more like a specimen and less like a spectacle. I climb onto the massage table, as Irena instructs me, while Valentina lights a series of candles and dims the overhead lights. I can smell the sulfur from the matches as the flames from the candles begin to flicker. Her strong hands commence massaging my lower back, and I quickly relax.

After about ten minutes of Valentina working on my lower back, Irena asks how I feel.

"I'm getting a little queasy," I tell her. It feels like I'm seasick but only in my back. It's a weird feeling and one that's difficult to describe. After a few minutes it subsides and Valentina continues with the healing.

"This is energy moving through areas that have been blocked," Irena explains.

It would be easy to chalk this up as fake, but Valentina's healing capability has been scientifically tested. Maybe she really can see energy and is able to move it around somehow.

As Valentina continues to move her hands over my back, I feel it becoming hot. Tremendous amounts of heat seem to be coming from her hands. At times it feels unpleasant, as though a hot water bottle has been placed on my skin. She moves from one area to another constantly moving her hands over various parts of my back. Her own hands seem impervious to the heat they're generating. After another ten minutes she removes her hands and steps away from the table.

"Lie here for a while," Valentina says in English when the healing is finally complete. She leaves the room. I happily follow her instructions as by now I am so relaxed I would just as soon take a nap. After a few minutes, I rise from the table feeling a little light-headed. I stretch out my neck and shoulders before putting on my shirt. The joints in my lower back feel better, almost numb.

When I join them again in the living room, Valentina suggests I come back for one more session. She says I'm fairly healthy and recommends another healing session to work on other areas of my body. Then, she says, I can treat myself with the exercise and diet she's suggested.

"Yes. That sounds fine," I tell her.

Irena and Valentina exchange words. Irena says, "Before you leave, Valentina wants you to know you and she have much in common in your beliefs. Valentina is Russian Orthodox, and you're a Christian."

I cock my head to one side and ask, "How is it that Valentina can see I'm a Christian?"

"Valentina's inner vision allows her to see and feel your deep religious feelings and your faith in God," Irena responds.

"Okay," I say, still a little skeptical.

"You have that type of spiritual energy around you," she says.

This intrigues me, but I'm still suspicious. Then Valentina reveals to me a large silver cross she wears around her neck. "I wear this cross for protection from other influences and harmful energy. Some people wear stones over their heart or even an amulet. Since you're of the Christian faith, you might wish to wear a cross yourself," Irena suggests, speaking for Valentina. "It would be good for protection and to strengthen your heart which is an area in your energetic field that she can see needs strengthening. A silver one, at least one inch long, would be most beneficial for you. The cross should hang down so that it is placed over your heart."

Her suggestion resonates with me for some reason. "I'll consider it," I respond, enjoying this unexpected religious quality about Valentina. I wonder what she recommends to people who need their heart energy strengthened and who are not Christians. Surely a cross would not have the meaning for them, but would it still be protective of the heart area?

"Valentina says also that you use a great amount of healing energy at the mental level, and this drains you," Irena replies. "You have a tendency to go below the 'energy red-line' and have symptoms brought on by the lack of a proper balance of energy in your system. Valentina suggests that you go to a quiet place for respite periods to regenerate your energy. Valentina does this herself on a regular basis, usually at a monastery or retreat center. She sees that a quiet area would be good for you since you have a similar need to recharge your energy."

"This seems like a good idea," I respond, feeling a warmth toward Valentina. She goes on to make a few more comments about the energy fields around my body and then interjects, "You're going to get more into the healing and spiritual fields."

I'm surprised by her comment. I'm a business person so I'm not sure why she would say this or what it means. I am intrigued by what has happened today, but I'm not ready to give up my day job.

At the very end of our session, Valentina leaves the room for a moment. She returns and gives me a gift, a large decorative ladle, painted in black and gold—a beautiful piece of Russian art. This is extraordinarily generous given that she has just met me. It's strangely touching for me, and I shake her hand warmly. I thank her, and the two women escort me to the door. "I've told you many things about your health and life today, but it is up to you to form your destiny," she says in English. "You have free will to bring about greater awareness in your life," she adds and closes the door.

I walk down the front steps to my car. I can feel the warm breeze from off the coast against my face. The session with Valentina has made me think about how polarized things are in my world. I tend to see things either black or white. Somehow she has been able to navigate through these opposites. I am amazed at just how effectively she has done this. For example, she is academically trained in areas such as Biology and Anatomy, yet performs hands-on healing. These seem like opposite ends of the spectrum to me. Also, she is extremely religious and faithful to her religion, yet she uses psychic energy. I wonder if I've just been blind to the idea of a middle way.

Sleeping Spells

I've often wondered if things happen as a matter of coincidence or if they're predetermined. This paradox between chance and destiny seems unanswerable. At times, something happens that clearly appears based on chance, while other times, it could be seen as fate. Did destiny lead me to Valentina, or was it merely a chance encounter?

After leaving Valentina's, I visit the pier at Fishermen's Wharf. A strong breeze has kicked up, and business people are combing their hair and straightening their ties. I've stopped by the wharf to have lunch before leaving San Francisco. It gives me time to consider my session with the Russian healer.

As I watch ferry boats shuttle people out to Alcatraz island, I wonder about Valentina's abilities. How was she able to pick up on my sleep disorder just by looking at my energy field? Is it really possible for people to see a human energy field? Until today,

I wouldn't have thought so. And what about this psychic energy she talked about. Was she using psychic energy to see these energy fields? There doesn't seem to be any other explanation. There were no clues, no advance information for her to know some of these things.

I sit on a bench near Pier 39 eating a small cup of crab meat. I reflect on what I told Valentina about my sleeping disorder. It's been a year now since I first couldn't wake up and get out of bed. How frightened my wife Vicki was about the whole ordeal. When the sleeping part subsided and some of the unusual episodes started happening, it really made Vicki nervous—me, too. A lot of these episodes I just can't explain. Moreover, something about today's session with Valentina reminded me of the things that have been happening to me. Maybe it's like Valentina says—it's a psychic energy that's just beginning to awaken.

I laugh when I think how my business partners would react to someone telling them their psychic energy is awakening. The unusual experiences I've had, like knowing when things were going to happen or what people are thinking, seem so peculiar. I've not talked about these experiences with my partners for fear they'd think I've gone off my rocker.

I really didn't know what to expect today from Valentina. I think about the session as I walk along the water park. Clearly Valentina has a most extraordinary ability. She saw a number of injuries that had taken place and that had left no visible scars. The inner ear problem I had as a child, for example. How was she able to see this? Her ability is uncanny. She couldn't have been reading my mind because I had very little recollection of the details of this incident. Valentina is clearly using some faculty that works on a different principle. This faculty fascinates me.

I finish my lunch and walk towards my car. The seafood meal reminds me that Valentina also had a lot to say about nutrition. I must have made two pages of notes on different food items she felt would be good for me to add to my diet. I wonder what she would say about crab?

One suggestion Valentina did have was to make a sort of pumpkin mash and eat it on a regular basis. She felt this would be beneficial for my digestive tract. It reminds me of some of the things my Grandma Ruby fixes. My grandma lives in a rural part of North Carolina. She has all of these home remedies for such things as an upset stomach, colds, headaches; just about anything that ails you. It strikes me that a few of Valentina's dietary suggestions might be Russian home remedies.

The one comment Valentina made that I'm still not sure about is the one on my dreams and something about the saints coming through in them. If she wasn't a religious person herself, I wouldn't give this much credence. Granted, my dreams are a lot different than before the sleeping disorder, but I'm not sure I would attribute this change to heavenly guidance.

I get in my car and begin driving in the direction of the Bay Bridge. Looking out over the city, I wonder whether or not there are any other people with talents like Valentina Tolstoguzoua. My meeting today with Valentina was really a transition of sorts for me. I entered a world as completely foreign to me as say... Russian art. Foreign but not unfriendly. I think I'll get a silver cross to wear over my heart, just in case. It feels right to me even if I don't truly understand how my heart energy will be affected. I do get the deeper sense that it is to help me open up my emotional heart.

The sun is high overhead by the time I cross the bridge and drive through the Caldecott Tunnel. I take off my sunglasses as a van with surfboards on top passes me on the left. With windows rolled down and beach towels draped over the seats, somebody has spent a day at the ocean. I'm certain my own kids are in the pool or running and sliding through the sprinklers on a hot day like today. The first thing I plan to do when I get home is to show my daughter Allison and my wife Vicki the gift Valentina gave me. They really like colorful things, and will enjoy looking at this beautiful piece of art. Maybe I'll hang it up in Allison's room.

Sex, Zinc, and Listening to Your Body

Every experience in life offers some value, I believe. The session with Valentina, the Russian healer, continues to intrigue me even weeks later. I'm interested in finding how she is able to do some of the things she does. I like a good mystery, and Valentina's unusual faculties bring up a whole slew of questions and paradoxes in my mind.

One area Valentina really emphasized was the importance of diet. Now diet and nutrition is the one thing that really seems grounded. It's so much easier for me to grasp the benefits, and the cause and affect, of good nutrition than Valentina's inner sight or hands-on healing. Although I'm still fascinated with her other faculties, I can't see or touch them, so diet is an easier place for me to start following her advice.

I realize that I haven't examined my own diet and food intake since college. Therefore, I've made an appointment with a professional nutritionist. Valentina said that diet can affect both your mental and emotional states. I'm curious how this will play out with the type of food I eat.

My appointment is with Dr. Joy Lasseter, a nutritionist who lectures and does consultations in health offices in the Bay Area. Vicki and a few of my business partners have expressed interest in also seeing a nutritionist provided I feel it is beneficial after my visit.

Joy analyzes my completed nutrition questionnaire in her office at the Wellness Center in Walnut Creek. Her eyes dart from page to page. She uses a yellow high-lighter pen to mark areas on the questionnaire that she wants to discuss with me. I intentionally left off from the questionnaire the whole sleep disorder issue so as not to have to get into a long explanation about it. In addition, it's still a little uncomfortable for me to talk about it since there was never a diagnosis of just what was going on with me. What do you tell someone? You fell asleep and couldn't wake up? Even my partners took to calling me "Rip Van Winkle."

With a Ph.D. in nutrition, Joy is serious about her work and thorough in her approach. Her slim figure and smooth complexion exemplify a healthy role model. I sit opposite her, writing answers to more questions about my eating habits, exercise, interests, and my daily routine. The depth and scope of her questions are different from what I have experienced with other doctors.

"Mark, I see that you have cereal just before you go to bed," Joy says after we have discussed my overall health.

"Yes, that's right," I confirm, eager to get her feedback on the completed questionnaire.

"How often does this take place?"

"Oh, I would say just about every night. I use it as a way of getting to sleep, sort of like warm milk."

"I would recommend that you eliminate it from your daily routine. In fact I would eliminate milk entirely," Joy says, marking down a few notes.

"Are you sure?"

"I believe it's causing the mucus that you noted here is forming in your nasal passages. By chance, are you allergic to any dairy products?"

"Cheese."

"That's what I thought. For some people, dairy products can cause the symptoms you're describing. Stay off the milk for two months, and see if you notice a difference. There are other ways you can get the same nutrients you get from milk."

"Okay," I answer.

Sensing my need for a little more assurance, Joy says, "Many people are unaware they have aches and pains caused by what they eat. Their health can be improved by simply learning more about the role diet plays. It is extremely important to our overall health to pay attention to the food we eat and to where that food was grown and what chemicals it has been exposed to."

"All right," I nod.

"There are certain things everyone should know about their body and how it's nourished," Joy continues. "If you think of your body as a car, you need to keep your body tuned so that it doesn't exhaust the machinery."

I like her analogy of the body to a car. Joy is very practical, and I take a few of her business cards to give to my partners. This is the kind of talk they can relate to.

"You need to know about the combination of particular foods

and food elements and adapt this information to your diet. And you especially need to *listen* to your body. I find most people I see are unaware of what their body is trying to tell them. Either that or they ignore what their body is attempting to say," she says.

I listen to Joy and make notes on the handout she has given me. She asked me to bring in the actual bottles of vitamins I take each day, and she evaluates each of them one by one as I sit across from her. She makes suggestions about which vitamin to increase or decrease or in some cases discontinue taking entirely. Her analysis of the vitamins I take daily is very helpful since I've never considered the balance between what I'm eating and the vitamins I take.

Joy continues, "Health and longevity should always be kept in mind. This will help you balance the need for exercise, sleep, and recreation along with work."

"Okay."

"I see on your daily food intake you enjoy fruits and nuts. All your fruits and vegetables should be as fresh as possible, and your nuts should be of the living kind," Joy says as she glances up at me.

Joy goes back to analyzing the data from the questionnaires I've filled out. I wonder what she means by the 'living kind?' Her comment about the role of diet reminds me of an upcoming lecture on health I plan on attending. The speaker is a local physician named Dr. Dean Ornish from UC San Francisco. I hear another client come into the center and speak with a staff person out front. I continue to watch Joy as she scans over the "daily routine" section of the questionnaire. I'm curious if she is going to ask about meditation which I've checked off under the question "things you do to reduce stress?"

"Another thing I notice about your diet," Joy observes, "is that you're not getting enough protein. In fact, you're considerably protein deficient, given your level of exercise."

"Hmm, I wasn't aware of that," I respond, wondering if this lack of protein contributed to my sleep disorder.

"I recommend you eat a minimum of 25 grams of protein a day," Joy suggests.

I make a note of this in the loose-leaf folder she has provided me. The folder contains information on nutrition as well as reprints of articles Joy has written for magazines and newsletters. In the interim, Joy reviews the questionnaires again.

"Let me see here," she says without looking up. "How often do you and your wife have sex, and/or how often do you masturbate?"

Her question catches me unprepared, and I stiffen in my chair. If she thinks I'm going to respond to that question, she's wrong, I tell myself while recovering from the shock of it. But then she looks up at me expectantly, and I can't ignore her any longer.

"Why do you need to know that?" I ask nervously.

"It appears to me that you're deficient in zinc, which can really be used up in a hurry by sperm production," she answers matter-of-factly.

I clear my throat to hide my embarrassment. She must be thinking I am a sex maniac or something, consuming all that zinc. "We probably are a fairly normal couple as far as sex is concerned," I couch my answer carefully.

"Fine," Joy says and moves on to another section of the analysis.

We proceed to the next questionnaire. The entire process

takes no more than an hour, yet I feel Joy has done me a great service by outlining a comprehensive nutrition program tailored to my lifestyle. My own awareness of the importance of nutrition and diet is expanding.

We set a date for her to call me for a follow-up in six months. I tell Joy I would like my wife to come see her. We exchange a few other opinions about the state of health and nutrition in America, and I leave with an armful of pamphlets and the binder Joy has prepared for me.

At a business breakfast meeting the next morning, I describe to my partners in construction, Gary and Dan, my encounter with the nutritionist. They about die from laughing when I get to the part about the zinc deficiency. I laugh right along with them. A week later, a bottle of zinc mysteriously appears in my "IN" basket at the office.

Floating a Trial Balloon

Is it possible that certain phenomena are based on scientific principles as yet undiscovered? If so, could this explain how the Russian healer was able to do some of the things she did? Clearly, there is no simple answer, but the possibilities intrigue me.

Summer is coming to an end, and the weather is beginning to get chilly. It won't be long before the leaves begin to change and drop from the trees. This is my wife Vicki's favorite season of the year. She loves that first sign of cooler air coming across the ridge near our home. Fortunately, the evenings are still pleasant enough that we can sit outside at our favorite restaurant on Main Street.

As Vicki and I enjoy an evening alone without the kids, a candle flickers on the table, providing a touch of romance. It's not often that we get to just sit and talk as a couple over a candlelight dinner. It's nice to be able to enjoy this other side of my wife. I'm still attracted to her thin features accented by graceful movements. Her long fingers reach out to clasp mine, and she twirls my wedding band almost out of nervous habit.

Vicki delves into her salad while she listens to me describe my experiences with Joy, the nutritionist, and Valentina, the Russian healer. Fortunately, I married a woman who is open to talking about my personal interests. Even though I try to dedicate the evening to relaxing, I make a few short notes about health and psychic energy on a cocktail napkin. Obviously, I have a hard time turning off my mind. The goal is always the same for me— *to apply* whatever I am learning. Deep in thought, I gaze off in the distance at the street lights.

After a long period of silence, Vicki touches my hand and says, "Care to include me in your thoughts?" She smiles and gives me a look with those large brown eyes of hers. We both laugh because she has, of course, caught me being with her but not *really* with her! I know this annoys her, and I bring myself back into the present. I wonder if this doesn't happen to most men who like to be up in their heads a lot.

I take a long sip of wine. The glass of white zinfandel is bittersweet, and the aroma works like smelling salts to clear my head. Vicki slides over next to me and, reading a line off the notes on the napkin she asks, "Mark, why the interest in psychic energy?" Why not medicine or science, something more down to earth?"

"You know I have a great respect for medicine. A group of

medical doctors literally saved my life once after an accident. I'll forever be thankful to them and the whole emergency room staff for their skills. And I believe modern medicine is very important to long-term health. But even with that said, ever since I met with the healer from Russia, I've felt there was something else at work here that's also important. You know what I mean?"

"Not exactly," she replies.

"It's the invisible component in these fields that intrigues me," I continue. "Even in my meeting with the nutritionist, I felt there was something else going on with her that helped her with her evaluation. It was more than just questionnaires and experience at work here."

"Did you ask her about it?"

"Not on my first visit, but I plan to on my six-month follow-up with her. It was more obvious with the Russian healer. The entire session with Valentina consisted of this interplay between the physical and non-physical element. It was quite fascinating," I say, taking a bite of my spinach salad. "You'll have to go see Valentina before she returns to Moscow," I suggest. "Then you can tell me what you think of her."

"There is this sign on a small office I used to pass every morning going to work," Vicki says. "It had the words 'Psychic/Palmist' on it and underneath had the symbols of a hand, crystal ball, and a deck of cards. Are these the type of fields you mean?" Vicki asks as our waiter serves our entrees.

"I don't know. I'm not even sure you can call them fields in the way that you can say 'the medical field,' for example. There doesn't seem to be one term that describes everything that's going on."

Our waiter returns as if right on cue to ask how our dinners are. With a mouth full of food, all I can do is mumble and nod my head that everything is fine.

"Mark, you like to call yourself a bottom-line guy. What do you think your real interest is, bottom line?" Vicki asks between sips of wine.

"I'd have to say it has something to do with looking beyond the physical to things unseen."

"In what way?" she asks.

"I'm not sure yet, but I'm becoming more fascinated with what lies behind the physical nature of a person; the inner aspects or inner resources if you will. There is definitely something attracting me, something that I can't quite put into words."

I catch myself and hold back from saying anything further. I'm somewhat apprehensive talking to Vicki about this because she has been through a lot with my sleeping ordeal. I don't want her to think I'm going off the deep end.

"I can't put my finger on anything specific," I confess. "I just find this stuff stimulating."

"You've never paid much attention to these areas in the past," Vicki persists.

"I know, that's the curious thing about it. That's why I relate it more to the sleep disorder than anything else. That's when I first started to look at health and my inner nature. Speaking of health, how about we splurge and share a soufflé after the main course?" I ask, changing the subject.

"Yeah, let's," Vicki replies.

We go on to talk about other things happening in our busy lives. We discuss the kids, a subject we can never seem to get away from, even when we try to. While we're enjoying our soufflé, I pose a question that has been on my mind for a while.

"I'm thinking I'd like to explore some of these psychic energy and healing areas in more depth. How would you feel about this?" I ask, floating a trial balloon.

"I guess we'd have to talk more about it, and of course I'd have to be wined and dined *a lot more* before I could come to a decision," she says with that splendid smile of hers.

I reach across the table and kiss her. She's at least open to my desire to explore these areas further.

"Perhaps it would help if you had a good idea about what you hope to accomplish," she says gently.

I appreciate Vicki's level head, and this discussion has been helpful. She is right. I sound kind of vague about what it is I want to find out and common sense needs to be applied here. I need more clarity about what it is that I want to do. I would never start a business without a plan. I need to choose a direction, set a goal and develop a plan in order for us to have more fruitful communication around this whole area.

Hidden Asset

Every experience happens for a reason; it's the reason that is not always easy to decipher.

Chapter Two

Venturing Inward

More Than Just a Job Offer

There is a phrase used in business known as "diminishing returns." It's a principle that in essence says the more resources put into a project, the less increase in the output. It's kind of like mowing the yard two or three times in one day. Each go-around there is less grass cut, and it's probably not worth the extra effort. Using this principle, I've begun to put my effort into other places, for example taking the problem or dilemma into meditation or writing it down on a pad on my night stand just before I fall asleep.

One person in the office who likes to razz me about my interest in meditation is Bill George, the founder and president of a regional distribution company. I've known him for fifteen years, and we've been partners in real estate and other business ventures for much of that time. While Bill is a fun person to be with away from the office, he has a brisk matter-of-fact business demeanor. He's bottom-line oriented and not one to accept other realms of reality easily.

Our companies share an offsite sales office, and I'm sure I'll run into him this morning. I see Bill's car as I pull into the office complex parking lot. The commute was lighter than normal, which is surprising given that many of the colleges like Stanford and Santa Clara have begun classes already. There's an early morning chill, and I walk quickly from my car to the office entrance. Bill spots me as I come in.

"Hey, Mark, what's up, bud?" Bill calls from the other side of the coffee room. He comes over and shakes my hand with his strong grip. "I haven't seen you for awhile."

Bill is strikingly handsome with jet black hair and light eyes; he resembles a young Elvis Presley. He's impeccably well groomed, tall, athletic and a rather formidable looking figure—the kind of guy I'd like to have along with me in the event I had to walk down a dark lonely alley.

"How have you been?" he inquires.

"Good," I reply. "How's your business?"

"Great! Can I offer you some coffee?" he asks.

"Sounds good," I answer as we walk together back into the coffee room. Freshly brewed coffee permeates the air. I pour myself a cup and lean up against the kitchen cabinet. I haven't seen Bill for a few weeks, and just this morning I received a strong impression about him during my morning meditation. I feel a strong urge to tell him what came to me, but I know some people are not receptive to information that comes to a person this way. It definitely took me a while to feel comfortable with thoughts that come to me during meditation. Even relaxing my mind in order to meditate took awhile. Actually, it was an article entitled "A Method of Meditation" that I got out of the *Catholic Update*, of all places, that helped me over the hurdle of meditating daily.

Bill and I talk for a few minutes about business and the stock market. He recommends investing in a company that's going great guns in the valley right now. Bill hears the fax machine receiving a fax and goes over to take a look. I take the opportunity to change the subject and say, "Bill, I had a strong feeling about you during my meditation this morning."

"Are you still doing that stuff before work?" he asks, looking over the fax.

"Every morning. It gets me off to a good start on busy workdays."

"So what's the information you got from the stratosphere, ...I mean your altered state?" he asks with a grin.

"I got a strong feeling that you're going to get a job offer to head up a company, and it's going to be soon."

As promptly as I voice this to him, I wonder whether or not I should have. I am getting more and more impressions of people and situations all the time. Once in a while these sensations are quite strong, as in this situation with Bill. When this happens, I feel I want to be honest in discussing the feelings that are coming to me.

He sets down his coffee on the table and stares at me. "Come on, Mark, you gotta be kidding. Are you sure you got the right person? Maybe it was another Bill," he says, cracking a slight smile.

"No, it was you. I just had the feeling of a job offer for you, that's all, and it was particularly strong," I add.

"You're right on a lot of stuff, Mark, but I don't know about this one. I have my own company to run. Who would offer me a job to run their company?"

"You never know."

"Hey, either way, I appreciate you sharing what came to you, and I'll keep my ears open. I have to head out on a sales call, I'll catch you later."

"See you," I call out as he leaves the coffee room. There are some people who are destined for success. Bill is one of these people. It doesn't surprise me that he might get a job offer. Still, I question again whether I should have said anything, and I decide there's no harm. I am close enough to Bill to know he won't judge the information I'm giving him. He will take it at face value, while other people might think they're dealing with information coming through a less-than-credible source.

Later that day, Bill catches up with me just as I'm leaving to walk out to my car. It's a windy day, and I stop under the eaves of the building to keep my folders from blowing away.

"Mark, hold on a minute, I need to talk with you," he says, catching his breath. "I just had to tell you. I had lunch today with a contact of mine who owns a company up the peninsula. He asked me, right out of the blue, if I would be interested in heading up his company because he's thinking about retiring. Can you believe it? And the offer was pretty generous as well. I guess you were right," he says excitedly, giving me a jab in the arm. "I know you have to run, and I was going to send you an E-mail, but I saw you heading out and just had to pass this on to you."

I feel excitement rise up inside me as I stare at him and say, "I'm astonished that this took place the actual day I talked to you about it, Bill. I've been feeling confident with some of my impressions, but this is really amazing to have it validated this way. If it hadn't happened the way it did, no one would believe it."

"Wild, huh, Mark?" Bill says as he heads back into the office.

"Are you going to take the offer?" I call out.

"No, but what a thrill, ...and you called it, Bud!"

It's not at all clear to me whether this incident with Bill is random or whether it has been brought on by some set of specific circumstances. Is there a cause and effect here? I try to think back to my meditation on Bill to see if I did anything differently. Nothing stands out. I feel excited and yet puzzled and am really only sure of one thing: the notion of exploring these types of experiences keeps getting stronger.

Bill's an amusing guy in a way. He's very logical and systematic like myself, yet sometime later he gives me a book titled, *The Way of the Peaceful Warrior* by Dan Millman. He said he read it and thought I might enjoy it. I think the incident with the job offer might have loosened his analytical mooring a little.

An Alternative View of Health

There are times in life when one event that appears minor, plays a significant role in a person's future. As I sit in a physcian's waiting room, I wonder if my visit with Valentina the Russian healer, is one of these times.

I'm here to see Dr. Stanton, a homeopath who was recommended to Vicki. Dr. Stanton's office complex, which is located against the hills and surrounded by trees, has a more natural feel to it than that of traditional doctors. I wonder if this is by intent.

As I wait in the lobby, I notice a list of other doctors' names on a physician's chart behind the receptionist. I'm curious whether or not they also practice alternative medicine. The door between the waiting area and the doctors' offices opens, and Dr. Stanton steps into the lobby to greet me. Her stature and features are small like those of a young girl. She wears bifocals on the bridge of her nose. Her hair is sandy colored with slight traces of gray on the sides. I'd say she is in her mid-fifties.

"Mark, have you heard of homeopathy before?" she asks me as we proceed to her office.

"I've seen the word advertised on the packages of cold medicines and such. That's about all I know," I reply, settling into the comfortable chair she offers me. She has a gentle quality and a radiance about her that makes me feel comfortable.

"Then let me start by telling you briefly about my practice and then homeopathy so you'll have a better idea of where I'm coming from and how I might help you," she suggests.

"I'd like that," I reply, noticing the large collection of books in her office.

"I was a general practitioner MD for a large hospital here in the valley for many years," Dr. Stanton begins while adjusting her glasses. "I eventually left the hospital and started a homeopathy practice because it enables me to work with certain processes that I was restricted from using by the larger hospital and insurance systems."

"Really. How long have you been practicing?" I ask, still feeling a little unsure about alternative practices.

"Twenty years as a traditional medical doctor and twelve years in homeopathy."

"Wow."

She smiles, noticing my reaction and launches into what seems like a script. "Homeopathy is a non-toxic system of medicine based on the principle of 'like cures like.' The goal of homeopathy is to alleviate the symptoms and re-establish internal order at the deepest level and thereby provide a lasting cure," she says, handing me a brochure on the subject. "With that said," she laughs light-heartedly, almost as if she can check this off her list, "let me begin by asking you some questions about your situation. What brought you here today?"

"Over the last year, I've had a sleeping disorder that had me taking rather long naps," I say with a slight smile. "The sleeping episodes have subsided for the most part, but I'm still interested in finding out what caused them. None of the medical specialists I've seen were able to determine a cause. You were referred to my wife, Vicki, when someone suggested alternative medicine. I've been reading more about alternative health lately, so I decided to experience it first hand."

"Were there any other symptoms besides sleeping?" she asks inquisitively.

I hesitate and shift in my chair. "Well, yes," I reply. "My dreams became much more vivid and real during this time, and that has continued. It's almost as if I'm aware of myself *in the dream* as I'm dreaming. Strange, huh?"

"It sounds a little like lucid dreaming," Dr. Stanton says.

I haven't heard that term before, and I make a note of her comment on my day planner. "And I started having what some might call paranormal experiences," I continue, now feeling more open.

"Oh, really," she says and leans forward in her chair. "That must have startled your doctors."

"Yes it did. I'm not sure they knew what to make of it. To be honest, I stopped mentioning it after a while. The other doctors primarily focused on the physical symptoms and bypassed these unusual experiences."

"Perhaps you can expand on these experiences later," she

recommends. "For now, I have several other questions to ask you about your lifestyle."

"Okay," I say. I'm hoping this was the right thing to say Dr. Stanton. I'm trying to be honest but not have her think I'm a nut case. She seems to take things at face value, but she's also not tipping her hand one way or the other.

Dr. Stanton begins by asking questions about my diet, relaxation, and work. We talk for a while about how I break up my day, what my routines are.

Then she asks, "What sort of physical exercise are you getting?"

"I run about twenty miles a week," I reply.

"How well do you handle stress?" is her next question.

"Running helps, but I also do self-hypnosis for relaxation. I took a hypnosis course given by Josie Hadley in Palo Alto."

"Hypnosis, hmm," she smiles. "Have you heard of Edgar Cayce?"

"No," I answer.

"I'll come back to him provided we have time when we're finished with the examination." She returns to her notes and continues down her list. "How do you react when you get mad?" she asks me along with many other questions about my kids, marriage, and childhood. I answer questions for about a half hour, impressed with her thoroughness. After the interview portion, I follow her to the examination room, which contains a variety of machines and medicines. I sit in a chair facing her. She asks me to remove my shoes and socks.

"Hold these," she says, handing me two metal cylinders—one for each hand—while she touches my bare feet and hands with leads that are hooked up to a machine. The machine appears to be a measuring device for electrical impulses.

"What does this do?" I ask while watching her monitor the meters on the machine.

"One of the things it does is tell me which parts of your body are functioning correctly," she answers and jots something down. "And we'll use it to identify which organs are causing you problems."

"I see," I remark, wondering if these machines are scientifically approved. Dr. Stanton continues to probe between my toes using the metal lead. The machine periodically gives off a small beep as she carefully watches the gauges.

"Do you have an upset stomach?" she asks, setting aside small bottles of substances as she tests me on the machine.

"Yes, I do," I admit, surprised that the machine can detect this.

"I'm looking for chemical imbalances or toxins in your body that might be causing your stomach to be upset," she says as she continues to work with the machine.

Dr. Stanton elaborates on a few of the substances she has set to one side. "These are composed of extracts from plants and minerals," she explains. "This one is for your stomach ache. Take it twice a day for three days. This one you can take when you feel a sore throat coming on. It'll be useful since you told me you frequently have a sore throat. The other two are vitamins and minerals to be taken on a regular basis. I'll write it all down for you."

"All right," I say, putting my shoes back on.

She has me take one of the substances right then and there. She wants to make sure I've gotten the hang of it. The medicine is in the form of small, white, bead-like balls. She has me pour three beads from the small, blue cylinder into its lid and then put them under my tongue. She tells me to keep them under my tongue until they dissolve. I've never taken medicine this way before.

"Now that we're done with your physical review, I have a few more questions to ask," she says.

As I follow Dr. Stanton back to her office I notice a familiar odor in the long hallway between offices—a sort of antiseptic smell. I can hear other patients moving about behind closed doors. Back in her office she continues her questions. "You mentioned earlier you were having some unusual experiences during and after your sleep disorder. Can you elaborate?"

"Sure. It's as if as a result of these sleeping episodes, I feel things and know things in a way that's different somehow," I venture, watching for her reaction.

"Do you have some examples of these occurrences?" she asks politely.

"As I said before, I've been having very real dreams. Before the sleeping disorder, I never used to remember my dreams. Now, some of them stay with me the entire day. This has been a real change for me."

"I see," she says while taking a manila file from the cabinet behind her. She takes a blue sheet of paper from her desk drawer and clips it to the left side of the file folder. I can see her write something on the blue sheet.

Slightly distracted, I continue, "Also, I've begun to know what people are thinking and feeling, especially the people close to me, like my wife and children."

Dr. Stanton acknowledges my comments by nodding her head. I further explain that sometimes I know the details of an incident that has happened elsewhere. I use the example of the day I told my wife that we'd have to postpone our appointment to have our family pictures taken because our son had had his face scratched at school. I had a strong sense of caution and concern, but I also seemed to know that it wasn't severe. It was as though I'd seen it happen before it occurred. Sure enough, our son Jonathan came home with a large scratch on his face from a playground mishap.

Dr. Stanton seems fascinated by the story. After talking about a few more of these types of episodes, including the recent one with my partner Bill George, I ask, "Dr. Stanton, do you think this was an awakening to a sixth sense in me?"

"What do you think, Mark?"

"It's hard for me to know since I haven't had this type of experience before. I'm just a business person. I deal in facts and figures, relying on management reports most of the time. Plus these occurrences seem almost random or at least I can't control them," I tell her. "Any suggestions?"

"It sounds a lot like you're having some form of intuition or clairvoyant experiences," she says.

"Intuition?"

"Yes. I spoke of Edgar Cayce earlier when you mentioned hypnosis. He discovered he had a very unusual talent while in a hypnotic state, and he was very, very intuitive. I think you'd find his information and experiences interesting," she says.

"What information?"

"He developed a sort of metaphysical psychology," she replies above the hum of the air purifier. "He was also instrumental in helping bring attention to the holistic health field in the early part of this century. He really helped broaden the understanding of body, mind, and spirit."

"Metaphysics?" I ask, thinking that I've heard the word but don't know what it means. I've seen it in the newspaper in the business section used along the lines of "the metaphysics of Wall Street" or in the sports section under "the metaphysical approach to coaching," but I've never taken time to look it up. Actually, I always thought it had something to do with mathematics.

"Metaphysics deals with the invisible and superphysical planes in their relationship to the physical universe," she explains.

"Okay," I respond, not really sure about all of this. I've been so interested in getting to the bottom of this sleeping disorder thing that I've focused strictly on the physical aspect. Maybe it's time to consider my overall health from a broader point of view. Dr. Stanton seems to have insight into some of the experiences I've been having. I'm not sure about all of this metaphysical stuff, but she definitely seems knowledgeable.

"You mentioned the holistic health field. What's the general idea of this field?" I ask, a little unclear on where she is going with all this.

"The key is not to focus on an individual body part but rather treat the whole person. Each system is different. The Ayurvedic medicine from India is different from the herbalism and acupuncture of China," Dr. Stanton says. "Yet each is a comprehensive system that combines natural therapies with a more personalized approach. The central supposition in each of these systems places equal emphasis on body, mind, and spirit or rather on the 'whole' human being."

Dr. Stanton continues to talk about documented cases where Edgar Cayce would enter periods of "sleep" in which he could diagnose illness, often in people he had never met, and then prescribe medical treatment. She says he offered solutions to people who had tried all conventional avenues of medicine and had been diagnosed as hopeless. Supposedly, the information was coming from the "universal consciousness," which Dr. Stanton personally believes is similar to Carl Jung's "collective unconscious."

I look at Dr. Stanton intently as she talks and realize there seems to be a lot of information out there that I haven't been aware of. I'm thinking, as I look around at the many degrees on her office wall, that I still feel somewhat skeptical about the effectiveness of these processes.

"Read some of the A.R.E. books," she suggests, noticing my skepticism. "They're based on the teachings and experiences of Cayce."

"What's A.R.E.?" I ask.

"A.R.E. stands for the Association for Research and Enlightenment. It's an open-membership research society that indexes and catalogs information," she informs me while searching through her files for some information on this organization. "Edgar Cayce has been called the father of holistic health in America. It's the sort of research organization that would be a good place for you to start if you want to know more about these areas. I'll give you their telephone number before you leave."

"Okay," I respond.

"Oh, it just dawned on me, Noetic Sciences is another organization that might shed some light on what you're experiencing. And they're local so you might have an easier time reaching them. They have some superb material. Noetic Sciences was founded by Edgar Mitchell, one of the Apollo astronauts," she says.

"Do you have their telephone number?" I ask.

"No, but I believe they're in San Francisco," she offers.

"Thanks," I say, making a mental note to look them up. "I want to ask you a straightforward question."

"Shoot," she says.

"I've always been a pragmatic business person and a logical guy. Do you think what's happening to me is strange?"

"No," she says in a matter-of-fact manner.

"Then do you think it's reasonable to look for an answer to what's been happening to me?" I query.

"Mark, there are mysteries in life that are not totally rational, and it's okay to acknowledge and explore them. You'll never find the answers at your business seminars," she says with a grin.

We continue to talk a little while longer about health in America, HMOs, and managed health care before I thank her and leave. As I walk out of Dr. Stanton's office, I look out over the hills at the horses that are grazing behind the office building. I find myself thinking how curious it is I never learned to ride a horse even though some of my uncles raise horses. All of the ranch equipment and tools seem so foreign to a kid reared in the city. In a similar way, Dr. Stanton brought up many topics that seemed foreign. I have to give her credit though. Her knowledge of western and eastern medicine as well as the topic of holistic health is extensive. The concept that excites me the most is treating the patient on all levels of being: physical, emotional, intellectual and spiritual. It's an intriguing philosophy. I wonder how practical it is, though. I leave feeling compelled to find out more about metaphysics, holistic health, and the whole body/mind/spirit field.

Metaphysical Bookstores

Can trauma change the human spirit so completely that one becomes more awakened? I keep turning this question over in my mind. I take Dr. Stanton's suggestion and go out to a local bookstore to peruse books on mind/body medicine, metaphysics, holistic health, Edgar Cayce, and so on. I also call the A.R.E. and Noetic Sciences people and get on their mailing list to receive their catalogs.

I make my first visit to a metaphysical bookstore. I am nervous at first, but when I find the large Christian section, I become more comfortable. I even buy books by some of my favorite Christian writers, such as St. John of the Cross and C. S. Lewis. It's odd to see the Christian section positioned between the sections on Dreams and Healers. Thinking about it, maybe it's not so odd. Many of the Old Testament prophets received prophecy through dreams, and the Disciples had great healing abilities.

I buy more books than I can read in a few weeks. Soon I find other booksellers with similar material and some in places I wouldn't have thought to look. For instance, I find a large assortment of holistic medicine books at my local health food store. Odd that I've passed this health section before and never taken notice until now. I also find an abundance of metaphysical books at the local Unity Church bookstore. Previous to this, I didn't even realize the Unity Church had a bookstore. The people behind the counter of the church bookstore are very helpful and order a book for me that Dr. Stanton suggested I get. For months, I stay up late reading various books. Most of the books are seeking to establish a body-mind-spirit connection. I'm fascinated with the recognition of more than just the physical aspect of health. One thing in particular I find intriguing is the belief that the body has the power to heal itself.

I find myself really striving to understand the body/mind/ spirit connection. I understand physical relationships very well. I work in businesses where labor and physical distribution costs are a large percentage of the Profit & Loss statement. I know I can trust what I can see and touch. Therefore, the physical component is easiest for me, but I'm less trusting of the mind/spiritual component. I remember there was a class on intuition in the Humanities Department, but at the time I wasn't interested in expending my electives on this form of study. And besides, my business school counselor frowned on studies outside the main business curriculum.

As I read more books, many questions are beginning to come to mind that I can no longer answer purely with my logical thinking: questions about the truths that lie beyond the physical world; questions about how to balance material well-being and spirituality and about what my purpose is in life. In the back of my mind, I've always wondered about these things. In the past I was able to stave off the desire to answer these questions by throwing myself into my career. With a wife and kids and companies to build, there was never enough time to contemplate these things. In the end, though, this very human need to find answers never left me completely.

Applications in Life

It seems to me the struggle to develop greater awareness looks different in each person. Maybe awareness is really just an *ideal* made up of individual goals, I think to myself as I sit perusing a book on the living room couch. I notice Vicki come out of our son's room at the top of the stairs. She tightens the sash of her teal robe and flips back her shoulder length hair over the collar as she steps quietly down the stairs. "I think they're asleep now," she whispers.

I put down my book and smile. She looks lovely in that color. "Come over here and talk with me," I say with a glimmer in my eye.

"Let me put the kettle on for tea first," she answers softly. Stepping into the slippers at the bottom of the staircase, she disappears around the corner, leaving me in solitude again.

"Mommy," a little voice calls out. "Mommy." I look up and see my son Jonathan peering through the banister.

"Mommy is busy now, Jonathan, it's time to go to sleep," I say as I walk up the stairs.

"I just wanted a glass of water, please," he says. "I'm thirsty."

"I can help you with that one, big guy," I reply, swooping him up into my arms. He wiggles his way down and scampers to the bedroom ahead of me.

"I beat you," he says triumphantly when I arrive.

"Okay, pal, it's time to settle in." Taking the empty glass, I tuck the blankets around him while he yawns and eventually closes his eyes. "Good-night, son,." I say as I kiss him one last time before turning off the light again. My daughter Allison's room is quiet as I walk by. I peer in quickly anyway. She has fallen asleep with a fairy tale book in her arms. The book is *Tam's Charge* by Jill Raiguel. It's not the regular type of fairy tale book but rather a fairy tale for adults. I read it to her at night along with the Bible and other assorted books. Allison is a little like me, I have to admit. She's fascinated with what are called "Fairy Fundamentals" in the book. Every time a fairy's wings change colors because they're mad or happy or sad, Allison gets all excited. She loves to be told which color matches which emotion. I gently remove the book from beneath her small hands and place it on her bookshelf. I pull the covers up to her neck and whisper a happy thought into her ear.

"All is well," I report, nodding towards the upstairs, when Vicki returns to the living room with a tray of tea things.

"Finally," she sighs as she curls up on the sofa next to me. "They've been going non-stop all day," she adds, leaning her shoulder against me. "Over all, though, it's been a good day."

"For me too," I respond, enjoying the softness of her hair against my face. "Hey, changing the subject, I've been thinking more about the direction of the exploration. Do you want to hear about it?"

"You mean the *personal quest* you're on?" Vicki says facetiously, turning to look at me.

"Personal quest—I like that!"

"I thought you might. Anything that involves research…," Vicki teases lovingly. She knows me so well.

"Actually, I'm eager to do more *primary* research," I interject.

"Primary research?" she asks.

"It's a marketing term for going out and interviewing people firsthand. My sessions with Valentina and Joy Lasseter are a form of primary research. Some people call it 'live' research."

"I'm getting an education in marketing here," Vicki says with a warm laugh.

I have to laugh right along with her. I'm glad Vicki can keep this a light-hearted affair because I can get too serious about some of this. I know I must sound very business-like to her.

Reaching down, I place my tea bag to the side of my cup and sip the tea with the tip of my tongue to make sure its not too hot. Having a hot cup of tea or hot chocolate at night has become something of a routine for us.

"And just what do you want to research?" Vicki inquires.

"I'm glad you asked that question," I say, smiling and sounding like a salesman. "I've been developing a mission statement, and I would really like your feedback on it. Do you feel up to reading it over?"

"Oh, oh," she laughs. "I'll read it, but really Mark, a mission statement?"

"Vicki, it's just like you intimated at dinner a while ago. I needed to get a more concrete idea about what I was really after in reading all of these books. I've continued thinking about this research venture idea, and I've come to realize that a mission statement will make things more clear on my real purpose."

"Oh, yeah. Do you think so?" Vicki asks rhetorically. "I hope you're not going overboard. I think, like a lot of men, what you really like is to apply techniques you've learned in business to personal things."

I retrieve a copy of the statement from my day planner on the dining room table pretending I didn't hear Vicki's comment. I hand the copy to her and suggest an analogy on why I need a mission statement. "It's similar to a couple vacationing across America who set short-term objectives and follow them but forget the real reason they went vacationing in the first place. They set goals to reach Arizona by noon on Friday and then Texas by Sunday morning. They want to be in New York by the following Saturday. Pretty soon the goals become so important to them, they forget that the original purpose of the vacation was to unwind."

Vicki nods her head as if to agree as she looks over the mission statement.

Mission Statement for Mark Bryant's Primary (live) Research

To gain a better and broader perspective of those inner processes that lead to greater awareness and develop a better understanding of my true nature.

OBJECTIVES:

1. Develop a conceptual map of how things are interrelated in the areas of:
   - Body/Mind/Spirit
   - Metaphysics
   - Holistic Health
   - Healing
   - Sense Perception and Extra Sensory Perception
   - Mind/Body Medicine
   - Paranormal
2. Identify useful information and tools in these fields for applying in my everyday life.
3. Determine how these areas connect with my notion of religion, spirituality, and my basic belief system.

"I like the analogy," she says. "But, are you sure that's not really how *you* are when you're on vacation?"

I give her that serious look and she retorts. "Okay, okay! So the mission statement is to help you stay on course and keep the big picture in focus, but I reserve the right to change my mind on this whole thing," Vicki remarks.

"Deal! Now any feedback on the mission statement?"

"Well, I think it's a little wordy," she says after a few minutes. "It seems to me that your main point can be boiled down into a single phrase."

"Which is?"

"Something about looking at inner processes for applications in life," she suggests as she pours herself a second cup of tea. "I know you—you're wondering how you can systematize some of these things? That's the businessman in you. Provided you can pull this off, you believe you'll be able to apply these inner processes better than before. Right?"

"Yeah," I respond.

"In addition, you've been seeking to find out how some of these things work. You want to know how applicable they are. That's looking for the applications in life."

Vicki extends her legs, propping her soft slippers on the table next to my bare feet. I lean over next to her and say, "Vicki, for a woman who's highly intuitive, your critique sounds very logical to me. I'll have to come up with an entirely new term for this. Let's see, ...how about *'feminine logic.'*"

"Oh, please!" she drawls.

"Seriously, I do appreciate your feedback," I acknowledge, giving her a gentle squeeze. Her input on all of this has been very helpful to me. It's not a subject that I can discuss easily with my business associates. I'm not sure they would see the value.

Without a direct profit motive, they'd likely advise me to keep my eyes focused strictly on business.

"What's your next step?" she asks.

"To be honest, I'm a little cautious about how to proceed," I reply.

"What about getting other people to help you?" Vicki suggests after an unhurried silence.

"We'll see."

"Mark, you know when you started your first business, how you searched for a mentor to teach you the ropes?"

"Yeah?"

"Michael Smith was there for you. He taught you things in business you might not have learned otherwise. Is there anyone in these fields who can act like a mentor for you?"

"You're reading my mind. You're not psychic, are you?" I laugh.

Vicki has hit on an important issue—guidance. I don't know these fields so I'm at a disadvantage. Everyone goes on these journeys at different times in their life and, it seems to me, we're all looking for someone wiser to help us through them.

"I'll have to go on faith that someone will show up for me," I say as Vicki goes into the kitchen to put her cup in the sink.

"Okay, but there's only one thing I ask," Vicki interjects.

"What's that?" I respond.

"No gurus!"

I laugh. "I don't think you have to worry about that. Remember, I'm an entrepreneur, ...a maverick! I don't conform too well to guru-type programming."

"Well, better men than you have succumbed to a guru,"

she says as she picks up a magazine and heads towards the stairs for the bedroom.

"You mean some beautiful female guru or any guru in particular?" I ask, putting my tea cup back onto the tray.

"You know what I mean!" she says turning and giving me a stern look.

"So, yes. Agreed. No gurus," I say, pretending to cower to her demands.

"Good," she says ascending the staircase.

When she arrives at the top of the stairs, I call out, "In case one follows me home, can I keep him?" She pretends not to hear me and continues into the bedroom.

As I rinse off the dishes before going to bed, I look over the objectives I have developed for this research — this "personal quest", as Vicki calls it. It seems less likely now that I'll wander off onto some unimportant tangent. I feel more focused. What was it that Vicki called it... "Applications in life" are the words she used as she perused my mission statement. I like that! It really comes down to the applications in life.

———————

Hidden Asset

It's easy to deceive ourselves into believing that the physical aspect is all there is, leading to a one-sided view.

Chapter Three

Seeking Paranormal Perspectives

Reality and Lucid Dreamers

I'm not convinced that inner processes such as intuition and dreams, by themselves, are enough to effect real change in a person. Research or not, a business person like myself is not going to be able to apply these processes without some help. It seems to me that there needs to be a way of translating these processes into things that are useful in everyday life. This thought occurs to me as I sit in a circle with eight other people who claim to be lucid dreamers. The session is being conducted by a woman named Beverly D'Urso.

As I wait for the meeting to start, I recall that Dr. Stanton had alluded to lucid dreaming in our initial meeting. Since my dreams were one of the things that began to change with the advent of my sleeping disorder, I decided to include dreaming as a topic to explore early on in my search. I contacted Beverly D'Urso specifically because she was the original testing dreamer for the book *Lucid Dreaming*. I was curious about her experience with dreams, and the role the dream state plays in overall awareness.

I distinctly remember Beverly's comment during a private session on lucid dreaming. She suggested that I come to an informal group session. "You'll meet other people who have developed the ability to be conscious in their dreams. This will give you a broader perspective," she told me. So I decided to take her advice.

As the meeting begins, I anxiously scan the room. I try to size up each individual in the circle. My eyes continue around the room and finally settle on Beverly at the front. Beverly appears quite young to have a Ph.D., although I'm not usually very good with ages so she could be older than she looks. She is very light-hearted, and her Midwestern casualness is comfortable to be around. Although well educated, she is down to earth and very responsive to members of the group. She has told me she leads these meetings one evening each month. I am the only outsider and the only person in the room who is not actively developing my lucid dreaming skills. "Who wants to begin?" Beverly asks the group in her measured speech.

"I will," says one of the young men sitting on the couch. "I've been using the new 'lucid dreaming' induction device for the last three months, and it's really working well," he says. "I like this model much better than the last version."

I'm in the dark, and I ask Beverly if I can ask questions during the meeting. She nods and I ask, "What's a lucid dreaming induction device?" sounding like a fish out of water. Some of the people here have been meeting together for years. Many are members of the Lucidity Institute. They're seasoned lucid dreamers and are used to discussing the more advanced nuances of their dreams. Even so, they take genuine interest in answering my questions.

"It's a device you wear when you sleep that may help you have a lucid dream," a young man, seated on some pillows on the floor, responds.

I'm astonished, although I don't let it show in front of the group. To think that there is a device to help you have a lucid dream is fascinating. Supposing it works, this must be a pretty ingenious device. I can't help asking, "Can you explain how it works?"

The same young man answers, "It's like a mask that you wear over your eyes. But it's not an ordinary mask. It's equipped with a small sensor that detects when you're going into a dream state."

As he's speaking, I realize there is one aspect of this conversation that resonates with me. It sounds like this device is grounded in technology, and this makes me feel more secure.

"Now just as you enter into the dream state," he continues, "the sensor sets off a small pulsating light on the inside of the mask. This light brings you to a semi-conscious state where you can become aware of the dream while remaining in the dream. That's about it in a nutshell."

Other members of the group nod their heads in agreement. One person adds, "There are a couple of firms making these devices, and they range anywhere from a couple of hundred dollars on up."

This is a novel idea. I like the energy of this group. They are very open with their comments even though they have never met me before. Some of the members look like grad students from the local university. Others are professionals who work for one of the many technology companies that permeate Silicon Valley. As I take notes, I ask, "How long does it take to become a lucid dreamer using one of these devices?"

Beverly speaks up and says, "Mark, that depends on how advanced a lucid dreamer you are to start with. I was a lucid dreamer as a child and have been conscious of my dreams my entire life. That's partly why I was selected for the studies at Stanford University. But most people have varying degrees of lucidity in their dreams. Even using these devices, it'll take some people longer to become proficient at lucid dreaming. Just training themselves to ask if they're dreaming when the sensor light goes on is a big task for some people."

"Supposing I wanted to buy one of these things, where would I go?" I ask.

The young man on the pillows jumps in, "Well, you can buy them directly from the Lucidity Institute, or there are a couple of mail order catalogs now selling them. I'd advise you get one of the less expensive models until you decide whether or not you're going to stick with this," he says while knocking on the floor.

I find this knocking on the floor curious. Certain people in the meeting have been knocking on tables or walls since the meeting began. I make a note of this as Beverly continues to talk about lucid dreaming. Off and on people in the group take turns talking about their dream experiences. At a break in the meeting, I'm attracted by the smell of herbal tea. A coffee pot and hot water dispenser sit on a small table in the corner of the room. As I make my way towards the coffee table, I notice one of the group members knocking on a door jamb. Here's my chance to ask about this unusual practice. I walk up to Beverly and ask her about the knocking.

"It's simple really," Beverly explains. "These people are performing the predetermined task of knocking on wood. It's a little technique we've devised to ask ourselves if we're dreaming."

"Okay," I respond as I mull over her answer. They knock on wood to help them tell whether it's a dream or not. But they're not asleep, so, I guess if they knock on the table and they don't feel the wood sensation, they must be dreaming.

Beverly interrupts my thoughts. "Mark, when we question if we're in a dream, and we're actually in one, we'll often get evidence that it's a dream. We practice this knocking while awake so that we don't forget to do this when we're in an actual dream," she says.

Interesting that they would need to practice this technique in a waking state to use in the dream state. I never knew you could go the other way where something you do while awake can help you in your dreams.

Continuing, Beverly says, "Our dreams can often appear to be very much like the waking state until we look at them and experience them with more attention."

The break is over and I return to my seat, reflecting on Beverly's explanation. They don't know if they're dreaming or not when they actually are, I think to myself, astounded that people can't distinguish the difference. Dreaming must seem very real for them if they mistake dreams for the waking state. I can't quite comprehend the full significance of this. I might have to re-read the dreaming books I have.

"Would someone else like to share a dream they've had?" Beverly asks.

I like the way Beverly is conducting these sessions. She is so open in listening to other people talk about their dreams. I make a note to initiate this type of dialogue with Vicki and the kids. With a little encouragement, the kids, I know, will really enjoy talking about dreams. I'm curious to see whether or not they can remember their dreams.

"I had a healing dream a few nights ago," begins a man

sitting near the window. My ears perk up.

"I dreamed I was a little boy and a beast was trying to get me. It chased me through the house and was just about to grab me when I became lucid, and its face turned into my wife's mother's face. I greeted her in the dream and left."

"What was the healing about?" asks the young man on the pillows.

"My fear has been that my mother-in-law would come live with us. In this dream I faced my fears by becoming lucid, facing my own anxiety around the situation, and the dream no longer seemed scary," says the man in the rocker. "The overall situation became so clear in my dream."

My first reaction is to think of my own mother-in-law, Carmen. Even though I love her dearly, there is a twinge of fright when I think about having Vicki and her mom in the same household. They're not exactly oil and water, but I can easily see how this type of situation could drift into one's dreams ... or nightmares.

When the man in the rocker is finished talking about his dream, collectively the group members give out a small cheer of approval as an unmistakable sign of camaraderie. I like that they can share in this man's healing of a fear or anxiety. There appears to be no judgment or criticism within the group as people discuss their dreams.

Next a woman in the group speaks up. "I dreamed of Bob last week," she volunteers. "In the dream, we met in a bar in downtown Chicago."

"Did you have a similar dream?" Beverly asks a man who apparently is Bob.

"Yes," he confirms, looking over at the woman. "Kathy and

I agreed to dream of each other ahead of time. It was on Tuesday. I dreamed that we met at a bar we both frequented when we lived back there. In the dream, I ordered a beer, and she had a glass of wine."

By this time I am thinking it's a good thing I met with Beverly beforehand and felt that the group was legitimate, or I would have had a difficult time believing this. Clearly they can articulate what's going on in their dreams, and I guess it's always possible that they could be dreaming about each other as well. Could this be some form of projection via the dream state?

"Yes, that's similar to my dream," the woman confirms. "In my dream, the bar was crowded, and there was a live band."

Bob nods to signify that this was true in his dream also.

The group continues sharing situations where they have intentionally dreamed of visiting specific places while I listen, fascinated. They refer to it as mutual dreaming. After spending some time with these people, I find out that there is more to dreams than I understood from just reading books. Lucid dreaming techniques that enable a person to be consciously aware they are dreaming during the dream-state are very appealing to me because of my own dream experiences.

Lucid dreaming and the study of dreams seem to go hand-in-hand. There is a mind/body connection here that I cannot quite comprehend, but I am excited about exploring lucid dreaming further. I'm also pleased that there is technology to support this process. What I got most out of this session is an understanding of the importance dreams play in our lives. Since everyone dreams, these discussions on dreams are universal in their applications.

I leave the workshop convinced that we can learn more about

ourselves through the study of dreams and remembering the last point Beverly made: "The key is non-lucid dreamers *think* the dream is reality, while lucid dreamers *know* they are in the dream and it's not reality."

In a strange way this makes sense to me. It used to be that when I dreamt I never realized it was a dream until I would wake up and say something like "I'm glad that was a dream." More recently my own dreams have become more like the comments I've heard here tonight. It seems as though these people know they're in the middle of a dream when they're actually dreaming so they know it's not real.

For a person who loves useful information, how ironic that I dream every night and rarely make use of my dreams. This meeting has spurred my interest in developing a better approach to my dreams. Beverly has helped me to realize my dreams deserve more attention, and I plan to act on a suggestion made in the meeting about keeping a written journal of my dreams. Interesting that my first application from this primary research is in the form of a writing journal. As a business person, I rarely write a letter or memo longer than a page.

The encounter with the lucid dreamers stays with me for a while. It's still hard for me to believe that things such as mutual dreaming actually exist. It's another realm of awareness I wouldn't think was possible unless I had sat in on this group. From this experience I can tell that this so-called research I'm doing is going to be more like an *adventure*. I like the freedom because it allows me to go with the flow and see what comes. This makes Vicki's comment about being on a 'quest' pretty accurate, since I'm not really sure what's around the bend.

Overlaying the Religious Template

I've read that it's better to begin an adventure without discussing it with anyone beforehand. Some say it takes away the excitement while allowing other people to give their opinion of the idea. My sense is that this is partially right. I agree that it's pointless to talk about exploration to people who would label it simply as fools-gold, ...worthless. On the other hand, there are certain people I trust for their advice and wisdom. The pastor at my church is one such person.

Over the years, the pastor and I have become good friends, and we get together for breakfast about once a month to discuss everything from preaching to sports. We're having breakfast this morning at a real grease-pit, but the food is delicious, and it's one of our favorite rendezvous places. I get out of my car and hurry to the front door of the restaurant to get out of the rain, which is pouring down and splashing against the windows of the building. I feel a sturdy hand grasp my shoulder. As I turn around to look, Pastor says, "Did you see the San Francisco Forty-Niner game last night?"

"Just the fourth quarter, Pastor. It was a close one, wasn't it?" I reply as we enter the small coffee shop.

"Yeah, and the Forty-Niners were down by two touchdowns going into the fourth quarter. What a come-back. Boy, can those guys play!" The pastor is a big man with broad shoulders, large hands and a powerful build. With his large frame, he could easily pass as a professional football player.

"May we have a couple of menus and some of the fantastic coffee you've got back there?" he asks the waitress.

"I thought you'd have memorized the menu by now," she teases him.

"Decaf for me," I say.

"You've switched to decaf, huh?" Pastor asks.

"Yes, a nutritionist I've recently seen suggested I cut back on caffeine."

I shift uneasily behind my menu, knowing I'll be approaching my pastor with questions around the whole body/ mind/spirit thing this morning. I'm in no hurry to get to this because I'm not really sure how he will react. I need to look for just the right opening. We continue to discuss upcoming church activities and when we've concluded our conversation on church topics, I ask, "Pastor, you know that a while back I was off work because I had a disorder that was never diagnosed?"

"Yes, of course. Why? Are you having the symptoms again?" he asks, his boyish face becoming more serious.

"Very seldom, thank goodness. But I'm still getting some really strong impressions about things that subsequently happen. These sensations I'm getting are still a mystery to me in terms of why and how they occur. It seems like these occurrences began happening after I got over my sleep disorder. I was wondering what you think happens to a person when they have an experience like I had?"

I hold out my coffee cup as our waitress walks by. The pastor looks at me for a moment and then says, "Well, if you look at the life of St. Ignatius, much of his work, which is the backbone of certain Catholic doctrine, was developed when he was laid up for a year with only two books to read."

"The Bible?"

"Yes, and a book on medieval courts of love," he says.

The pastor begins to talk about the life of St. Ignatius. He explains how St. Ignatius was able to get in touch with the divine during the year he was bed-ridden, and how his calling was to minister to the poor and to develop a system to help teach them. The pastor believes St. Ignatius discovered a lot about his calling in a year on that bed.

I wonder if my experience was as simple as getting in touch with the divine. If so, what was the inner calling about? Clearly I did read my Bible more, but this was just because I was afforded the time. I do feel closer to God, but other things seem to be happening here also—things beneath the surface that I don't quite understand.

"Mark, your circumstances may be similar in that you were incapacitated for a while, and in that time, developed a better intuitive sense. You can find many people in church history that have had setbacks that caused profound changes in their lives. They all had some form of connection with the divine that provided them with insight into what they should do."

"Interesting," I say.

"These days we give it the name intuition," the pastor continues. "You know the root meaning of intuition is to 'dwell in God'."

"No, I didn't."

Our food arrives hot off the skillet. The plates are extra large just like the pastor likes it. He breathes in deeply to get a better whiff of the bacon and eggs. We bow our heads, and the pastor blesses the food. His comment about people from church history intrigues me. One of my partners, Peter, owns a Christian bookstore. Since Peter set up the bookstore's entire inventory, he'll know if there are some books like this from church history. I'll ask him when I see him at the office. I smile with admiration as I think about Peter. He supported me throughout my ordeal without ever complaining about the time I missed. He managed the firm and took on my responsibilities in addition to his own. He truly epitomizes the term "partner" when it comes to helping other people.

"Pastor, how do you think intuition works?"

"I truly don't know, Mark. The important thing to remember is the Bible tells us that we're not able to understand all of the mysteries in the world. There's a book in the church library about beliefs and the paranormal. I've enjoyed reading it, and I don't pretend that I can explain all of the mysteries in it with the word of God. It's beyond my comprehension as a human being. It would be the same as saying I could solve all the mysteries of the Bible or of the Universe."

"Can I borrow this book?" I ask.

"Sure. I believe paranormal phenomena exist even though I don't have a clue as to why and how."

I enjoy the pastor's honesty. We begin to share stories about unexplained things that have happened such as the shroud of Turin and apparitions of Mother Mary. We talk as we eat and are caught up with different mysteries of the world and forgotten powers. Near the end of breakfast, I feel it's time to ask the pastor about my desire to explore some of these phenomena. I shift in my chair and motion to our waitress for more coffee. "What do you think of the idea of me taking time to explore some of these paranormal phenomena first-hand?"

There's a long silence as the pastor looks at me intensely. I can feel the energy shift. Up until now all the talk about defying science and impossible feats has been light and somewhat distant. Now I'm throwing my hat into the ring as it were.

"Mark, are you really asking if it's a sin to delve into this stuff?"

I don't answer immediately. I think we're both trying to adjust to the situation. We've been friends a long time. Finally, I say, "Yes, that's more to the point of my real question."

"First of all, I want to counsel you on staying away from anything that is in conflict with Biblical doctrine. If these sensations you're having lead you astray from the Bible or what you believe to be right, then yes I would say it's a sin. Do you understand what I'm saying here?"

"Yes, I think so," I reply.

"If there is no conflict with doctrine and it doesn't take you away from your responsibilities to your family and God and the church, then I would say it's probably okay," the pastor adds.

"And you see the conflict as dangerous?"

"Yes, I do," the pastor says. "The danger is that much of the paranormal can lead to the wrong ideas. Satan can produce paranormal activity to deceive. Jesus warned us that his miracles could be copied by 'false prophets.'"

The pastor has launched into his Sunday sermon. He's doing his job. He doesn't want to see me stray from the flock. He's the shepherd watching over the sheep. For the next five minutes our conversation is very awkward. Neither of us wants to damage our relationship, but clearly the pastor can set our friendship aside in order to counsel me. Quoting from the parable of the "sower and the seed," he tells me to follow the straight and narrow and not to fall by the way side.

Finally, he lightens things up by saying, "Mark, let's take me for example. You know I love sports. I love to play sports, watch them, read about them, you name it. Are sports a sin? No. But if I start to let sports keep me from God, then yes, they'd be a sin for me," he clarifies.

"I bet it's a real conflict when the kick-off begins at the same time as the sermon on Sunday morning," I say with a smile.

"Not as long as I have them in the right priority..., and a reliable VCR," he says and grins.

The pastor has provided some very good advice. He's not suggesting how I should proceed as much as he has emphasized the need to keep my relationship to God in focus. We go on to talk about some doctrinal issues on good and evil. As we finish our breakfast, the pastor admonishes me to be careful in whatever course I take. The irony is I want to follow his advice, but I don't want my belief system to prevent me from finding the answers.

Intuition Over Intellect in the Boardroom

Working in the heart of Silicon Valley provides me with a unique perspective. Hewlett-Packard, Intel, and Apple Computer are just a few of the successful companies that have sprouted where once cherry and pear orchards grew. The two biggest groups of financial winners have been those people who have started companies and those who have developed the land. Entrepreneurs and developers top the *Fortune* list in the Bay Area every year. These people are respected for their courage to act on their dreams. They have capitalized on their imagination and creativity.

During a year-end meeting for a company where I serve on the board, I look out over the valley to the hills behind the high-rise buildings across from me. My chair is turned away slightly from the round walnut conference table, positioned to give an optimum view out the large south window. The sky is an unusual blue today, I notice, while the meeting goes on without me. I can barely make out a flock of Canadian geese flying over the nearby foothills. They're getting a late start on flying south for the winter. My eyes continue to pan over the scenic backdrop when suddenly I hear a topic that brings me back to the meeting at hand.

"Now, we're ready to discuss the geographic expansion," states the president, standing at the overhead projector. I shift my attention to where corporate financial statements are being displayed. Discussions of quarterly reports, sales projections, marketing strategies, and operational budgets permeate the room. My mind begins to wander again while talk of a financial budget and business strategy fades in and out. My thoughts vacillate between the boardroom discussion and contemplating exploration and research into the areas of body/mind/spirit and awareness.

I used to be the most noticeably driven of the corporate group, priding myself on the fact that no one could work harder than me. This was the standard for an entrepreneur like myself, I believed. Yes, I loved these meetings, discussing competition and markets. I had a great enthusiasm for making money and building businesses. However, something is different now. I feel a strong urge to explore my inner nature and inner processes. I still enjoy the feeling of being industrious, but I would rather split the time up in a way to include exploration time or what some call inner work.

Deciding to explore goes against pure intellect because it adds little value to my career. My intellect seems to be saying, "Whoa, slow down here, pal, you're headed toward a precipice," but my intuition is speaking with a stronger voice, saying: "This is the right thing to do."

As the advisory board meeting continues, I think how there have been mixed messages from my friends and business associates about my researching fields that traditionally have no place in business. One partner was supportive but said, "Don't go off the deep end on us." An interesting side note to this is how this exploration is changing the way I deal with power. As with many entrepreneurs, I have issues around control. I like to be king and control everything in the kingdom. Yet, I don't see how I can control everything and open up at the same time.

It seems to me many people in business have systematically limited their growth and awareness by keeping totally focused on the bottom-line. "Consciousness" is the buzzword human resource people like to use, yet most managers discount the value of such a concept working in business. "You know this is going to set you back, Mark," one well-meaning business associate warned me. This comment is not completely unconvincing. Even a business colleague seated across from me at the table told me in private, "You've taken five steps forward in your career; now you're taking two steps back."

Comments like these lead me to examine whether searching for inner resources is really a backward step. In a way, this sort of talk is good for me because it really brings out my emotions. The more I hear these statements, the stronger I feel that I'm doing the right thing. There is this inescapable feeling that if I don't spend time exploring these fields now, I never will.

Soon it's time for me to talk to the group of executives seated around the table. I put away my exploration ideas and pull out my findings on business expansion. As I move to the podium, I'm quickly brought back to the demands of business. One thing is clear. I'll need to plan my time wisely in order to handle my business responsibilities along with any exploration. A balance between my work and the research is essential; a little like balancing the intellect and intuition.

———◦———

Hidden Asset

Working with non-physical dimensions such as dreams can help influence the way we live our lives.

Chapter Four

Moving Out of the Comfort Zone

Chop Wood, Carry Water...

Vicki zips up our daughter Allison's lavender jacket against November's chilly air. Late autumn gusts swirl eucalyptus and poplar leaves into temporary patterns along the paved trail. Our son Jonathan has already taken off on his tricycle ahead of us. "Good thing I checked his jacket before we left," Vicki says, half to herself.

"Yeah, he'd be a tough one to catch up with now," I respond, watching our son pedal a hundred feet in the distance. Allison is still new to the pedaling thing, and we walk slowly behind her as she zigzags her way along. Next to the trail, about ten feet to the south, a river runs full and slow. Pea soup green and deep, the old river winds along the north boundary of the town, creating a haven for birds and other wildlife. Sun filters through the trees along its banks, visible as translucent gold streaks across the path in front of us. Vicki zips up her jacket as well. Then, taking my arm, she huddles close to me. "Brrr," she says, "it's colder than this time last year."

"Winter came early," I reply, feeling the chill on my ears. "Are you warm enough?" I pull her closer to me.

"Barely, but the walk will get my blood moving."

We walk keeping one eye on Jonathan, who has nearly

disappeared on the horizon, and the other on Allison, who threatens on occasion to get too close to the river's edge.

"You'll be interested to hear what Val, my hairdresser, told me while she was cutting my hair yesterday," Vicki suddenly says.

"Tell me."

"Val has a nine-year-old son who has been having problems in school since kindergarten," she explains. "She took him to the school counselor at first and then to an outside psychologist. Val tried everything, but nothing seemed to really change anything. Today I asked her how he was, and she said he's doing a lot better at school."

"That's great," I respond, bending down to tie Allison's shoes again. "What created the change?"

"Well, that's the exciting part. A few months ago she heard about a psychic who had helped people. Val felt she had nothing to lose, and she really needed to help her son so she was open to trying it out. Well, it turns out that the psychic, her name is Mary Coleman, could see things about Val's son—desires and fears and such—that the psychologists couldn't see. The information has helped Val to understand her son in a different way. He's already shown improvement at school. His teacher even commented about it."

"No kidding," I answer, beginning to get excited about her story. "Could you call Val and get Mary's telephone number for me? And maybe the sort of questions Mary can answer?"

Vicki looks at me with surprise at my desire to get the psychic's number and my unexpected enthusiasm. "Sure, Mark, but what's your interest in calling her?"

"Give me a push, Daddy," Allison interrupts as we approach a small incline.

"There you go, Allison." I nudge the back of her trike carefully, then return to Vicki's question. "As you were relating the story, Vicki, a thought occurred to me. If this woman can help people with deeper issues, possibly she's a good person to add to my research."

"Maybe Mary can tell you what brought on the sleeping disorder," she says with a slight shivering in her voice.

"That question will definitely be on my list," I reply. Although I don't say it to Vicki, I suspect this psychic will say it has something to do with making a person look inward. If you don't have a trauma happen to you, then it's hard for me to believe you'd look inward on your own.

Jonathan has abandoned his bike, and I watch him race recklessly up a steep slope. I keep a watchful eye on him as we continue to walk along the river. What's ironic is that if you look around, many people today are having something happen in their life that's motivating them to look deeper within themselves. It's presumably not a sleeping disorder, but it might be losing their job, or depression, anxiety, divorce, or the death of someone near to them. I'm thinking about a lot of our friends who are going through turmoil in their lives.

"And what about the intuitive occurrences you've been having since the sleeping spells? Maybe Mary could help you in this area," Vicki says while pushing Allison's tricycle with her foot.

"That would be nice, wouldn't it?" I step off the trail. "I'm going to skip a couple of rocks down by the water, Vicki. I'll join up with you on the other side of those reeds." I take a small fisherman's path cut narrowly at the water's edge while Vicki and the kids keep on along the main trail. The distinct sound of a blue jay can be heard amongst the tall trees.

As I walk, I feel rather excited about this Mary person. For a while, I've felt as if I had squeezed out the emotional and intuitive part of myself, which I am now rediscovering is an important part of me. In an emotional way, it's similar to a marriage. When I'm away from Vicki for any length of time, I miss her a lot. I miss the kids too, but I miss Vicki in a different way. She's like that other side of me that is absolutely necessary to make me feel complete. When I'm apart from her, I'm without certain qualities that she brings to our relationship. When I think about the intuitive aspect of myself, it seems similar. I realize how much I've missed this side of me. It feels as if I have shut down the more intuitive side of myself over the years, and as a consequence of that, it's as if I've been away from my partner for a long period of time. I'll be interested in Mary's perspective on this.

"Were you thinking about what I told you about the psychic?" Vicki asks when I join them on the trail again. She can see how anxious I am about all of this.

"You bet!" I answer excitedly. "It certainly seems worth making an appointment to see this Mary Coleman woman."

"You're right, I suppose," Vicki admits. "Who knows? Maybe she'll end up being the mentor you've been looking for. Isn't it amazing that this person has shown up so soon after you made a commitment to move forward on this stuff!"

"No kidding," I reply. "Who would figure I'd get a lead through your hairdresser! What is it the people who practice Zen say? 'When a student is ready, a teacher will appear.'"

"That and 'chop wood, carry water,'" Vicki says and laughs.

We walk in comfortable silence for a while, each involved in our own thoughts about what's around the bend for us. Fear of the unknown comes up in me. What will this exploration really do for me? Am I going to change? A visit with this Mary Coleman could help answer some of these questions. Fascination compels me forward, offsetting any fears I may have.

A Mentor for Metaphysics

For every person there are memories of the first time they experience something. Whether it's the first ride on a roller coaster or taking their first airplane flight, first time experiences are often the most memorable. I have a feeling this first encounter with Mary Coleman is going to be one of those firsts I remember for a long time to come.

The late afternoon sun is low in the sky and blinds me as I drive toward my appointment after work. I reduce the speed of the car and concentrate harder on my driving. The road veers to the left, changing the position of the sun's glare on me, and I return into my thoughts. Mary Coleman's house is easy to find: large, white and majestic on the open country road. It is a beautiful place, I notice as I walk up to the side door as I've been instructed. It's not what I imagined at all.

As I stand at the side entrance, I look out over the open fields across from Mary's house. I can smell the tilled sod drenched by recent rains. There's a moisture in the air that has me zip up my jacket. I hear a tractor in the distance as I knock on a large oak door.

"You must be Mark," a woman says warmly, opening the door for me. "I'm Mary Coleman. So nice to meet you."

"Yes, I'm Mark Bryant. I'm pleased to meet you, too." Mary shakes my hand gently and invites me in. Her hands are very warm, and she has piercing eyes that seem to almost look through me. Her hair is jet black without a trace of gray.

"You have a lovely home here."

"Thank you. Please, have a seat," Mary gestures toward the chair next to the large bay window. "Those are my grandchildren," she says as she sees me take a quick look at the photos on the desk.

"You have a nice looking family," I state politely, taking a closer look before moving to the chair by the window. The face of Jesus smiles at me from the painting across from where I sit. I settle into the chair and take out a notepad and my list of questions from my day planner. "I've only met one other psychic before," I admit. "How are these things done?"

"I refer to myself as an intuitive and not a psychic," she clarifies, handing me her business card from the table next to her, "because my intuition is what I use in my work."

"Intuitive Counselor," I read out loud, "I like that." I remember Vicki saying that Mary is well known for helping law enforcement agencies solve difficult cases. It's interesting to me that someone can make a living focusing on their intuition. I am quite the opposite. I have made my living focusing on my analytical skills. "I have some questions to ask you, but go ahead and do what you normally do," I say, wanting this to be authentic.

Mary sits across from me, her brown eyes looking deep into mine. "I suggest you hold your questions until I've done a complete reading for you."

"Okay." I'm anxious but my face shows a calm exterior.

She closes her eyes and begins; speaking for nearly half an

hour, she tells me one thing after another about myself. She talks about my physical body. "You need to take calcium and eat more dark leafy greens," she suggests at one point. I wonder if this has anything to do with me giving up milk? "And you might want to cut back on your running to decrease the impact it's having on your hip joints," she says. This is interesting because I haven't said anything about running. "Drink more water and fruit juices to help your digestion."

Mary continues speaking, only occasionally stopping to ask me a question. "Were you ever lost in the woods when you were a child?" she asks about midway into the session.

"Yes, I got lost on the side of a mountain," I confirm.

"Was there a white flag involved?"

"Yes," I repeat, surprised she picked up on this piece of detail. "I made a flag out of my white T-shirt on a long branch and climbed up on a large boulder in a clearing to wave it for my rescue."

"The emotional trauma of the incident still affects you," she explains, and we discuss it. My confidence in her is building. She tells it like it is but very respectfully and without judgment.

While Mary has her eyes closed, I take a quick glance around the room. Potted plants and green ferns are placed throughout the room. She must have a green thumb the way these plants are flourishing. Either that, or they like the abundance of psychic energy that must be in this room.

"You're holding on to resentment towards your wife in two areas," she says boldly. "This is keeping you two from being more intimate." I look at her with surprise and slightly ashamed that she sees something not in order.

"What are these two areas?" I ask cautiously.

"One area is the differences you two have around your current house. The second area is your wife's cautiousness about something you want to investigate." I feel uneasy about her comments, and I shift in my chair as she continues. "I highly recommend you take this feeling of resentment into prayer and begin to eliminate it. Mark, you don't need such a heavy heart around this, and you would be better served by spending more time communicating with her." I continue my silence. "Visualization techniques can also help with the resentment issue," she says.

I don't respond to Mary's comments about me being resentful, but she is absolutely right with her assessment. The truth is painful to hear. She continues to tell me things about myself in an almost script-like manner. It's as if she is reading everything off an invisible paper. Most of the time her eyes are closed. One comment after another flows out of her unrehearsed. She is remarkably candid and direct with her comments. Near the middle of the session she says, "I can see that you're a religious man."

I think about what she has said. I haven't told her that I go to church. It's almost as though she can see me in church, she is so good at this. A picture of Mother Mary hangs over her desk with rosary beads around it. Other religious relics are about the room. I wonder how someone can tell when another person is religious just by looking at them.

"So now, what are the questions you have for me?" Mary asks, opening her eyes. I sit back in my chair overwhelmed and contemplate my list. I'm somewhat unfocused for a few moments.

"I guess you've answered most of them already," I admit

truly amazed.

Mary laughs, her face softening at my bewilderment.

"Actually, I do have one question," I finally say. "It's one of the main reasons why I came here today. Some time ago I became ill. Can you tell me what that was about?"

"My sense about what you're asking, Mark, is that it wasn't really an illness at all—not a physical illness, not something that could be cured by a doctor. It was an illness from God to get your attention so that you'd make changes in your life. That's what I notice."

"Sort of like I fell asleep in order to wake up from a deeper sleep," I declare with a slight smile on my face.

"Exactly."

I listen intently to what she says, pondering the changes I have made since I first fell asleep. Can this be right? I ask myself.

"You know, there's one more thing, Mary," I say. "I'm interested in exploring areas such as metaphysics, holistic health, and the mind/body connection first hand. My wife calls it my personal quest."

"What's it a quest for?" Mary asks.

"Inner processes," I respond.

"I can see they're important to you, Mark."

"Mary, can you tell if this exploration is a positive direction for me?"

Before she can answer, the gold crucifix around her neck catches my attention. "Excuse me," I say to her, feeling more at ease. "Do you mind if I ask you a personal question?"

"Go right ahead."

"Are you Catholic?"

"Born and raised."

"How can you be Catholic and believe in this other area—this metaphysics?"

"The way I look at it, Mark, we're given these gifts from the Holy Spirit—the gift of healing, prophecy, second sight, telepathy, clairvoyance, etc. I have chosen to develop these gifts to help people. Still, I go to church every Sunday and believe in the Holy Trinity. Metaphysics does not interfere with my beliefs as a Catholic or vice versa. In fact, metaphysics enhances and brings alive the whole concept of God and my Catholic belief."

As Mary says this, I look around the room at the different religious artifacts. I hope that my own Christian beliefs can stay intact through this exploration. It's one of the main concerns I have about exploring metaphysics. I do feel that her Christian background and her being active in the Catholic Church, together with her understanding of metaphysics, are going to be very beneficial for me. There seems to be a match here already and an inescapable feeling that I was led to her by some greater force. Maybe it's the Force from "Star Wars," I think with a smile.

"Mark, this research, this spiritual growth looks like a very good thing for you. You could go a long way with it."

"Great."

"And just a suggestion," she adds. "As you start meeting and talking with other people in these fields, it's important that you proceed with a certain amount of caution and discernment. Be aware and careful about people's motives. And most importantly, keep it simple. Be patient with it. Some things take a while to understand."

"That makes sense," I reply, knowing I can't master this

overnight. "You said I could go a long way with it. What did you mean?" I laugh at myself and how naturally I ask this question. I want to know the future just as much as anyone. Does she see something coming up for me?

"Mark, all I mean is that I sense you have the will and commitment to collect higher knowledge and put it into practice," Mary responds. "Otherwise, I would have told you to think carefully before exploring metaphysics. One has to be ready to make sacrifices in the way they live. You have to be ready to align your agenda with God's agenda."

I like the idea of aligning with God's agenda, but I wonder what she means when she says you need to be ready to make sacrifices. Mary launches into a mini explanation of her comment. She tells me once you open the door of metaphysics and begin using the universal principles, you can't go back to the way you were. She says working with the spirit of God forces a person to shift gears and look at life in an altogether new way. Mary seems very committed to what she is saying. She's sort of fiery and compassionate at the same time.

Sounds a little like Pandora's box to me. If there really is no going back once you open the door, it's even more critical to do things gradually. I don't want to jump into things irresponsibly only to find I can't undo something. However, I do like the idea of using universal principles.

"You'll find that you see and feel events in a different way," Mary says. "That's really what I meant when I said that I saw you going a long way with it. It'll become part of your everyday life and you'll learn more about patience. Through patience, understanding is possible."

"All right."

Mary continues, "Remember, you're trying to understand the seen and unseen. Some things will sound sophisticated and others will appear esoteric. So try to see through them and get down to the spiritual basics. Keep focused on your spiritual growth and the course you've chosen for yourself."

Mary makes several other suggestions and counsels me on what to expect. She senses it would be better for me to do my exploring in a broader way rather than focusing on one specific area. In other words, don't get side-tracked on just one thing. She says there are a large number of areas that might not be worth my time and won't be useful to me. According to Mary, I'll know for myself which ones are useful and which aren't. She explains this is what she meant by discernment.

At the end of our session, Mary adds a final bit of advice. "One more thing is that it's important for you to take good notes, but it seems you already know that for yourself," she chuckles. I laugh too, tapping my pen on the notepad. "Take good notes, and be very precise with the information that you get. I'm not exactly sure why that is, but that's what I'm sensing."

"Thank you Mary, you've been very helpful. I really enjoyed our session," I say, reaching out to shake her hand when the session is over. She takes my hand then hugs me warmly.

"I know you're going to do fine with this," she says as she opens the door for me. "Just remember the importance of taking what you learn into prayer with you for guidance and inspiration from God. And again, keep it simple."

I walk to my car feeling the cool winter air against my face. As I get into my car to drive away, I feel exuberant. I don't know if I could have found a better match to help me with what it is I wish to learn. I like that she has a humble way about her.

Mary's comments are on my mind the entire drive home. It seems to me there is a fundamental difference between metaphysics and Christianity that somehow Mary has solved for herself. Metaphysics is a point of view about the universe and how it works. According to Mary, people into metaphysics seek a personal knowledge of the spirit of the "Higher Self" or God within. However, as a Christian, I've been taught to believe that God is external to us. Somehow, Mary is able to retain the relationship to God through Jesus Christ as well as believe God is within. It's going to take a while for me to decipher how this belief is possible.

Brotherly Advice

I often find myself thinking about the second half of my life. It's almost as if the sleep disorder happened during the half-time festivities of my life, and I still have the third and fourth quarters to play. It was a real wake-up call for me. I could easily have reached the later part of my life, still hard driving and possibly with serious health ailments. Instead, I'm meeting people like Mary Coleman, Beverly D'Urso, and Dr. Stanton, who are helping me to become more open to other aspects of my inner self.

As I consider adventuring further into unseen realms, I seek the advice of my older brother, Thom, short for Thomas. He is an architect by education and helps develop corporate campuses for large firms in Silicon Valley. He is exceptional at taking complex ideas and breaking them down to simplify them—a clear mark of genius.

At my brother's home to celebrate Christmas, I pull him aside. "Thom, I'd like your advice on something."

"Sure, let's go into the other room while the kids play in here," he suggests.

I follow Thom into the den just off the dining area. Everything in the room is laid out very precisely, which is very much the way Thom is. Even Thom's physical features have a sharpness to them, sort of like his mind. He's tall and has a lean muscular build. His physique still resembles that of the young carpenter framing houses during summer vacations from college. His eyes are steel blue, his hair dark. All in all he has taken good care of himself physically.

"So what's going on, Mark?" he asks. "Everything okay with you and Vicki?"

"Vicki and I are fine. You've probably heard I've begun to look into metaphysics, holistic health, and the whole mind/body connection field.

"Yeah, Vicki mentioned something about it at Thanksgiving," he says as we hear the muted sounds of the kids playing in the back yard.

"Any brotherly advice for me before I get caught hook, line, and sinker?" I say with a smile.

"Sounds like a spiritual awakening to me," Thom says.

"I guess that's one way to define it," I reply.

"I believe everyone goes through some kind of change as they approach mid-life," Thom continues. "It's a natural shifting into another phase in life. Gail Sheehy talks about this in her book *Passages*. It may be happening a little early for you, that's all."

Thom's comment makes me wonder if a spiritual awakening

is just a mid-life occurrence or crisis depending on the turn of events. The Lord knows I've seen a number of mid-life crises with work associates and friends. Even people who have spiritual guidance or religious support are likely to seek change at this point in their lives. It seems to me that when people approach their 40s and 50s, it's an irrational time for many. I have seen people doing some crazy things almost unconsciously, like changing cars, changing houses or spouses to try to satisfy themselves. They're always trying to change things on the outside, like the clothes they wear or their hairline, as opposed to changing something incomplete within themselves.

Breaking my train of thought Thom says, "Mark, I have three separate pieces of advice for you. Number one, while you're exploring, just remember that first and foremost you're a householder."

"A householder?" I question.

"Householder is an eastern term signifying the responsibility you've taken on as husband and father," Thom explains. "If you always keep this in crystal-clear focus, changes will be easier to handle. You've got young children, Mark, who will still be in school during the second part of your life, so you need to consider this as you explore these other areas."

"Seems straightforward enough."

"Yeah, it's simple really. Just stay focused with a purpose and explore these fields using your common sense."

"Okay."

We can hear all of the excitement and laughter that the Yuletide brings coming from the other room. The noise has risen to the level where it's hard for us to talk. Thom stands to close the French doors.

"Now, little brother, I have a question for you. You mentioned metaphysics. What's your definition of metaphysics?" Thom asks.

"Just like it sounds, meta....beyond, physics....the physical." I say. "I'd like to explore those areas that are beyond our everyday senses... like dreams, intuition, etc."

"Why?"

"I believe there's some connection to my sleep disorder, but I'm not quite sure what the correlation is."

"That's old news! Mark, you're beyond those sleeping spells."

"That's true, but I keep thinking that the sleeping disorder was a wake-up call of sorts. Kind of like an alarm going off to get me to pay attention to other areas of my life. It's caused me to begin to look for some inner processes out there that I can apply to my life. Processes that I haven't come into contact with in the business world."

"How do you expect to unearth these processes?" Thom asks, leaning back in his chair.

"That's the adventure part. I have to branch out and find them."

"How do you plan on handling your householder duties?" he asks.

"I'll work in the mornings and explore later in the afternoon. That's the plan right now," I say, unconvinced my brother is buying into this. He has that skeptical look on his face. It's that look that says, "I'll believe it when it happens." I'm not deterred. Most younger brothers are in competition to some degree with their older brothers. It's as if we're always striving to prove ourselves to them. Thom sits quietly sizing up the situation.

"Thom, you said there were three pieces of advice you had for me. You gave me one, the householder advice. What are the others?"

"One is to use caution as you explore the spiritual aspects of these fields," he says with a straight face. "In this unseen world beyond the physical, I firmly believe there are spiritual entities around, and they're not all out there looking after your best interest. Bottom-line, Mark, all spiritual entities have their own agendas."

Why did he throw that in? I ask myself. This seems as if it came out of left field. "What do you mean by that, Thom?"

"All I mean is don't be disillusioned if these forces work for their own purpose and not for yours."

"Trying to scare me off, huh, big brother?"

"Just make sure it's your own inner guidance and not the influence of another unseen force. Don't get taken in by a spirit working through a channeler or fall into the habit of employing a psychic as a crutch. Go with what sounds right to you!"

"Okay."

"I just don't want you to lose sight of the things that are important to you, Mark. That's the key issue here!"

"I appreciate that. And the last piece of advice?"

"If I were you, I'd read up on spirituality in business in parallel with these other fields you have in mind. You know you're always going to be in business, so why not try to make your research inclusive of this."

"That's a good idea, Thom."

"Margaret Wheatley's *Leadership and the New Science* is a good example of a book that bridges two separate domains. In her case it's business and science, but you know what I mean. If you can find books on business *and* spirituality, I think your research will be more satisfying because you can apply some of this stuff in the workplace too."

"I like it. And I've always enjoyed these types of books to boot," I add.

"Tom Chappel's, *The Soul of a Business* is a another example of what I'm talking about. Now then, I have a couple of contacts who might be of help," Thom continues. "I believe Buckminster Fuller wrote a book on intuition. You might want to call his institute in Santa Barbara and check on this. Another person I think you may find interesting is a friend of mine who publishes the national magazine *Gnosis*. He publishes articles in several of the areas you're looking into. I'll get his telephone number for you."

Thom gets up to get the number.

"Just don't tell him you're my brother," Thom says facetiously. "He might cancel my subscription."

———

Hidden Asset

There are times when we have to be willing to change our frame of reference in order to learn.

Chapter Five

———❦———

Experiencing "Whole Life" Processes

The Whole Life Movement

It has always fascinated me to see which profession a person chooses for their career path. What it is that motivates a person towards one career when clearly they might do just as well or better in another field? Is it some form of childhood desire, or is it more opportunity driven? This then has made me wonder if there is some greater life plan for everyone and how attuned or aware we are of this plan. These are some of the questions I hope to explore further.

It has just stopped raining, and the sun is breaking through and reflecting off the windows of the Transamerica pyramid building in the distance. It's rather cold for this time of year in San Francisco. Usually, you can expect milder weather during the winter months in the city by the bay. Even the ubiquitous seagulls have taken to warmer shelter. I turn to the map inside the brochure I received at the entrance to the Whole Life Exhibit Hall.

"Anything here interest you?" I ask Gary.

"A lot of interesting and different stuff," Gary replies, reviewing his brochure. "Uhm, I probably lean more towards the health-related topics."

Gary Robinson is my partner and CEO of a construction company we founded. He has been a trusted friend of mine since high school, or as he likes to say, "we have a long term unconditional friendship." His personal interest in maintaining good health led to his decision to accompany me to this weekend exposition. Gary is fun to have along because he is good-natured and open to new ideas. He has a stocky build, curly and often ruffled brown hair, and a ruddy face. In a way he is like a kid in a man's body.

Whole Life Expos are held across the country in various large cities. The concept behind the Whole Life Expo is to bring together, in one facility, people and companies with products and services that enrich a person's life. These include everything from companies that sell blue-green algae and spirulina to psychics and healers.

"Gary, I'm thinking about this lecture on intuition in the workplace and the one on chakra therapy. Maybe there's a third one in the health category that we can sit in on together," I propose.

"This one on nutrition looks like it might be worthwhile," Gary says with a smirk. "I'll ask the nutritionist to check to see if I'm low on zinc."

"Very funny," I counter. "It's early. Let's look around awhile."

As we enter the pavilion, I distinctly recall the first of these Expos I attended. Originally, I had thought they might be on the outer fringe of practicality, maybe even a bit of a farce. In actuality, I was able to find out about quite a few different practices that have been very good for my family and me. I think if this hadn't been the case, I would never have asked Gary to come along with me to this one. As we continue through the ticket counter area, the director of the Whole Life Expo, whom I have recently met and interviewed, approaches and gives me a hug.

"It's good to see you again, Mark," the man says.

"How are you?" I respond, now accustomed to this form of greeting in the whole-life community, although I am still not one to instigate a hug with another man. Gary, standing nearby, is taken off guard when my acquaintance turns to him. I wish I had brought a camera to record the expression on Gary's face as this man wraps his arms around Gary's six foot one, linebacker type frame. Judging by his expression, I would guess that Gary must be wondering something like, "What's happening here? Who is this guy?" Gary handles the situation in a friendly way even though it's an awkward moment for him.

"See ya," I say to the man afterwards, and we begin to maneuver our way through the large room filled to overflowing with a variety of booths. I'm glad we ran into this guy. He explained the Whole Life movement as an environment that showcases services and products on natural health, personal growth, spirituality, and global change. Since there are almost a thousand booths to choose from, Gary and I shouldn't have a problem finding things that are interesting to us. The first thing I notice as we enter the large pavilion is the smell of incense and candles in the air; a sort of sweet fragrance with a touch of burning smell.

"Would you like a free ten-minute Reiki treatment?" a young man asks as we approach his booth. "You'll feel great afterwards."

"No, thanks," I reply, "I've already tried it, and you're right. It's very nice," I add, recollecting my first Reiki treatment. The Reiki practitioner had been able to pick up on an energy blockage near my right elbow. It didn't occur to me until after the treatment that the practitioner had focused on a troublesome nerve injury sustained years ago in a college scrimmage.

"How about you, then?" he asks Gary.

"What's Reiki?" Gary asks suspiciously, giving me a quick glance.

"Reiki is a form of healing based on utilizing life force energy," the young man explains.

"Sure, why not?" Gary says. "You go ahead, Mark, I'll catch up with you." Gary climbs onto the massage table. I am immensely pleased Gary is keeping an open mind. This makes the entire experience more enjoyable for me.

I wander around looking at the people attending the Expo— there are people of all ages. I soon discover a booth displaying colorful stones. "That's lapis azul," the woman behind the table informs me when I hold the cool, smooth stone in my hand. "It enhances your intuitive abilities and your communication when you wear it against your skin."

"Really, that's interesting," I reply. I don't say it, but I've always been of the opinion that stones and crystals were what made this show sound too new-age. The term "new age" has a really negative connotation these days, possibly due to the commercialization of what was once believed to be sacred.

Further down the aisle I notice a colorful poster. "Reflexology," it says, as I get close enough to read it. "Each area of the sole of the foot represents and corresponds to an organ within the body," a friendly woman informs me. I pick up a flier and read the top line: "Reflexology is used to relieve stress and tension and promotes the unblocking of nerve impulses to normalize and balance the entire body." This might be good for me to try out on Vicki and the kids.

"I also have a corresponding chart for the hands," the woman says.

I examine the charts and purchase one of each. "Is it related to palm reading?"

"No. By the way, palm reading is called 'hand analysis' by most people today," she clarifies. "Have you ever had your hands analyzed?"

"No, I was just curious if there was a possible association between the two."

"Stop by the hand analysis booth at the end of this aisle. I'm sure you'll find a reading interesting," she says.

At first I'm put off by this woman's suggestion. I guess I've always associated things like palm reading and tea leaves as techniques for predicting the future. Right now I have enough to work on in the present without being worried about the future. But there is something about this woman's honesty that catches my attention. I continue meandering through the booths before stopping at a psychic's booth. After a short reading, I continue my travels through the aisles, stopping at one or two more booths. I take the advice of the reflexologist and stop at a hand analysis booth. A woman is sitting at the side of a small table. Her card and brochure say she is a television host for a local cable channel. Her program is about psychic phenomena. She is not busy at the moment and is observing the crowd. I step up to her table and ask for a reading. For the next fifteen minutes she lets loose with everything from my personality to what is going to happen to me in the next five years.

Gary catches up to me as my reading concludes. "How did it go?" he asks.

"It was interesting," I reply. "She told me I had two major gifts."

"Two? What are they?"

"In a nutshell, she said I have a ruthlessly judicious mind that would serve me well in the business world and also that I have a compassionate heart."

"No way," he says and laughs. "Just kidding. Actually, that does sound a lot like you."

"Thanks, Gary. The lady went on to say these two gifts could work together very nicely, or they could contradict each other, and one might dominate. She said to be aware of that."

"Sounds like a challenge to me," Gary says. "Did you hit any other booths?"

"I had another psychic reading and also talked with a sound therapy practitioner."

"What did the psychic say?" Gary asks.

I shrug. "She said I came from a planet where they like to argue a lot."

"Another planet! Come on, you're kidding me!"

"She was dead serious about it. She said she could see into these other worlds."

Gary laughs, "I always wondered why you were so argumentative. How do you use this type of information?"

"I can't. What would you do with information about being from a different planet? But I'm not dismayed. I've come across a number of people whose information I just can't use effectively. It's good for me to find out that you can't utilize everything," I say.

"How about the sound therapy? Any luck there?"

"This lady was much more interesting to me. I've scheduled an appointment for next week to see her at her office. She has a sounding device hooked up to a table."

"What's it supposed to do?" Gary asks.

"According to her, certain sounds can do things like slow your breathing and reduce blood pressure and muscle tension."

"No kidding."

"Somehow, she uses a 'sound table' to produce a frequency that's beneficial for your body. She said after the session she'll make me a tape of this sound to take home. That way I can get this same sounding benefit at home. Pretty neat, huh?"

"I guess it is if this stuff really works. I'm not sure you can measure its effectiveness. Mark, how do you know you're getting your money's worth and that the tape really works?"

"That's the 64,000 dollar question, isn't it?"

As we weave in and out of aisles, we separate again and Gary heads towards the nutrition section. I hear a large clapping noise one aisle over. I make my way through the crowds and spot a large muscular man and an athletic looking woman together demonstrating a type of cord used for stretching. As I stand in front of them, I recall how several intuitives, including one today, suggested that I stretch more to complement my running. One thing that I'm discovering is that when I hear the same thing a number of times from different sources, I should pay attention to it. Some say it's the universe speaking. My own sense of this is that other people are using their inner guidance to give me advice. Nevertheless, it does make me wonder about God's use of other people to help me change areas of my life for the better.

I watch as the woman with the athletic build does an exercise with the cord wrapped around her wrists and the soles of her feet. I know how much Vicki enjoys stretching so I buy one of the cords.

"Hey, there's one of those neck massage benches," Gary notices when he finds me again. "I'd like to give that a try."

"Sounds good to me. I can go for some relaxation. By the way, did you get any more of those hugs while I was gone?" I tease him. He holds up his fist to me, and we laugh.

We place our names on a list next to the massage table and are told to come back in thirty minutes for our turn.

"Let's grab one of those tofu burgers while we wait, " Gary suggests.

"I think I'll stick to fruit smoothies!"

"Oh, that reminds me. I want to check out those juicers I saw back over there," Gary points behind us. We move towards the whirring sound of juicing and see a man on a stand with a hands-free mike hooked around his ear. He offers Gary and me a sample of a blend of banana, strawberry and kiwi in small paper cups. I drink mine down quickly, telling him I like the combination. Gary picks up literature on juice therapy from the counter and reads it. It is titled, "The Use of Raw Juice of Fruits and Vegetables to Nourish and Replenish the Body." The information persuades him to purchase a juicer. Gary has always loved fresh juices for as long as I can remember. I had talked to him about juice therapy as part of regular health regimen, and I am glad to see him take an active step in this direction.

Later, as I sit in the lecture hall, I thumb through the Expo program guide waiting for the speaker to appear. I recognize the importance of screening the information and determining how I can apply it. A lot of systems and information are enticing but not applicable to me, and there could be a temptation to dabble. Many of the systems like astrology, numerology, I Ching, and others, seem to be based on a mathematical model of some sort. These systems are a departure from the intuitives and healers who appear to be employing a form of psychic or healing energy.

I don't plan to spend as much time with these ancient esoteric systems. Although it does seem clear that some people are able to strengthen their intuition by using these age-old systems. It's a paradox of sorts to me. For example, how does an astrologer see the characteristics and temperaments of my children from looking at my chart? It is not at all clear to me how this can be done mathematically, so there must be something else at work here. Is it their intuition? I should have Gary evaluate these systems, since he was a math major in college. I'm sure this would be quite an encounter for him, just like the hug earlier today.

Creative Intuition in Counting Balloons

There is something about mediocrity that can bring out the worst in people. It seems my entire life I've been overly concerned about making mental mistakes at the risk of being less than perfect. It's a quality just short of being a perfectionist. I find spending time with children has helped me overcome some of this attitude.

It's my scheduled day to help in my son's kindergarten class. Early morning sunlight shines through the classroom window. It's chilly outside, and the children hurry inside to get warm. I've swapped the morning time period with another room "parent" because I have a corporate luncheon in San Jose and need to leave mid-morning. My son Jonathan and his classmates put away their coats and lunch pails and rush to their designated squares on a large colorful mat. Sitting crossed-legged on the rug, Jonathan leans forward to gaze down at the paper his teacher has handed him. A drawing of a clown, holding a bouquet of circus balloons, fills most of the page.

"All right, now count the number of balloons in the picture," the teacher instructs the children. Jonathan examines the picture closely, as do all the other children.

"Just do your best," their teacher instructs. Many kids raise their hands for help, and that's where I come in. As a parent-helper, I guide the kids without giving them the answers. After about five minutes, she announces, "Okay, everyone turn in your paper now." They finish counting and pass their papers to the front of the room where the other parent-helper collects them.

"Let's count the balloons together," the teacher says. "Here are four in front, then this one behind the tree makes five, and see these others here on top of the sign—six, seven, eight…. So, there's one more, can anyone find it?"

"The red one that's mostly covered," one girl calls out.

"That's correct. Thank you. All together we have twenty-seven balloons. How did we do?" the teacher asks, looking toward the other parent-helper.

"There was one child who got the correct answer," she replies, "and that's Jonathan Bryant."

"Very good, Jonathan. Would you please come up front and show us how you counted the balloons?" He grins and gallops to the front of the class where he turns to face the other children. "Now, Jonathan, how were you able to count the balloons correctly?" she asks in her teaching voice.

He digs his hands into his pockets and answers shyly, "Oh, I didn't count the balloons."

"What?" she says with surprise. "You didn't?"

"No," he replies, looking up at her, "I counted the strings."

"You counted the strings?" she says, looking at me. "That's very clever, Jonathan," she says. "It's a very creative solution."

Later that afternoon when we're at home I ask my son, "Jonathan, how did you know to count the strings?"

He thinks for a moment. "It just came to me, Dad, to do it that way," he replies with a shrug.

I am both delighted and awed by the incident. It reminds me of how open children's minds are. It's so hard for me to see these childlike qualities in myself. Although, instinctively I know I had them at one time. I hope Jonathan never loses the open mind of a child.

I make an effort to wrestle Jonathan down to one knee to capture the spirit of child's play. Jonathan is very energetic and has a long angular body similar to Vicki's younger brother Rich. He wraps his arms around my neck and pulls me over backwards. I grab hold of his leg and pretend I'm giving him a body slam.

"What's that pledge about mistakes?" I ask Jonathan, letting him escape from my hold.

Jonathan jumps up and calls out confidently, "I'm not afraid to make mistakes because I learn by them!" He tackles my legs and shouts triumphantly as I let him pin me.

We've created pledges as sort of affirmations. With these pledges we're trying to help the kids not be afraid to try new ways of doing things. If they get so caught up with worrying about making a mistake, they won't grow. Some of the time growing is about making mistakes. I am happy that Jonathan is putting this pledge into practice (as his answer to the balloon problem so clearly indicated).

I have to laugh to myself, though, when I wonder how the kids feel about their dad bringing home new pledges. Recently Vicki told me our children think all dads go on adventures like this, which made me roar with laughter. But behind all the fun, the main thing I'm learning is how our fears around making mistakes can inhibit our natural intuitive approach to solving problems. This is a critical thing for me to remember whenever I get down on myself for making a mistake. To think I'm learning this concept through my son makes me feel good inside. Kind of like my dad must feel when he learns something from me.

I suppose some people might say that Jonathan's incident was more imagination than intuition. What is the link here? Does creativity come from the desire to find a solution which then leads to an intuitive answer? Is intuition really just psychic impressions put into creation? Perhaps business acumen is intuition in disguise. It seems to me that it was intuition that helped Jonathan exercise his imagination.

As I review the situation, Jonathan's assignment was to find the correct answer, NOT to find a new way. Yet he did discover a different way of doing something. This is very much how intuition seems to work for people in everyday life. It enables them to discover new and different ways of doing something.

Teaching the Right Brain to Talk

The illusion of instantaneous enlightenment is often heightened by market-savvy individuals and companies. They would have you believe you can have enlightenment overnight. As part of my continuing quest to venture inward, I'm careful to look for people who understand the larger, and often times, longer process of increasing one's awareness. If it's possible, I meet with people in person whenever I can. But there are times, when I talk to people by telephone.

With my agenda in front of me, I shut my office door and dial Karen Kenney's Arizona phone number. Karen does intuitive counseling over the telephone. I distinctly recall it was a business person who gave me Karen's name as a referral. I remember it surprised me that a business executive would have such a number. Maybe this is more common than I realize, and business people haven't come out of the closet yet.

I turn the thermostat up, loosen my tie, and lean back in my chair. As the telephone rings, I think how Karen's biggest influence has been helping me to understand myself. She sees my inner self so well that she can give me counsel on how a particular situation is affecting me at a deep level. She does all of this with a marvelous sense of humor that keeps our meetings light-hearted. She has a tremendous amount of experience and wisdom and many techniques to draw on for use in our sessions.

"Are you ready for our two o'clock session?" I ask her as the connection is made.

"Of course," Karen replies.

I'm still amazed at how young her voice sounds. The first time we spoke on the telephone, I assumed she was in her twenties. In reality she is closer to my age and is a mother of two teenagers. The resonance in her voice is very soothing.

"Karen, I meant to ask you last time, how long have you been doing intuitive work?"

"For about twenty years, full time. And, for the record, being

intuitive simply means teaching the right brain to talk," she
clarifies.

"I haven't heard intuition described that way before."

"It's the way I like to describe it. Intuition is a right-brain
skill, just as analytical thinking is a skill associated with the left
side of the brain," she explains. "Many people think that the right
brain can't talk, and that's not true. You can teach it to talk. One
of the things I'll do for my dissertation is to demonstrate how to
teach the right brain to talk."

"That sounds intriguing."

"I believe it's a skill that would benefit more people if they
developed it," Karen says.

"How so?"

"People's minds would be so much more flexible if they
developed their right brains. What's needed is to teach the right
brain how to think laterally, in a consecutive way, then put
language to it. That's what being intuitive is really all about."

I remember a book I read many years ago called *Drawing
From the Right Side of the Brain*. I really liked that book. I wonder
if the concepts in it are similar to what Karen is talking about. As
I recall, the exercises in the book are all about helping you to
integrate the two sides of your brain in order to become a better
artist.

"Mark, intuition is a right-brain skill. The same is true for
clairvoyance," she continues. "Remember the Renaissance artists
who painted auras around holy men and women? These guys
really sensed or saw those auras using their right brains. The great
thing is that anyone can do it. Everybody does it, in fact. They
just don't have the language to communicate it. So in many ways,

it doesn't become conscious."

It's coincidental that Karen should mention this. Recently, the kids have been asking about these halos or auras around the saints on the cover of the church bulletins. I've told them basically the same thing Karen has said. However, the kids want to know why they can't see these auras around people. It's a fair question for me to explore with Karen in the future. I move the receiver from my left ear to my right and shift in my chair.

"What you're doing, Mark, is trying to discover and express who you are by exploring some of these areas," Karen explains.

I consider this and then ask, "Why is discovering who I am important?"

"Let's keep it simple," she suggests. "You have a lot of validation in business. You can set up reliable structures, set up a good business, make money, feel secure, feel successful, and there's still a part of you that says, okay, who am I? There's been a lot of success for you in business, but, in a way, it's not enough for you, is it?"

"That's true," I confirm.

"Okay. Now if I put this on a totally physical level and relate it to the brain, you've worked with your left brain and become successful. You know your way around your left brain, and there aren't too many secrets. Right?"

"Right."

"More recently, you've been working on the right brain a lot," Karen continues. "You're finding that you need to understand and develop this side of yourself. Eventually, you will find you'll need to go back to the left side again because the left side is what creates things in the world. What I see is that you're not really interested in or willing to work on just one side or the other. In a way, what you're trying to do is get both sides to work, which I think is optimal. There is that left brain that says: 'Hey, I'm handling things fine' while the right brain is kind of an explorer for you. Does that makes sense to you?"

"Yes, it does."

"You're working with the whole brain," Karen elaborates. "The best thing is to be able to go back and forth at will. This is the same way you'd work with your children, wouldn't you? You don't want to say, 'Now just be in the left brain, and give up all the right brain and don't go back.' If you said this to your children, you'd be creating a barrier in them."

"Yes, I see that," I say, recognizing the significance of the "whole" in Whole Life Expo for the first time. This hadn't really dawned on me when I was at the Whole Life show but now it makes a lot of sense. I lean back in my chair and wonder if it's people like me that the Whole Life Expo organizers are trying to reach.

"Now, you've been meeting some right-brained people who don't incorporate the left brain, and what do you see?" she asks.

"I see some people who're highly intuitive, yet are struggling to make a daily living," I reply.

"They aren't creating a whole lot in the physical sense, are they?" Karen asks.

"No."

"Why do you think this is?" she demands.

I hazard a guess, "I suspect they've done the exact opposite of what I've done. They've worked with their right brain and become highly intuitive, whereas I concentrated on my left brain and became successful in creating physical stuff."

"What do you think needs to change?" she asks.

"I suppose the right-brain people need to work on the left-brain skills in the same way I'm working on the right-brain skills," I answer.

"Bingo!" Karen exclaims. "And yet you've also met plenty of left-brain people who're creating a lot of physical things, but they forget why they're creating them. The answer is that it's not really one side or the other, you really need both ways of thinking—working together. Somewhere along the way you thought you had to choose one over the other. In doing this," she continues, "you left a big part of yourself out. You hadn't quite learned the ability to step outside your comfort zone in order to expand and create. This is another attribute of whole thinking."

Karen asks me to hold on while she turns over the tape. Even though I can't see her, I imagine she has this intricate recording process all set up in advance. She seems very efficient.

When she comes back on the line, I ask her, "So the goal is to be able to use both sides of my brain and become a whole thinker?"

"Yes, I think that's your underlying purpose: to be able to have a good integration between the right and left sides, and to be able to shift freely," Karen concludes.

We continue talking for another twenty minutes before I hang up. Five years ago I would have said this right brain/left brain stuff was irrational; it isn't useful in business. But now, as I keep on learning, I feel that it's important to incorporate more whole thinking in business.

Hidden Asset

**Very often we feel we have to choose
intellect over intuition.**

Chapter Six

Acquiring an Intuitive Edge

An Experience with a Guru

It's always hard to pinpoint the exact moment when winter changes to spring. One reliable sign is the appearance of bright orange poppies on the hillsides and meadows. On what's starting out as a beautiful day, I've been invited to have a private audience with a spiritual teacher with a local following. Accompanying me is a friend named Julie. Julie and I originally met at a talk given by Barbara Marx Hubbard, the well-known speaker with books on concepts like the *universal human*. Julie is a member of the local Unity Church and has introduced me to the pastor and other members of her church. Even though I am a member of the Lutheran Church, I find the people at Unity very warm and friendly.

As we drive along, we talk about the exciting work that Barbara Marx Hubbard is undertaking. I've known Julie now for about six months. She is in her thirties and extremely attractive. She has the type of looks that can make you feel self-conscious and almost uncomfortable to be around.

The private meeting we're attending is being given by a spiritual teacher visiting from the Southwest. He has a celestial name, but I'll call him Monk. He was big in the 70s and has since dropped out of the mainstream spiritual movement. He still has hundreds of followers. Monk has a spirit that he channels and this spirit is supposed to be a very high being. We're both excited as we understand it is very rare to have a private session. Yet, I'm still wondering why we were given this opportunity, and to be honest, I'm a little suspicious. This special session with Monk came about because he came up to our group after a talk he gave in San Francisco. Julie and I were with a group of other people from the Unity church. Monk said he was willing to give Julie and me a private audience later in the weekend before he headed back down south. It surprised me that he picked Julie and me out of this group. I wondered if he was going around the auditorium doing this with other people.

Despite Vicki's admonition about 'no gurus', I'm eager to have a session with Monk to find out what he has to offer. Ordinarily, I'm not into movements like this but this is an opportunity to find out more about a spiritual leader. It's not like meeting the Pope or the Dali Lama, but Monk still has a large following within the spiritual community. Julie and I continue to talk as we drive to a private residence in Marin. Monk is staying with some of his followers in a large, magnificent home in a remote wooded area.

We pull up to the home and find a place to park. There are cars everywhere. Many of Monk's followers are staying here for the weekend. We are escorted into the home and asked to take our shoes off. When we were asked to visit I assumed that Julie and I together would sit and talk with Monk. However, I quickly find out that the group has other ideas. We are to see Monk separately. Well, no big deal, it will give me more of a chance to ask the type of questions I'm interested in.

One of Monk's helpers, a young woman dressed in a

flowing gown, escorts me in first to meet with Monk. The smell of incense is strong as I enter a room at the end of the hall. I sit on a throw rug in front of Monk, who is sitting on a large variety of quilted pillows. I ask him how he wants to do this. He invites me to ask my questions first. I'm glad, because I like to control the agenda. I immediately launch into my typical questions. How long has he been into this stuff? What does he offer people? Why did he get into the spiritual movement? etc.

Monk answers my questions but tires of them rather quickly. He then has his own questions for me. His first question surprises me.

"Are you and Julie together?" he asks.

"We came together, but we're not a couple if that's what you mean." My inner voice sets off a little red flag. "Julie is happily married and so am I. We came together only because it's a two-hour drive here and we thought it would be nice to drive together."

"Good," he says and leaves it at that.

For the next thirty minutes, Monk proceeds to ask me about my business endeavors. He is very curious about my financial holdings. Again I find this odd, but I am very straight forward with him. At the end of our session he asks me if I would like to partner with him in a warehousing business in Arizona. I thank him but say I have my hands full with my current ventures.

Then there is a knock on the door, and I am escorted out of the room. Another of Monk's helpers takes me to a room on the other side of the house. I pass Julie in the hallway as she is being led in to see Monk. I roll my eyes up as if to say "big deal" and continue to walk on. I'm taken into a room and told to listen to angelic music. I'm a little bored but I expect it's the normal treatment one gets at this type of community. I sit quietly on a couch for what seems like an hour before the attendant returns. She tells me it is time to go. As I follow her back down the hall to the front door, I am struck by the fact that I've seen only women attendees.

I put my shoes on and walk outside. Julie is outside waiting for me. She looks frightened and asks very softly if we can leave. There are several people hanging around outside on the deck, and I assume she doesn't want them to hear her. Since I drove, I tell her sure, and we walk to my car.

As we're driving down the long windy road back to the freeway, I ask her how her session went.

"I'd rather not talk about it," she says.

"All right," I say, a little surprised by her demeanor.

We drive on for about ten minutes without talking. We don't even talk about the weather or kids or our spouses. It's not like Julie; she's a very gregarious person. Finally, I ask, "Are you okay?"

"No, I'm not," she replies

"What's the matter?"

"I feel Monk tried to take advantage of me." she says quietly.

I'm stunned! I don't know what to say. I grip the steering wheel tightly. Immediately, I think back to the question Monk asked me about Julie and me being together. "What happened?" I ask, beginning to get a little worked up about this.

"He told me that he could see my soul and that I was attracted to him," she says slowly. "Mark, did you sit next to him on the pillows?"

"Of course not!" I reply. "You didn't sit with him up there, did you?" I ask, now really getting mad.

"Yes, I did. The attendant said to sit there and then Monk came in and sat by me."

I tell Julie I'd like to turn the car around and confront Monk about this. I have a temper and in situations like this its hard to control. I'm mad at myself for not picking up on some of the signs that this was happening.

"Let's just get out of here," she says.

We don't talk for a long while. I'm steaming inside that this happened. Julie is happily married with a son and a daughter. I feel as if I should have turned around even when she said not to.

"What else happened?" I demand to know.

"All I can say is I could feel him trying to get inside my head. I know that sounds crazy but that's what it felt like. He asked me to lie there with my eyes closed. I really felt he was going to do something. I believe he might have if you hadn't been down the hall." Julie begins to cry.

My heart is ripped. I enjoy Julie as a friend and should never have let her go in there alone. I should have used my intuition to sense Monk was up to something. I felt something wasn't right, but I couldn't put my finger on it. Monk is headed back home tomorrow so there isn't time to say anything to him. What would I say, anyway? I can't bring myself to ask Julie about any more details because I can see she's really shaken by all of this. After about twenty minutes of silence, Julie speaks up and changes the subject to talk about her children. She tells me about the drawings her son is doing in school. She asks me not to say anything to Rob, her husband, when I see him next. I agree to this but feel cheated somehow in my heart.

My mind jumps back to my brother's admonition that everyone

has their own agenda. I don't know if this action was that of Monk's or the spirit he channels, but it clearly was about a physical attraction to Julie. Sure, Julie is attractive but it doesn't give anyone the right to take advantage of her. How would I feel if this had happened to Vicki? I learned a good lesson today. People who are spiritual face the same temptations as those who are not.

Telepathy: An Uncharted Arena

What is it that enables two people to connect deeply with one another almost right from the start? This has always been a mystery to me. The process is usually very gradual and is normally built on a combination of things, such as time spent together, common beliefs, etc. However, occasionally a strong connection with someone seems almost instantaneous.

While sitting in a movie theater waiting to see the latest blockbuster, Vicki and I talk about people in our lives whom we have liked right off, almost as if we have known them for a long time. We agree this is how we felt about each other when we met for the first time. My relationship with Mary Coleman is another example of this instant connection. There seems to be a bond between us not based on the way relationships are usually formed.

My sessions with Mary have been of particular interest to Vicki, so much so that she decided to make an appointment herself. I am pleased that Vicki has chosen to do this. I coach her beforehand on how to ask questions and inform her about Mary's unique gifts. By having Vicki see Mary, I get an objective view of her abilities.

"I actually enjoyed my session with Mary," Vicki relays to

me while the local advertisements flash across the movie screen. "I have to be honest, it took a lot to convince me Mary had the type of gifts you talked about."

"I'm glad you were convinced," I say.

"Oh, that reminds me. I have to tell you the intriguing part," Vicki adds.

"Yeah?"

"About halfway through the session, Mary stopped talking mid-sentence and informed me that something else was coming in. She said information was coming in about gymnastics. I was puzzled at first because I really didn't know what she was talking about. Then I glanced at my watch and realized all at once I'd forgotten Allison's gymnastics lesson. I used Mary's telephone and called the gymnastics teacher to say Allison wouldn't be coming. The teacher said she had just been wondering where Allison was moments before I called. When I told this to Mary, she said that it must have been the teacher's thoughts that she was picking up on. Then she continued with the session. Fascinating, huh?"

"Yes, it is," I reply. "Mary is so used to being telepathic that she doesn't think twice about it." The movie theater is just about full. I look around to see if other people sitting close to us are listening to what Vicki has said. I'm still a little uncomfortable talking about these phenomena in front of other people. Especially people I don't know. No one seems to be paying attention to us, and most people are enjoying quiet conversations.

"Vicki, it appears to me that a number of evolved intuitives have this ability similar to Mary's picking up on the gymnastics teacher's thoughts. It's an occurrence where a person can send and receive information by means other than the normal senses."

"I don't know if I'd go that far," Vicki replies.

"Seriously. Remember a month ago when I was really irritated with an incident at work? A potential client had done something that I thought was underhanded—saying one thing while doing the opposite. I was pretty stressed over it, and it was really affecting my concentration and emotions. Remember?"

"I remember."

"Well, there's an interesting footnote to the story." I look around the theater to make sure I'm not talking too loud in my excitement. "That evening when I got home, there were messages from both Karen Kenney and Mary Coleman. When I checked the time of the calls on my message unit, they were within ten minutes of each other."

"You're kidding," Vicki says.

"Isn't it interesting that both of these women had picked up on my vibration almost at the same time?"

"Sounds more than just coincidental," Vicki offers.

"They both sensed my hostilities around this incident. Somehow they were using telepathy or a hypersensitive ability to accurately perceive thoughts and emotions. It's quite a remarkable faculty that they've developed."

"Amazing!" she agrees.

"Wait-a-minute...I'm getting something telepathically," I utter. "It feels like pop..pop, yes it's popcorn."

"Oh, stop! Okay, I'll go get some popcorn," Vicki says as she steps into the aisle.

When she returns, I talk about other unusual experiences I've had over the past few months. Some are strange, almost scary, while others are quite remarkable. It is much easier for Vicki to accept some of these things now that she has first-hand experience of them.

Meaningful Road Signs

I've come to believe there is a warrior element in my nature that made it essential for me to go into business. This Mars-like characteristic took hold of me early and continues to shape my life even now. Nevertheless, as I've continued my adventure, a second element of a more intuitive nature is stirring within me. This intuitive nature might well have always been part of me, yet now I am seemingly more conscious of it. Even my old friends can detect a change in me.

Following a business meeting, I have lunch with my business mentor, Michael Smith, who is the founder and CEO of a large national distribution company. He is an astute businessman who has been successful in several ventures. We have known each other now for twenty years. Most people see Michael strictly as a successful businessman, and they don't realize he has worked tirelessly behind the scenes to support a battered women's association for many years.

Michael was the first person to take a chance on me and invested in my first company. His manicured good looks and thin physique give him a very youthful appearance. He could easily pass for my age or younger, I think as we make our way to a table at a local Chinese restaurant. It's a balmy day so Michael and I choose a table by the window across from a large salt-water aquarium.

"I'll have the chicken salad," I order.

"Make it two," says Michael. He hands the menu back to the waiter who returns quickly with a pot of green tea. "Any sleep episodes lately?" he asks.

I sip the tea. "No, not in a long while, thank goodness. I'm back to my normal self, although I'm paying much closer attention to my overall health. I only wish I had been more mindful of my health earlier."

"You always seemed like a fairly healthy guy to me."

"Yeah, but there were road signs along the way that I didn't pay attention to."

"Road signs?"

"Yes. Things that happened where my intuition was trying to help me along, and I chose to ignore it." I say feeling much more at ease in talking about this now.

"Your intuition?" Michael asks.

"Looking back, and aware of what I know now, I believe my intuition was attempting to break through and warn me to take time for myself or suffer the consequences. I just plain ignored it."

"Are you saying the repercussion was the sleeping disorder?" he asks.

"I think so," I admit. "It's like the saying, 'pride goeth before a fall.' I was too proud of myself and the life I had built to pay attention to the road signs."

It's a whole lot easier to be open with Michael about this situation. I'm feeling less invincible than I once did. I find it soothing to talk about this subject to my mentor, a man who invested so much time preparing me for the business world.

"What were some of these road signs?" he asks between bites.

"One unmistakable sign was the lack of intimacy with people, even with you—and I owe you so much," I confess. Mike graciously acknowledges what I'm talking about. I go on to explain how I began to work incessantly by starting more companies that required a reach for me to be successful. I admit to him I always felt like I was behind and not doing enough. I felt I just could never catch up. Mike and I both realize these comments aren't unique but are general signs of stress.

Mike pours us some water from a pitcher on the table. I tell him the road signs involved all aspects of my life. I was exercising less. My diet deteriorated to snacking and eating in my car while on the run between meetings. My spiritual life had stopped expanding. I admit remembering how linear and narrow I'd become.

"I thought I would have been the last person to fall into this trap of becoming too narrowly focused," I say.

"How's it that you see these road signs now?" he asks.

"Partly it's hindsight, and partly it's making better use of my inner voice. I can see the mistakes I've made in the past, and I've learned by them. One of those mistakes was shutting down my inner guidance when things were getting stressful in my life. Paradoxically, that's the very time I should have been listening to my inner voice."

"Ouch," Michael says with a grin.

"Yes, and the double 'ouch' was not taking heed of Vicki's intuition. There have been so many times she had the right sense about something, yet I proceeded to bull my way along a different path. In some cases I went headlong into trouble."

"Hey, I've never been that way," Michael says with a smile and we both laugh. I guess in a way most men can relate to this.

I tell Michael about a recent trip to the snow in the nearby Sierras. "It had been a while since the family and I had been to the snow, and we were taking a route we hadn't traveled before. Vicki wanted me to stop and put on chains, and I refused until the snow was so heavy I could hardly see in front of the car. I was bound and determined to make it to our lodging without putting the chains on."

"Finally," I continue, "at Vicki's insistence I stopped at a service station to put on the tire chains. The station attendant told me it's a good thing I put on the chains when I did. When I asked him why, he said, 'If you don't have chains on, there's a hundred-dollar fine for every sign you pass that says *chains required.*' I counted the number of signs to our lodging—there were seven. Needless to say, I kept quiet the rest of the way."

Michael laughs at the story while I admit how thankful I was for Vicki's persistence.

We go on to talk about current events and how each other's company is doing. Gradually the conversation drifts back to intuitive faculties.

"Sounds like you learned some things, Mark."

"You're right, I have. I've broadened my decision-making so that I evaluate situations with a more inclusive, longer view."

"And you think your intuitive abilities brought on by your sleeping disorder are responsible for this change in your decision-making process?"

"I do. However, we're all intuitive, it's just a matter of how much focus we put on it. I was going down the business highway at

100 miles an hour, I wouldn't listen and didn't hear it. I never let my mind rest long enough to listen."

"That describes a lot of people in business," Michael says.

"It does, doesn't it. Speaking of people in business, I've just ordered an advanced-sales copy of a book called *Intuition at Work*. It's due out later this year and is supposed to contain different peoples' view of intuition in the workplace. I'm looking forward to reading it and to finding out how others see intuition being applied in today's business world."

"Let me know when it hits the bookstores; I'll pick up a copy," Michael says.

"I'll do that."

Our conversation slowly drifts back to business and to some of the mergers going on in the valley. It occurs to me that one thing that's always impressed me about Michael is his intuitive sense. He's always used his inner sense, or instincts as we might call them in business. He was into some of these right-brain techniques long before it was the popular thing to do.

"Mark, I have a suggestion for you."

"What's that?"

"A professor friend of mine, Dr. Daniels, runs a group class each semester around the enneagram system. Are you familiar with enneagrams?"

"No, I'm not," I say, shaking my head.

As if on cue, Michael jumps into explaining enneagrams. He says it's a system made up of personality types that helps us understand ourselves and other people in our lives. He advises me to sit in on one of the enneagram sessions. He points out that the class is about 90% business people.

I acknowledge that I would be willing to do this, and Michael suggests I get the definitive book on the subject called *The Enneagram* by Helen Palmer. He explains the group classes are at night, and the professor puts together a panel of people from a specific personality type. There are nine personality types in all so personality Type 2 might be on Tuesday night and personality Type 3 might be on Wednesday night. The panel sits in front of a larger group of, say, fifty or sixty people and answers questions on their specific personality type. " It's a great discussion," Michael says.

"Is this enneagram system practical?" I ask.

"Yes, it is!" he affirms. "It's becoming more accepted as time goes on. The key is how one uses it. The enneagram system was first brought to the West by Gurdjieff. He used it to diagram the potentials in people. The use of this system has gradually expanded as more and more professionals have applied the information."

"I see," I say thoughtfully.

Michael continues, "The other reason I'm suggesting this is because of your interest in intuition. I suspect at some point that you turned your attention away from your inner perceptions. Working with the personality types of the enneagram system can reintroduce this connection with intuition."

"Thanks for the suggestion. Can you leave your professor friend's number on my voice-mail?"

"Sure. Hey, ...speaking of intuition, will it help me win a car race on Saturday?" Michael asks with a laugh.

"Only if you read the road signs, ...and have a very fast car!"

We both laugh and continue to talk about many of the

techniques that Michael has tried over the years. I have discussed with Michael some of the same information that I expressed to my homeopathic doctor and other people, yet this was a business setting. I like that I have been able to be authentic at this lunch. It feels good to speak openly about intuition. During my exploration, I've learned an important lesson about integrating those areas that I previously compartmentalized. I now firmly believe that if a person is able to guard against an over-concentration of logical thinking, they'll have greater awareness of the road signs.

Chakras and Businessmen's Egos

Whether I'm willing to accept it as fact or not, many healers have a perception uncommon among the general public. I remember watching Barbara Brennan, the renowned healer on the East Coast, work with a man describing the most minute details of his illness. She knew, long before he spoke, what ailments he suffered and even what measures he had taken. This was quite remarkable to me. She really mesmerized the people in attendance, myself included.

During the past months, I have uncovered other healers similar to Barbara Brennan and different forms of healing through referrals, expositions, conferences, and reading material. One of the healers I've chosen to have a session with is Gina, a healer and a homeopath from New Zealand. She is a Christian and has studied Buddhism with lamas in Tibet. I'm eager to see how she uses these two different philosophies in her practice.

I stand on the steps of a health center. A wind chime is hanging just outside the door. I open the door and walk into a small lobby filled with brochures and magazines. Gina had instructed me to go down the hall to the room on the left. As I make my way down the hall, I see a large Native American dream-catcher hanging on the wall just to my right. A candle flame and the sweet aroma of burning sage greet me as I enter the room where Gina will do the healing session. She has soft features, reminding me somewhat of my mother. Her skin is very light and smooth. Her long, lavender skirt sways as she closes the curtains and turns on soft music while I climb onto the table. "Are you comfortable?" she asks softly. "Would you like a pillow?"

"I'm fine except I'd like to put something over my eyes," I reply.

She places a soft cloth over my eyes and dims the lights. "This healing process will balance your energy and your chakras. Are you familiar with chakras?"

"Somewhat," I say. "I am interested in how chakras work." I'd first heard about them at the Whole Life Expo, and I remember the book *Anatomy of a Spirit* by Caroline Myss, explaining the chakra system.

"To put it simply, chakras are energy centers in the body," Gina says. "The seven major ones are located along the spinal column. The first chakra is located at the base of the spine, and it's called the root chakra. The other chakras are located at the abdomen, solar plexus, heart, throat, forehead which is sometimes referred to as the 'third eye,' and top of the head. When these centers are blocked, or out of balance, physical symptoms can result." As I listen intently to Gina, I wonder if she is going to find any blocked chakras. I can just see myself now with a clogged chakra. Uhg!

She continues, "If a person has a blocked throat chakra, for example, they may be having some difficulty in communicating, expressing themselves, and so on. Unblocking this chakra and balancing it with the others will help. Of course, if they continue with the same patterns of behavior that caused the block in the first place, the block could return. It depends. It's unique to each person."

I like the idea of these chakras representing an external aspect of a person. This system seems to connect the inner person with the outer, more expressive part. I begin to wonder if the sore throats I often get are related to a blocked throat chakra and if so, what it is that I'm not expressing or communicating.

As I ponder this I feel myself smiling inwardly as I remember a funny incident that happened before I had heard the word spoken. Not knowing it was pronounced "Sha-kra," one night while I was at a restaurant with some friends and business partners, the conversation turned to the subject of spiritual centers in the body. We began talking about chakras and mispronouncing the word as "cock kra." After the conversation had gone on for a while, someone at another table leaned over and whispered, "It's pronounced 'sha-kra' or in some cases 'cha-kra,' but there's no 'cock' in chakras." The memory makes me laugh when I think of a group of business people talking like experts when we couldn't even pronounce the terms correctly. Needless to say, the conversation changed almost immediately to a new topic!

Interrupting my reverie, Gina brings my attention back into the room as she says, "I'll show you some exercises when we're through so you can learn to balance and clear your chakras on your own. Right now, just lie here and relax as there's nothing for you to do. Do you need anything before we start?"

"No," I answer, thinking about her choice of words: "just relax." Relaxing has always been hard for me to do in a situation where I am not completely in control. Part of my quest is about letting go of the need to maintain an ironclad control of any situation. At first this was an uncomfortable feeling, but I'm working at it. Gina has the situation well in hand, and she has been doing this healing work for many years. Still, my natural reaction is to try to control the situation or the healing somehow.

"I'll begin with your feet, then work up your spine ending with your crown chakra at the top of your head. If you need anything during the process, let me know. Don't worry about interrupting me," she instructs.

"Okay, I'm ready. Can you tell me what you see or feel as you go?" I ask partially for the knowledge but primarily to maintain some element of control. If part of developing my intuition is about learning to let go of a controlling nature, then I have a big step ahead of me. I have to be honest with myself on this. There is a lot of strong emotion around being in complete control.

"I'll do my best, but usually it's difficult to talk and focus on healing at the same time," she tells me. "Breathe comfortably and allow the music to relax you while I take a minute to clear myself." She steps away from the table and closes her eyes. "I ask for guidance from the Light, and I ask Mark's guides and angels to assist in this process to serve his highest good." I find her prayers to the guides and angels appealing. I wonder if it's her Tibetan training that speaks to the guides and her Christian training that speaks to angels.

"I feel heat on my feet through my socks," I mention a few

minutes after she has placed her palms on the bottom of my feet. It's a feeling similar to the one I experienced with the Russian healer.

She takes a moment to respond. "I see the energy moving up your thighs and into your hips. Allow yourself to unwind now. Drift back into a peaceful place in nature. With each breath, you will relax more deeply. Allow any thoughts or concerns to be put to the side now." After ten minutes she moves to my ankles, then to my knees and hips. Mentally, I drift between a dream-like state and the reality of the room. I am conscious of her presence moving all around me. I don't ask any more questions and lose a sense of time.

I'm brought out of my restful state by Gina's gentle voice. It seems as if we just began the session, but I realize by looking at the clock that 45 minutes have passed. Feeling light-headed, I slowly move to a chair across from Gina.

"I felt a real strong vibration around your heart chakra toward the end of the session," Gina says softly as she gently leads me back to a full wakeful state.

"It might have been when I was dreaming," I admit. "I was very lucid. I felt this really strong tug on my emotions. I remember I was dreaming I was a little boy standing in a meadow all alone. For some reason I felt a deep sense of loneliness even though there was a lot of beauty around. What this means or why I had this dream, isn't clear to me, but the dream experience itself was very real."

"Do you meditate?" she asks.

"Yes, I do."

"I'd advise you take your dream into meditation and ask

what it means for you. Your Higher Self, that place where you're with God, will help you sort out what you need to know from this dream," she suggests.

"What do you mean when you say higher self?" I ask. I've seen this word in quite a few books, still, I'm interested in how Gina defines it.

"This is where your soul can unite with its spirit and work in harmony with the will of God. With this transcendent power from above, you can interpret the meaning of this dream. This is the way to the kingdom within." She encourages me to remain relaxed for several minutes more.

I sit quietly acclimating myself to the surroundings. Gina sits in another part of the room with her eyes closed, possibly in prayer. I think about Gina's comments on the chakras and how these spiritual centers within the body are readily accepted in the East. I'm still curious how a person can make practical use of these spiritual centers if they can't see them. It's an inner resource that seems hard to apply.

I also recall my brother Thom's comment about chakras. He told me he could *feel* his chakras, really feel them in his body. He said that when I could *feel* my chakras, then I would be ready to work with these spiritual centers. Maybe that's the key to applying these inner resources, you have to be able to feel them if you can't see them. I'm not there yet; I can't feel my chakras. But I am beginning to get an idea of the role these centers play inside the body.

After about ten minutes, Gina comes out of her meditative state and says, "It's important to drink at least three eight ounce glasses of water today and again tomorrow to complete the cleansing process."

"I'll do that," I affirm.

Afterwards I reflect on the session as I sit in the small ante-room. Gina will be heading to Europe shortly, and I take down her address in New Zealand before I leave. Silently I ask myself what I got from this session. I remember experiencing an unusual violet light near me, but I wonder how I sensed this light since my eyes were closed. Maybe I was experiencing my third eye she spoke about earlier—that imaginary eye that can see things with the mind—the mind's eye.

I remember feeling extremely warm under Gina's hands, which made me a little nervous at first. I wonder if this heat translates into healing power. Maybe a machine or some scientific equipment could measure this heat and its effectiveness?

My skeptical side wonders if there is any assurance that a healing actually occurred. Are there really natural gifts of healing which science cannot explain? I remember as a child, witnessing a number of faith healers at evangelical rallies. I have always believed that abiding faith in God is needed for healing to take place. I wonder if Gina's healing abilities, which had been documented, would be effective on my body if I had no faith in her. Does the healing result because of the *faith* of the patient in the healer or because of the healer's energy? Or is it a combination of both?

Hidden Asset

*Letting go of our controlling nature
stimulates the intuitive process.*

Chapter Seven

Believing in the Process

Second Sight and the Very Young

I'm finding that this adventure is full of rewards—from developing inner awareness and discovering untapped abilities, to learning new applications for personal growth. That's the business person and avid self-help student in me talking. From time to time, however, there are situations that are just pure enjoyment. Many of these enjoyable moments revolve around my children. Their energy is so fresh and clean and innocent. I'm always after ways to involve them in my exploration.

Jonathan and Allison clamber out of the car with excited anticipation. They have a week off for spring vacation, and I'm taking them to see Maria Strauss, a highly skilled body worker. I've noticed the kids have an easier time understanding physical or bodily things at this age. I have brought them with me to see Maria as a way of helping them understand spiritual/holistic processes by way of their own bodies.

Maria is in her twenties, is fun-loving and a touchy-feely person. She has raven hair brushed straight back and milky white skin that makes for an attractive combination. She wears wonderfully colorful clothes, always loose fitting and flowing. She has a rich voice and often hums to the music that's playing in the background. She is also clairvoyant. This ability to perceive objects not present to the senses is a real gift. Her gift complements massage therapy because it allows her to see and work with energy in the body.

Allison scampers up the steps ahead of Jonathan. She turns around to smirk down at him, clearly pleased with herself for reaching the top before her older brother. Jonathan nonchalantly keeps pace with me, pretending he isn't interested in the game.

We are seeing Maria at a holistic health center. It's one of the many centers throughout the Bay Area that I've used to learn more about the alternative healing culture. Although it's a distance from my home, I've found many of the practitioners to be genuine and helpful. Coincidently, since I began my search, a holistic health center has opened in my own town. It has body workers, chiropractors, Reiki practitioners, and is run by two nurses with forty years of medical training between them.

"Is this the door? Is this the door?" Allison asks, wanting to be the first to knock.

"It's the next one, sweetheart, the one with the big doorknob." She stands in front of the door waiting for us as patiently as any pre-schooler can and knocks softly as we approach. "It's okay, Allison, we can just go right on in." She wrestles with the doorknob, turning it one way and then the other. "Do you need some help there?" I ask her.

"Nope, I've got it," she says. Finally the door gives way, and Allison enters the room first. Finding no one there, she climbs into the white wicker rocker, her legs dangling over the edge.

"Where's the lady?" she asks me.

"Maria will come out in a few minutes."

Allison surveys the waiting room from her chair, admiring the candles while I scan the bookshelves for a new book on healing.

Harp music plays in the background.

"Mark, are these your kids?" asks Maria, as she appears from another room.

"Hi, Maria. Yes, this is Allison, and this is Jonathan. Kids, this is Maria." Jonathan moves forward cautiously and shakes Maria's hand. Allison climbs down from the chair, reaches for my hand and is completely quiet for the first time that afternoon.

"It's nice to meet you both," Maria smiles warmly at them. "Let's get started." She leads us into another room, modestly furnished with a massage table, two folding wood chairs, and a floor lamp. Maria adjusts the massage table and sits down to speak to the kids about bodywork.

"Massage is very important because it helps to move energy that sometimes gets stuck in places in your body. It helps you to feel better," Maria explains.

"Is it like when my dad rubs our feet at night?" Jonathan asks.

"Yes, like that. Do you feel better when he does that?"

"Oh, yeah. It's fun," Jonathan says.

"Well sometimes instead of just your feet, having your entire body massaged helps to move energy away from darker places in your body so that these places can become lighter. When this happens, you feel better. Your dad has tried this before."

"Is it true, Dad? Did you feel better after?"

"Much better, Jonathan. After a massage, I feel relaxed and clean inside," I tell him, tousling his hair. I remember a time not too long ago when the notion of a massage seemed just ridiculously self-indulging. It was okay at vacation health spas, but I had no time for it as part of my regular health maintenance.

Oh, how things have changed. I'm more convinced now than ever that there is a relationship between my body and my energy.

"You know kids, Maria has a special gift that is sometimes called 'second sight.' This means she can see the energy inside you and the aura around your body."

"Ooh, what does it look like?" Jonathan asks.

"It appears as different colors of light. Some energy looks brighter than other energy. Brighter energy is usually healthier energy," Maria explains.

"Is it dangerous?" Jonathan asks cautiously.

Maria laughs. "Oh, no. It's very safe."

As Maria prepares the massage table and arranges things, the kids watch her intently. "She has power," Allison interrupts after a long silence. "She has power in her hands," she says, pointing to Maria. I glance down at Allison, puzzled, as I haven't heard her use this language before. I pick her up and hold her.

"Allison, you're right. Maria does have healing energy in her hands," I confirm.

Maria looks gently at Allison. Allison relaxes upon being acknowledged, then asks to get down.

"Okay, now, who wants to go first?" Maria asks the children.

"Me," they both say together.

"Jonathan, you seem like the more anxious one to get in and out while I suspect Allison wants to relax and enjoy everything. Why don't I take you first?" Maria suggests. As Jonathan gets up on the table, Allison and I sit back and listen. Maria talks to Jonathan as she works on his body. I appreciate the way she explains everything she sees and also what she's doing. She takes her time and answers each one of the children's questions. Then she takes a few minutes of quiet time and also asks the kids to be quiet. She tells them that she is going to do some healing. She runs her hands lightly over their bodies to perceive any energetic blockages. She then transmits energy to those areas to re-establish balance.

When Maria begins to speak again, she explains to the kids that this is a practice also known as therapeutic touch. It is based on the theory that humans can transfer energy through their hands to help induce health. The kids are fascinated and ask Maria to teach them how to send out this healing energy. Maria takes time to show them, and they practice on each other on the way home.

In the car, I ask Allison why she said Maria had power in her hands.

"Uhm, it's like I just knew that about her, Daddy," she answers from the back seat.

"Allison, how can you see power?" Jonathan asks.

"It's like something was coming out of her hands," my daughter says.

"What did it look like?" I venture to ask.

"Daddy, I couldn't really see anything, I just knew it was there."

We merge into the diamond lane, heading for the Discovery Museum. The kids take out their pads and color markers we always keep in the car. They begin to draw people in our family and add colorful auras around them. I hear them in the back seat talking about the colors they sense around their friends and relatives. They're imagining they can see the auras that Maria talked about. Funny how kids immediately use new things they discover.

As we drive on, I think about the many people who have told me how young children have the ability to see into the spiritual realms. This belief seems to cross over cultural and religious backgrounds. I have been told this by healers from Russia, Europe and Asia as well as by people from different religions. This session with Maria and the kids (and especially Allison's comment) leads me to believe there may be some truth to all of this.

Taking Health for Granted

Late April, early May is one of the prettiest times in California. Wildflowers are in bloom, and orchard blossoms can be seen throughout the central valley. The hills are emerald green from the winter's snow runoff. Against the backdrop of this lovely season I have recently received some disheartening news. My long-time friend and former co-worker, Randy, has been diagnosed with a terminal illness. The doctors don't know how long he has to live.

When he told me, it hit me like a ton of bricks, but gradually I'm adjusting to the situation. It's difficult for me to see Randy so thin and weak and slowing down. He has always taken good care of himself physically. His youthful body is now wafer-thin from the medical treatments he is receiving. His black hair is a little longer in the back but still parted in the middle and falls to the sides of his face just above his glasses. I visit him at home since he is on disability.

"Hey, Mark, it's nice to see you," Randy says happily. "It's been awhile. How are you?"

"Fine, and yourself?"

"I'm feeling pretty weak, but I can't stand being cooped up. I'd like to get out of the house. How about a short walk down by the canal?"

"Sure, let's go," I agree.

We leave the house and walk slowly towards a trail that runs along a nearby creek. Randy's movements are slow and sure. He doesn't have quite the flexibility he once had. He still does Tai Chi every morning to relax his mind and to try to keep his body limber. Randy is Chinese, and he's told me this form of exercise was taught to him at a very young age. We continue to walk toward the water, enjoying the cool breeze.

"How is your research into the spiritual and holistic communities coming along?" Randy inquires.

"Good," I reply.

"What happened to the no-nonsense, hard-driving business person?" Randy asks with a cynical look.

"That hard-driving person is still inside me, maybe just a little gentler than before," I admit.

"This I'll have to see for myself," he says with skepticism. "What made you decide to choose this area to research?"

"I guess because it deals with both the spiritual and physical side of things," I reply as I try to pinpoint the exact reason. "I believe there is something to this body/mind/spirit connection. I've set my sights on trying to find out what it is."

"We haven't lost you to the New Agers, have we?" Randy asks.

"If you mean in the narrow sense of ancient concepts and philosophies being brought forward, no. I'm more interested in the 'new thought' aspects of the New Age."

"Sounds like a new mindset," Randy says.

"Yeah, it is," I respond. "Transformation is another word that could describe what it is that I'm after. In meetings with Marilyn Ferguson, the author of the book *Aquarian Conspiracy*, she explained the implications and scope of this period of transformation that we're living in. I found her to be a very clear thinker."

"I have to tell you, you really sound serious about all this."

"I am. I passed up starting another company in order to do this exploration."

Randy puts his hand on my shoulder. "That's not like you, Mark. You always seemed so focused on making money and getting ahead, I'm more than a little surprised by all of this. Besides, you were born to start companies!"

"Maybe so, but taking time to find out about inner resources is sort of like starting a company," I answer calmly.

He stares at me with a "sure" sort of grin and says, "Mark, we've known each other a long time, and I don't see how looking into these areas is like a start-up company. Unless of course you're going to start 'Mind/Body/Spirit, Incorporated,'" he says with a weak laugh.

"That's just like you, all business," I say, grabbing him by the scruff of the neck and feeling the closeness between us. I try hard not to think about him not being around. He steps ahead of me so that we can walk single file to allow a group of children on roller blades to pass.

"I've been meaning to get a pair of those while I can still put them to use," Randy says, glancing back at the skaters.

Randy's comment surprises me a bit since he is getting more

frail all the time. The medical treatments have made it extremely hard for him to gain weight. I can't see him learning to rollerblade given his condition, but the hope of learning does seem to raise his spirits. Skaters and people on bicycles continue to pass us as we walk along. The creek has a clean, grassy smell with water moving swiftly from last season's rains. In another few months the water-line will be down and small ponds will begin to form.

I can tell Randy is not completely convinced of my intentions around this exploration. He has known me for years, and other than a strong interest in the human resource side of business, there has never been any indication of interest in these other fields. Looking at it from his perspective, it probably does seem a little unusual.

"Mark, why are you even spending time on this?" Randy persists. "Remember the old business cliché—'what's in it for me'—the WIFM? Well, what's in it for you?"

"Integrating inner processes that balance out my life!" I recite without hesitation. "The more I can integrate many of the processes I'm learning, the more balanced I become. And the process seems to be quickening."

"What do you mean by quickening?"

"When I'm out of balance, the feedback seems to be happening faster. Five years ago, if I lacked balance somewhere in my life, it seemed like it took longer for it to have an impact on me. Now if I'm out of balance, I feel the impact within a couple of weeks or so. Does that make sense to you?" I ask.

"Not really. I don't know if I can measure how out of balance I am," Randy says honestly.

"Yeah, it was really a hard concept for me to understand at

first. It was kind of like I was 'reaping what I was sowing' in less than a month."

We continue to walk along the narrow path on what's turned out to be a beautiful day. The sight of birds making their nests can be seen along the creek. Randy doesn't get out a lot now since he always has to have someone with him in case he becomes too weak to get home. I decide to change the subject a little to cheer him up.

"That reminds me of something funny that happened last weekend. You want to hear about it?"

"Sure," Randy says.

It's a good chance for me to amuse Randy. He has, of course, a lot to be depressed about right now. I relate a story that ties into the holistic health field.

"You know me. I have to try out all the technical gadgets and products. One natural product I started using was a hair cleanser made from certain plant extracts. You use it once every two weeks. It's supposed to restore balance to your hair in a natural way."

"Uh huh."

"Here's the kicker. This product has one unusual side effect. It makes your scalp really feel cold, freezing-like, almost a stinging cold. I don't want the kids to get into this so I put it up on a high shelf in the bathroom next to Vicki's face creams and mascara, things she doesn't want the kids into."

"Sounds safe," Randy cuts in.

"Yes, it is. Well, Vicki and I went away last weekend, and Vicki's sister, Carla, and her aunt Lena came to stay at the house and watch our kids. Lena stayed in our room and used our bathroom. She saw my scalp product up with Vicki's facial creams in our bathroom, and thinking it was face lotion, she put it all over her face," I say grinning.

"Oh, oh," Randy says with a big smile.

"In about five minutes, her face was like an ice cube. Then she tried to wash it off. Well, guess what? When you apply water, it makes it even feel colder. Needless to say, my name was mud for the rest of the weekend. Lena has still not let me live this down."

Randy bursts into merry laughter. His laughter is contagious, and I join in. It is good for me to hear Randy laugh. I glance at my watch. Randy has told me his doctor doesn't want him to get excessively tired, so I keep track of the amount of time we've been on the trail.

As we continue to walk, I tell Randy I'm beginning to break the research down into categories. I'm really just seeking to comprehend the scope of what's going on in these fields. So far I've broken the categories down into "what they do"— for example, a healer, an intuitive, a teacher/lecturer, a technician, and so on. Each person falls into one of these primary categories. Then I try to reason "how" they do what they do. Are they employing a system or a gift, for example, or are they using energy somehow, or do they work with a tool? As we walk along, the canal trail opens up to a park with a small lake. We find a bench with a view of the water and continue our conversation.

"Randy, I'm trying to determine what each practitioner is doing and what they're working with. For example, is an intuitive using psychic energy or is she using some system to help her? I'm really just looking at what the process is and I'm attempting to break it all down in a way that's easy for me to understand."

"And we know that it has to be moderately simple for you to be able to understand it," Randy says with a laugh.

I reach across the bench and grab him by the shoulder. "Okay, let me show you something simple. I'm going to practice a little 'applied kinesiology' on you. Let's see which one of these muscles of yours are weak." I remind him of an applied kinesiology lecture at a business seminar we took that focused on the power of the physical body. I clearly recall getting up in front of the room and having the instructor perform a muscle test on me. He demonstrated the neurologic difference between a strong and weak muscle. I pretend to be trying to do the same with Randy as I bend his arm behind his back. The instructor went on to talk about the link between imbalances in the body's organs and glands and the weakness in specific muscles. I don't think most of the businessmen in the room understood what was going on, myself included, but it was a nice break from evaluating income statements.

I loosen up my grip on Randy, remembering he's not to get too worked up. After I let go of his arm, Randy asks, "You were speaking about these practitioners and their processes. I mean does this stuff really work?" He bends over to pick up flat stones and skips them across the water.

"Yes and no. There are obvious issues such as quality, accuracy, and scope of ability," I reply while watching the ripples on the water. I pick up a stone too and throw it the way I used to as a kid.

Randy considers what I have said. "This is valuable stuff if you can put it to use. I'm not convinced yet that you can," he admits. "I'm getting a little tired. Do you mind if we start back?"

"Not at all." Maybe I shouldn't have roughhoused with him, I think to myself. His disease is withering his strength away. The doctors don't give him a long time to live, but I'm holding out for a miracle. With difficulty, I hold back my emotions so that I can be upbeat around him. I throw my last stone into the water and we begin to walk back to Randy's house.

"Mark, I can see that you've changed just by your decision to explore these areas—they're so dramatically different from your past ventures," Randy points out as we walk on. "To me it's an indication that you're more open-minded."

"Thanks, Randy, that makes me feel good. Hey, before I forget, I wanted to mention I have several really good books on healing. Would you like to borrow them?" I'd brought them with me hoping he would want to read them.

"Yes, I'd like that, I have plenty of time to read."

"I'll get them out of the car when we get back."

"You know what, Mark? Even though I may sound cynical, I'm glad you're taking time to do this research. I firmly believe we all are on a journey of some form or another."

When we get back to Randy's house, I walk out to the car to retrieve the books. I say to myself that this whole quest business would be worth it if I knew it could make Randy better. The old proverb "God helps those who help themselves" comes to mind. I believe in miracles, and I'm praying for one for Randy. At the same time, I'm sharing the information so he can help himself.

Trusting Another Person's Hunches

It would be nice to point to a specific turning point when I could say I believed in all of this body/mind/spirit material fully. However, I can't. It's not like a light switch going off and on where suddenly I believe in other realms of reality. Rather, it's a gradual unfolding of events and experiences that enables me to have faith in the overall process and move beyond cause and effect.

This unfolding process is further enhanced by interaction with Vicki. I'm taping most of my interviews and conversations which gives Vicki a chance to review them. I usually have the tapes transcribed so I can highlight the key points.

"Isn't tomorrow your regular breakfast with the pastor?" Vicki asks me one evening.

"Actually, we met this morning because he's going to a synod conference in LA tomorrow."

"How is he?"

"He's fine. But it seems the church's lease will come to term soon, and he's talking about possibly moving to a larger facility. He talked to me about the increase in seating capacity since I'm on the evangelism committee. He was pretty excited about it."

"Where will they get the money?" she asks, flipping through a direct mail catalog.

"It has to come from the congregation. I was hoping we could adjust our family budget and give to the building fund," I respond, feeling enthusiastic and satisfied in my own mind that this is the right approach. Vicki's stare tells me she's not in agreement.

She returns to her catalog without comment. A few minutes later, she says, "I don't feel we should give any more to the church, especially the building fund."

"What?" I protest.

"I just don't think it's a good idea."

"Why?"

"I don't know, Mark. I have a strange feeling about doing this. It's not the money. It's just something doesn't feel right."

I feel disconnected from her even before she finishes her sentence. We don't usually disagree on church matters. When we've been able to give, we gave. What's different in this case? Determined to hold on to my position in this matter, I ask, "What exactly is it that you don't feel good about?"

"I'm not sure. I just don't feel good about it, that's all. I can't really explain it," she says hesitantly. "It's probably just my intuition. You know, one of the areas you've been studying," she says somewhat sarcastically.

My exuberance subsides momentarily. Vicki's comment has let the wind out of my sails. Somewhat defeated in my effort, I am completely quiet.

Here we go, I declare to myself. Intuition being used *against* me when there is something I want to do. "Hold on!" I say to myself. Here's an opportunity to look at intuition from another angle. Isn't this the very reason I'm exploring, ...to find out how these inner processes work? And what if this is a premonition of sorts ... Vicki's awareness of some impending problem with the church. I can't let my strong desire to give more money to the church negate Vicki's inner sense.

Then Vicki asks, "When are you going to see Mary Coleman again?"

"Next month."

"Why don't you ask Mary how she feels about this?"

"Great idea, Vicki," I respond, getting up from the table to make a note of it. "I don't usually talk to Mary about this sort of thing, but it's important enough to me to bring it up to her. And besides, it seems like your picking up on something even if you can't explain it."

Vicki goes back to reading. I can sense a slight rift between us even though we end our conversation on a positive note. I suppose it's a natural occurrence when we disagree on something. I know when I don't get my way, it's easy for me to tune her out. Still, I've learned it's important to listen to Vicki's intuition. More than once it has helped keep me from getting into hot water like the incident with the snow chains.

I take Vicki's advice and make a note to discuss this issue in my next encounter with Mary Coleman. Mary has become somewhat of a metaphysical consultant for me, helping me to understand how everything is connected in this field. Although she still helps me by using her intuitive capability and clairvoyance, she continually encourages me to use my own inner sense.

At a typical meeting with Mary, I go through a list of practices and people I have met with during the month. We talk about the spiritual/physical viewpoint. Since she has been in this field a long time, she's a good source to use for this.

After Mary and I talk about the practitioners and healers, we usually spend time on general topics. I use Mary's wisdom to get a better interpretation of these areas and to validate what I'm hearing from other practitioners. During this particular meeting we talk for about thirty minutes before I come to my note regarding the pastor and the new church building.

"Mary, there's one last thing I need to ask you about before we end today. It's about my church. Vicki and I are considering an increase in our tithing in order to help the church get into a bigger facility. What are your intuitive feelings about this?"

She changes her position slightly and takes a deep breath.

"You're not thrilled about the idea, are you?" I ask, noticing her hesitation.

"Mark, I don't have a good feeling about this," she says, placing her hand over her solar plexus. "I feel it right here."

"Why?" I ask, disheartened.

"I don't think it's a good use of your money," she says.

"But, Mary," I protest, "this church has been a wonderful place for us to learn and grow."

"It's not the church!" she continues with her expression changing slightly.

I'm confused about Mary's comment. Could there be something else going on, and if so, was this what Vicki was picking up on? "If it's not the church, what is it?" I ask worried that something might happen to Vicki or me.

"It's the pastor. He's not going to be with your church in a year," Mary says matter-of-factly.

I put down my pen and gaze out the large bay window on my right. I look out towards the farming fields. There's a lump in my heart, and the beginning of a smaller one in my throat. I hope Mary is wrong. Selfishly, I'd like her to interpret the pictures she sees in her mind's eye in a different way. The pastor is my close friend, and my emotions are getting more intense around this.

"Mark," Mary gently says. "I know how you feel about this man, but you have to let it go. He has his own lessons to learn."

The pastor and I have spent so much time together. I've enjoyed our late evening talks about growing up in the church and the responsibilities of being a Christian. If the pastor were to leave, I would miss our monthly breakfasts where we just talk about anything and everything. I'm caught off guard by Mary's comment about "lessons to learn." What does she mean by this? What lessons?

"So, is the pastor going to go to another church or leave to teach at the seminary? Is that it?" I ask, attempting to make sense of things.

"No. Unfortunately, I feel your pastor is going to leave the church and also the ministry within the next year."

I am at a loss for questions. Mary's revelation is stunning. Again I turn toward the window. Mary must be off today, I tell myself. She can't be right about this. This man is related to famous men in the church. His family has had pastors in it for centuries.

"I know that's not what you wanted to hear, Mark, but I trust the information I'm getting, and I need to be honest with you. Besides that, I feel you'll need the resources for your own spiritual search," Mary says, sensing my sorrow.

Mary has confirmed in a way what Vicki had been sensing. Now I feel there is a good possibility that what Mary told me could come true because both she and Vicki have a similar uneasy feeling about it. "Thanks, Mary," I say turning my attention back to her. "I'll see you again soon," I add, my emotions still somewhere else.

When I arrive home from Mary's session, I am confused. Vicki is there and eager to find out about the meeting. We had briefly spoken about the church situation again just the night before.

"It's not great news, and I'd rather talk about it later tonight after the kids have gone to bed," I confess to Vicki when I see her.

That evening, Vicki begins our conversation with, "I feel bad about this and don't even know why yet. I sense it has something to do with you and the pastor. I know you two are close."

I go on to divulge to Vicki everything that Mary said. She is as bewildered as I am at Mary's comments about the pastor. Vicki reaches out and holds my hand as we talk. We discuss Vicki's original feeling about the situation and her sense that something was wrong. Eventually, we come to another decision on the new church building and handle the financial contribution in a different manner.

I'm sad to say, not long after my meeting with Mary the pastor does step down from the church and leaves the ministry for undisclosed reasons. I can't help wondering if this was a premonition on Vicki's part. Somehow the small church is never the same after that, and within several months, my family and I start attending another neighborhood church.

Hidden Asset

*At times our minds are unusually receptive
as to what is about to occur.*

Chapter Eight

Eliminating the Dividing Lines

Scout Out the Inner Body

There are no "economies of scale," when it comes to the experiential side of an adventure. Each moment must be enjoyed for the fullness and richness the experience has to offer. One person I've met recently who is quite inspirational is Scout Bartlett, an intuitive who hosts a local weekly radio program on a San Francisco station. He has several offices in the Bay Area, and I first met him at an office in the heart of Silicon Valley. He has a wonderful gift of insight and is immensely talented. Two gifts stand out most in my mind when I think about Scout. One, is his ability to see inside the body. The other, is his keen perception into business ideas and his talent for following these perceptions to fruition.

Scout and I have spent a number of hours working through business strategies. Somehow he is able to see the marketing streams in his consciousness; it's as if he can astutely perceive different paths of a product or service. I've found this to be a very difficult task for an intuitive. He is also able to look at business models and organizational issues for me. It is quite remarkable. He personally has a good head for business, which makes working with him that much easier. He even looks like a business person. Tall and distinguished looking, he has a short haircut and is clean shaven. If he were wearing a business suit, you might think he worked in the financial district.

Scout and I once developed a completely new archetype for my partnering relationships. It was based on the functional roles of the partners—for example, visioning, producing, actualizing. When I stop to think about how I have used this in my business dealings, I am still amazed at how well it worked.

Today, I meet with Scout at his office in the East Bay. We sit across from each other in comfortable armchairs while he adjusts the microphone to tape the session. I take out my notes and review my list of questions. Scout is extraordinary in identifying areas in the body that might not be functioning properly. The popular term for this today is *medical intuitive*, although Scout doesn't profess to be one. He just seems to have a unique understanding about what's causing weakness in different areas of the body. He gives his usual disclosure statement that he is not licensed to practice medicine, etcetera, before we begin.

"Could you look at my father-in-law, Len, this time?" I ask.

"Of course, I'll be right back." He closes his eyes and retreats into another form of consciousness. I observe quietly and think about the earlier sessions we've had together. He has told me a little bit about himself and his life growing up in Kansas. It strikes me as peculiar that he has always been aware of his intuition and never closed it off. He seems to have been able to keep a childlike innocence about him. It makes me wonder at what age I started closing down my own intuition.

In a few minutes Scout speaks, his eyes still closed. "I see your father-in-law has a problem with his left hip. It's as though he has maintained an awkward position for years so that his hip has turned and is cutting off the blood supply. If he doesn't correct this, it could affect him in the future."

"Could this be serious?" I ask.

"Yes, if he continues to cut off his blood supply, things could get more severe."

"How specific can you get in the area of the hips?"

"It's mainly that his hips have turned inward from being in this awkward position for long periods of time," he explains. "That's as specific as I can get on this. I'm not concerned about his heart. He's got a heart like an ox. It's his hip that could affect his blood flow."

"My father-in-law has owned a tile company for the past thirty years. Of course he's laid tile during much of that time. Do you think the position he takes to lay tile could be what you see?" I ask, becoming concerned.

"It's likely," Scout says.

I am amazed that Scout was able to peg the "awkward position." I've laid tile with Len, and you often have to work in cramped quarters in a squatting position. It's fortunate Len is so physically strong and that he owns the company so he doesn't do as much of the physical labor as when he was first starting out.

"Do you have any suggestions for correcting this or reversing it?"

"Would your father-in-law be open to a chiropractor?"

"I really don't have a clue about that. I'll have to ask my wife," I reply, writing a note to talk to Vicki about this.

"Okay, let me look at his spirit. I'm going to go away for a moment," Scout says and is quiet again for a short while.

I wonder what he's doing when he's off in that silent world.

His eyes are closed, but he seems to be looking at something in his mind. What does he see in there? Does he really see my father-in-law or his spirit or what? Maybe he manages somehow to suspend reality and draw on other hidden resources.

"I'm looking to see if I can tell whether your father-in-law would go to a chiropractor," Scout says as if he knows what I'm thinking. "Nope, I don't think so. He doesn't look as if he'd go. Tell your wife it's worth a try at any rate because she can at least plant the seed for him."

It is remarkable to me that Scout, like many other intuitives, can sense the way other people feel. It's as though he can see their very being at another level—at a spirit or energy level. Then somehow he gets impressions from this energy. Amazing!

"Any other suggestions then?" I ask, hoping there are other avenues to helping my father-in-law.

"Yes. First thing I would recommend is for him to be aware of the effect of this crouching while he's laying tile. Also, drinking lots of water and taking certain herbs will help."

Scout closes his eyes. "I'll be right back," he says again. While he is off mentally searching, I think about why I'm posing these sorts of questions. One reason is Vicki and I feel good we can make suggestions to family members to help them have healthier, happier, and longer lives.

"I see your father-in-law also has a problem with his left shoulder, and his right knee has been busted in the past. The knee looks like it's getting progressively worse."

"Anything else?" I ask.

"No, those are the main things I see," Scout replies.

"I want to move on to having you look at my father's health, but first I've got a reminder here on my day planner to ask about the *baby poll*. Did I ask you about this the last time I was here?"

"No," Scout says and grins. "What kind of baby poll am I participating in?"

"It's not really a poll exactly, but you know the old saying, 'You're either pregnant, or you're not'?"

"Uh huh."

"Well, I'm putting a slight spin on this. My wife Vicki and I just got some good news! This month we found out that she's pregnant with our third child! In addition to my excitement as a father, I also see an opportunity. This presents an ideal chance to do a mini-study on the accuracy of intuitives. It's a right or wrong sort of question; it can't be both. I'm doing a little poll of the intuitives I'm seeing to determine what their take is on the sex of the baby."

He chuckles. "Now you're so professional and all; is this poll from your analytical side, or are you really just interested because you're a curious dad?" he asks.

"Probably a little of both," I admit.

"Okay, I'm going to go away for a moment," he says closing his eyes again.

Unless Vicki has twins, the baby has to be a girl or a boy, and this requires the intuitive to choose one or the other. It's a good test to measure the accuracy of the intuitives. So far, I've found most people possess intuitive abilities imperfectly. I'm curious as to why this is. Scout really pegged my main interest, though. Deep down I want to know from my own curiosity.

"It's a girl. I see a girl who eventually is playing with your other kids. She has really blond hair with a sort of a curl at her shoulders when she's two or three," he says with a proud feeling of being correct.

"Really," I utter, feeling excited, almost as if I can see what he's seeing.

"Definitely a girl! By the way, I'm curious, how does the poll break down so far?"

"Just about fifty-fifty. Half the intuitives see a boy and half see a girl."

"Well, let me know. But only if I'm right," he says and grins.

"I will." It sounds peculiar, but intuitives really do see more of the essence of a person than their physical form. That would explain why many intuitives can see the emotions and feelings around people yet may not be able to make out their physical form. Most of the intuitives have described the baby's spirit while seemingly making a guess of its physical gender. I'll be interested to see how Scout does.

"Can you look at my dad's health now?" I ask, hoping to get the same type of evaluation that will identify things to help my father.

"Sure, what's his name?"

Scout goes on to talk about my father, again using his skills to look inward at my dad's physical body. His only real concern is for my father's digestive tract. Scout can sense some of the difficulties my father is having in this area. Other than that, Scout feels good about my father's overall health, given his age.

As with Vicki's father, Scout suggests a few things to consider talking to my dad about. One of the recommendations is to investigate certain herbs that will help my father's digestive system.

Later that evening, I evaluate my session with Scout. I have already sat down with Vicki and told her all the information about her father, hoping that she can pass it along to him. Scout is an intriguing dichotomy. He uses his intuitive ability alongside his business training. He's not a touchy-feely kind of guy but very pragmatic in the use of his gifts. He actually would be good at training business people to use their intuition, especially men.

Scout has one other quality that I've noticed in many of the people in the spiritual and mind/body fields—dedication! Even though Scout could earn much more in another field, he continues to stay involved in the mind/body/spirit areas. It's an interesting attribute.

The Paradox of Healing and Wholeness

It seems to me a person's mind works differently when liberated from inhibiting attitudes. My own thoughts now take place in a new way. Things crop up that I've really never thought about before. Just such a thought arises as I make my way through freeway traffic. The bright California sun glistens off the front windshield. It occurs to me that I've always been drawn to sunlight. Sunlight seems to always give me extra energy and brighten my disposition, while winter skies and cold drab days affect me in the exact opposite way. When I can't see the sun or feel it against my body, I tend to become moody and withdrawn. In an odd way I'm attracted like a magnet to the sun.

This fleeting thought reminds me a little of the practitioners I've seen who work with magnets and other electromagnetic devices. The whole idea of a magnetic field affecting the human body is fascinating to me. I'm drawn to these types of therapies like the proverbial fly to honey. All in all, I really am enjoying this adventure, I think to myself as I pull into my driveway.

Once at home, it's time to take off the tie and spend time with the family. The kids are out back playing, and before they see me, Vicki and I have a moment to catch up on the day's events. She is mixing up a batch of brownies for Jonathan's Tiger-Cub den meeting and the kitchen is filled with the aroma of chocolate. I open the oven to take a deep whiff while hugging Vicki around the waist.

"How's your research coming along?" Vicki asks.

"Good," I reply, dipping into the chocolate batter. "I'm getting a better grasp of how intuition works. I met with Penney Peirce, author of the upcoming book, *The Intuitive Way*."

"Sounds like *The Artist's Way* ... but for intuition instead of writing," Vicki says.

I nod, adding, "She's a very talented intuitive. While I was meeting with her, she introduced me to the editor of *Intuition* magazine. I liked the editor and her vision so much I signed up for a subscription."

"Just what you need, another magazine," Vicki says with a laugh.

I tug on the string to her apron in response to her comment, and she gives me a little shove with her hip before I can untie it. We both laugh.

"Actually, a different feeling has come over me recently about intuitives," I confess.

"Which is?"

"The more I meet with intuitives, the more I want to place them in the healing category," I go on to I tell her I believe counselors using intuition are really healing a person, too. Often it's a mental or spiritual healing, but they're still healing with information or energy. It seems to me that the goal of people in the holistic/spiritual community is to develop further awareness in other people. I remark that I've learned from a psychologist that the root word of "heal" is "hale" which means "whole." Intuitives are really giving a person the whole picture of themselves. So they're healers in this sense. "Our society is so down on the concept of needing to be healed," I continue. "It's the same fear and guilt people have when they hear talk of a 12-step program. I was always that way myself."

"Tell me about it," Vicki says.

"Now I'm beginning to look at healing as a way of becoming more complete by knowing all sides of ourselves. When I look at it this way, my idea about what healing really means changes 'completely,' ...pun not intended."

"It sounds like you need a pledge to remind you about this," she says teasingly, reminding me of the daily pledges with the kids.

"That's right, Vicki. Let's see now, what would be a good pledge for this concept?" I ask, teasing her back.

"Oh, stop," she says.

"How about, 'Healing is a way of becoming whole and complete.' Yes, I like that. I'm going to put this saying on the refrigerator. Maybe I'll have it printed on my business cards too," I say, still kidding with her.

"Stop, Mark, before you make me spill something."

The kids spot me through the large kitchen window. "Ooh,

I gotta go. I promised the kids I'd do some integration routines with them."

I learned some of these routines at a workshop with drum circle enthusiast, Arthur Hull. I call the kids in from the back yard.

"Do you mind if I watch?" Vicki asks, amused at my excitement.

"Sure, we love to perform. Okay, kids, who wants to use which instrument?" I ask.

"I'll take the drums," Jonathan shouts.

"I'll take the flute," Allison jumps in.

"Okay, I'll take the maracas," I announce. They know that the object is to play their instrument in an individual way and then for us to play together and make music as a group. I'm trying to show them they can be unique within the whole. I want them to find their way in the world while holding onto their individuality. And, just as important, I want them to be able to interact with other people in a group effort. This exercise helps them accomplish both. In essence, this game is about integration without losing sight of one's individual self.

"Now, one at a time. Let's share our rhythms with each other. Allison, you're the youngest, you go first."

"It goes like this," she says with an intent look on her face. "Toot, Toot, Tooooot, got it?"

"Yeah," Jonathan and I scream out.

"Jonathan, you're up!"

"Everyone watch me carefully," he says in a grown-up manner. Boom, boom-boom-boom, boom, he drums loudly. I tell him it sounds like a Latin dance number.

"Go, Dad, go," Allison says as she can't wait for all of us to play.

"Let me think. Okay I've got it." Cha-Cha, Cha-Cha-Cha, ...Cha-Cha, Cha-Cha-Cha.

"Are we all ready?"

"Yes," goes up the call.

"Then hit it!"

Toot, Toot, Cha-Cha, Boom, Toooooooot, Boom-Boom....

Vicki covers her ears and heads for upstairs. She is sensitive to loud noises, and this is too much for her. But I can see she is smiling.

"How long are you all going to play?" she yells from the top of the stairs.

"About fifteen minutes," I yell back, and we play on. After a few minutes, we begin to add variations. We change our beat. Then we change instruments. We play sitting. Then standing. We try for every conceivable combination to this integration game. A lot of it has also been about creativity and letting the kids make up the rules of the game. They really light up when they get to set the rules. We stretch fifteen minutes into twenty before Vicki calls out "bath-time," and the kids hurry up the stairs. I reflect on how I learned this integration process at a seminar on spirituality— spirituality in business, no less. I haven't gotten around to attempting this at the office, but it sure is fun to do at home.

These types of processes are important for the children. Instruction and understanding are of far greater value to them at this stage of their life than purely material things.

The Programming Says "Business Isn't Spiritual"

By the middle of June, I'm seeing as many practitioners as possible in the time I've allotted each day. The kids will be out of school soon and enjoying the endless days of summer. It won't be long after that before Vacation Bible School begins, and that means church ice cream socials can't be far behind. Recently, a businessman and friend of mine suggested, as part of my research, that I see a psychologist he knows. I take his suggestion and make an appointment with Daniel Epstein, Ph.D. I'm hoping to get a different perspective on healing. Dr. Epstein is also a certified hypnotherapist. He works as a psychotherapist at a hospital and has a private practice which is located in a professional center near the University of Santa Cruz.

After we handle introductions he asks me to call him Daniel and tells me about his background and his practice. He seems very progressive, well educated, and informed about his field. I feel comfortable with him. His office is large with an oak desk and chair adjacent to a small sitting area. After having me fill out a brief client form, he motions to me to sit in the more comfortable chairs in the sitting area. There are no windows in the room, but it is well lighted and very clean.

I spend the first twenty minutes telling him about myself and a little about the exploration I'm doing. I finally say, "Daniel, many of the intuitives and healers have said that I'm healing myself. What do you think they mean when they say this?" I'm a little tentative with Daniel because I don't want this interview to turn into a psychoanalysis session. I'm not interested in "I hate my third cousin on my mother's side of the family" kind of thing.

"For many people, healing is about *programming*," he says. "From what you've told me about yourself and your business life, I'd say you've created some barriers for yourself. Does this surprise you?"

"No, not really," I respond, liking the way he gets right to the point. I've come to see Daniel to get a psychological view of healing. At the same time, I want to be able to talk about spirituality. He seems to afford me a nice solution since he has the traditional psychological background and training while he is also open to spirituality. I also want to be able to talk about the association between business and spirituality. Since Daniel often works in the business community giving workshops and seminars, he seems like a good choice as a discerning person with whom I can discuss the balance of spirit and business.

"You see, Mark, from what you've told me, you've always thought that if you went into this world of business, you couldn't take what you've learned spiritually. By thinking this way, you've created a war with yourself because you turn off your spirituality while at work. You don't think that part of yourself belongs there. But guess what? It's going to turn on again sooner or later. You can't suppress who you really are at work or wherever."

As he speaks, I wonder if my sleeping disorder had anything to do with my inability to bring my own spirituality into the world of business. I look around the room as Daniel continues to talk. It's your typical office except for a few items that seem out of place, like an unusually large mask hanging on the far wall.

"I'm trying to show you the pattern of programming that's gotten you into this either/or way of thinking," he says. "You're trying to integrate these two sides by exploring these mind-body-spirit fields. It's going to be awkward for a while because you aren't used to it. What you're doing is exercising a muscle. That muscle says you *can* go between these two worlds of a spiritual guy and a business guy and not lose yourself. Does that make sense?"

"Yes, I guess I just don't see how to incorporate spirituality if I'm concentrating on business," I admit. "That's been a problem all the way back to college. I've been known to tune out everything but the project I'm working on."

"See, ...that's another part of your programming! You're focused, and you'll always be focused—it's part of what has made you successful. But you can also shift back and forth. What happened in your early training and schooling is you developed a program that said: if you're focused, this means you can't be flexible in your thinking. It's the programming that says business isn't spiritual; you can't use the spiritual principles for business; you can't use all of who you are in business. Change the programming. Or, to answer your original question, heal in a way that you're using all of yourself in business," Daniel says.

"So, what you're saying is healing is about changing the programming?" I ask while thinking how scholarly Daniel is. He has diplomas all over the place but still seems grounded.

"Right. The programming that says 'business isn't spiritual' is what the healing is about for you and business people in general. I'm not saying this is all-encompassing because there are many other aspects of healing on the physical, mental, and spiritual level. But for you, your early programming is the healing you're after," he explains.

Interesting, his choice of words about "early" programming.

I can't ever remember anyone explicitly saying "don't be spiritual" in business or school or church. It doesn't seem to happen that way. There must be some other way that this programming builds up over the years. It would be easy to say he's wrong with his analysis. But his comment is accurate because I do believe it's hard to be in business and be spiritual at the same time.

"Again, being healed or becoming whole for you is about bringing your spiritual self into business." He adds, "It's an emotional issue for you."

"I'm surprised at some of the emotions that have come up for me while I'm trying to incorporate my spiritual ideas," I confide.

"I'm glad you're thinking about it this way, Mark. Would you like my take on why these emotions are coming up?"

"Sure."

"Mark, you have strong ideals and unwavering convictions. They're your personal truths. Each of us has personal truths. You work in Silicon Valley so let's take a computer analogy. Truths are somewhat like our computer operating system. It's what makes everything work in our brains. Now when I talk about programming, I'm talking about a program that's been inserted in this computer of yours. It's like a picture. For example, the picture you have about not being able to be spiritual and in business. That's a program you picked up somewhere."

"Okay."

"Programs are like pictures in your mind. It's not your picture originally, and it doesn't work, and it doesn't feel right. Yet, you believe it to be your picture and your reality, so you're not willing to look at it or let it go. And it was put there with some emotions to cement this program in place."

"It sounds like you're saying I got this program from an external source," I remark.

"That program is someone else's diskette in your computer! That's all it is."

"Whoa, that's a totally new perspective." I almost laugh. Someone else's diskette in my computer—it's a strange analogy. The word "virus" comes to mind. I have caught a virus, I repeat to myself. Let's see what Daniel has to say about an anti-virus program. I doubt if it's a quick fix program like I have at home on my computer. I'm curious though about how he sees me getting this foreign diskette, with a program that doesn't fit me, out of my internal computer.

"What you've been attempting to do is quite beneficial to becoming who you are," he says. "In addition to working on your spirituality, you've been working at the technical level of programming."

Oh, oh, the "technical" word, I say to myself. Daniel begins to explain what he means. He believes that using the proper techniques is beneficial to the process and the programming process is valuable when directed correctly. He describes it as taking one picture and placing it on top of another and hoping that top picture will be strong enough to replace the first picture. They're called affirmations in business.

"Now Mark, in the spiritual community, you're learning meditation techniques, guided imagery, lucid dreaming steps, and intuitive communication. You're learning about sounding and energy and chakra systems. These are all ways of helping you to re-write your original programs," he explains.

"It sounds easy when you talk about it. But how do you

know when you have an original program that's faulty?"

"Simple really," Daniel says. "You can discern it's a program because it doesn't really work. It doesn't allow you choice. It says black or white, yes or no, right or wrong. The solution is getting the proper computer disk—the right program. Let's go back to one of your programs—the correct program for you is that you can have spirituality and business. That's the appropriate disk for you. You don't have to compartmentalize them. Church on Sunday, work on Monday, that sort of thing. You can integrate and be who you are, the whole you in both places."

"Daniel, I like your explanation of this entire process."

Daniel continues and tells me about other clients he has who are facing the same dilemma. I appreciate his advice and honesty, and the fact that there are other people dealing with the same issues. In the past, I've been very selective about receiving advice. I'm not sure if it was a pride thing or being overly sensitive to criticism. I was usually more concerned about the person's motive, than the advice itself. Sounds a little like a *program*!

Hidden Asset

*When we stop compartmentalizing our lives, we can
respond from a more universal perspective.*

Chapter Nine

Uncovering Tools for Transformation

Turning Nightmares into Poems

"Allison," I call out. "Allison!" The sharp sound of my voice awakens me from a deep sleep, and I bolt upright in bed. Moments pass in the darkness before I fully realize that it was a dream. I feel relieved and grateful. Even so, I get out of bed and walk quietly down the hall to Allison's room. It's not until I see her face illuminated by the night light that my uneasiness subsides. I pull up the blankets, which she has kicked off in her sleep, and cover her again. She stirs, flinging one arm overhead as I lean over to kiss her.

The inescapable feeling of losing Allison clings to me as I return to my bed, and it remains for the next several days. It's the kind of dream that is so frightening, you wake up with your heart beating fast and adrenaline flowing. I consider telling Vicki about the dream but decide against it so as not to worry her unnecessarily. Her pregnancy is a big enough concern for her right now. Instead, I interpret it the best I can on my own and finally, still dissatisfied and feeling that I might be missing something important, make a note to talk to Mary Coleman about it during our next appointment.

The weather has gotten considerably warmer. The flowers in front of Mary's house that get indirect sunlight are doing well. Mary gives me a warm hug as I enter her office. She asks about

Vicki and the kids. I believe this is more than just a cordial line. She is always interested in my family as much as, or more than, in other things I bring up in our meetings.

"The kids are fine and Vicki is great!" I say. "I really appreciate how much support Vicki has given me on my exploration." Although Mary hasn't mentioned it, quite a few practitioners have told me that Vicki is my soul-mate. I'm not sure I understand this in the bigger cosmic picture, but I can say she is the right mate for me in the here and now.

Mary nods as if in agreement and says, "Through you Vicki is opening to some of the spiritual concepts and principles. Not only that, but she's your grounding cord."

"Grounding cord," I repeat with a laugh.

"That's right. Occasionally, you complain about her desire for a bigger house or new car. This is Vicki's way of staying grounded and keeping *your* feet on the ground."

"By that, I suppose you mean we shouldn't have two Christian mystics in the house at the same time," I say somewhat facetiously.

"Precisely! This wouldn't be good for you or the children. God knew Vicki was just the right person for you and the path you've chosen," Mary says in a firm tone.

"That reminds me of a great book I read recently by Angeles Arrien, called *The Four-Fold Way*. In the book she talks about walking the mystical path with practical feet. That sounds a lot like me, doesn't it?"

"It does," Mary answers.

Now a little more serious, I say, "I do refer to Vicki as my standard, the foundation that keeps me upright and strong."

"She's all of these things and still more," Mary says emphatically. "She's your standard and also that presence in your life that gives your marriage balance. You see, your quest isn't only balancing or spiritualizing yourself, but it's also about developing balanced relationships. Vicki is the right balance for you."

"Mary, I appreciate your saying this; it makes me feel good about our marriage."

Mary stands up to close the curtains a bit. There is something about Mary that makes me really enjoy being around her. It's a quality easy to like but hard to describe. I remember it's the same feeling I had as a teenager for my pastor at the First Baptist Church. He always treated people with great respect. Mary sits back down and asks where I want to start today.

"You asked about the kids. They're fine, but I did have this dream the other night about my daughter Allison that really scared me. It felt so real that when I awoke, I actually thought it had happened. It's left such a strong impression on me, I thought we could talk about it."

"Did you write it down?"

"Yes, I did," I say to Mary. I tell her how I used an interpretation method I learned from Charles Thomas Cayce, the president of the A.R.E. I mention to her that I still feel there are some important things in the dream that I am missing. Mary asks me to retell the dream as I remember it. I start by describing the scene in the dream: how I was at a convenience store, and Allison was with me. Allison was playing hide and seek in the aisles and then, suddenly, I couldn't find her. At first I thought she was playing a game with me so I paid for the milk, but I became even more frightened when I realized Allison was no longer in the store. I began to panic, and I quickly asked the people in the store if they had seen her. Finally, I found her. Then I woke up. I was immensely relieved, but the terror of losing my daughter stayed with me even after the dream was over.

"At first I was frightened that this incident had really happened," I say to Mary. "Then when I realized it was a dream, I was concerned that I might be seeing something that was about to happen. I interpreted my dream using these steps," I add as I hand a list to her.

STEPS I USED FOR DREAM ANALYSIS

1. Write down as much as I can remember about the dream.
2. Write down how I felt in the dream
     (was I afraid? Worried? Happy? etc.).
3. Determine whether characters are literal or symbolic.
4. Is there an influence of God in my dream?
     What is it telling me?
5. Restate the dream in some form
     (poem, narrative, etc.)

"I like your steps, Mark. Did you restate the dream in some other form as it says to do in point number 5?" Mary asks looking up at me.

"Yes, I wrote it in the form of a poem. Would you like to see it?"

"Yes. A businessman writing poetry, …this is something you should frame," she says with a friendly laugh. "You've come a long way in your development, Mark."

I hand her a copy of the poem I wrote about Allison's dream.

POEM I WROTE FOR ALLISON'S DREAM
(Step 5)

There was a man,
who couldn't stand
to stay connected to ones near.
He'd rather be
up in his mentally
created castle where things were clear.
Were others too dull,
or maybe it was the pull,
of fantasy that had him in his head...
that cherished cranium dome.
Finally a dream
in his real life seemed
to shake his foundation down to his bones.
He soon realized
that others relied
on "both his head...and his heart" being at home.

"What made you think of writing a poem about this, Mark?" Mary asks.

"Charles Thomas told me that it's a way to integrate the dream. It takes the analysis of points one through four and adds a creative interpretation to it."

"Isn't that interesting," Mary says. She continues to read my notes. I lean forward in my chair and stretch. The smell of fresh-cut flowers attracts my attention. There is a vase of red roses beside Mary's desk. I get up and go over to smell them. There is a bit of irony that Mary should have red roses in her office because my nickname for Allison is Allie-Rose. I always tell her she's my little rose, and whenever I smell roses I think of my daughter.

"What do you think your dream is telling you?" Mary asks after rereading what I have written.

"I've thought a lot about it. I think it's showing me or reminding me how much I love Allison. Also it seems to be reminding me to really be with my daughter when I'm with her and not be thinking of something else. I think the dream is a lot about staying in the present."

"Good, that's good," Mary nods. "Can you remember anything else about the dream?"

I think for a moment. "No, not really—just that I felt a real terror at losing Allison. It seemed like such an important dream."

Mary knows I'm asking her to use her clairvoyance to look at the dream. "Okay, Mark, do you remember going out of the store? As I look at your dream, I see Allison leaving the store and something about a telephone."

As most true clairvoyants do, Mary sees things in pictures. She's developed an interpretation process to help translate these pictures. In this case it doesn't need much interpretation. "A telephone?" I ask, puzzled at first. "Oh, I do remember going outside, now. Yeah, that's where I found her, outside pretending to be talking on the phone. A telephone, yes, she was near the phone. I forgot about that."

"So what does '*Allison and the telephone*' mean to you?"

"Well, normally I would think it's something she couldn't do on her own. It's too high for her to reach. Then, of course, the telephone is a way of communicating," I reply. I am pleased that Mary brought up the telephone because it sparked my memory of other things that took place in the dream. I had a feeling that I didn't have quite all of it.

"Let me look at Allison's energy around this," Mary suggests, closing her eyes briefly.

Now I am getting the full use of Mary's gifts. First she sensed that there was more to the dream. Now she's looking at Allison's essence or spirit to see what's going on with her. Combining the two should provide a well-rounded look at the dream and what it means.

"I see that at a deeper level, Allison wants to be more independent and responsible even though she's only a pre-schooler. She's also trying to tell you she wants to be considered as special and not just one of the gang. So, Mark, your dream was symbolically expressing Allison's desire."

"Wow! This feels exactly right." I've learned to be more aware when something feels right—when it's a fit—almost like the feeling when you hit a ball on the sweet part of the racquet or golf club.

My heart warms when I think of Allison wanting more responsibility. "Seems like I need to think of some things for her to do to help her develop this responsibility she's yearning for," I think out loud, "and to feel special."

Mary nods in agreement. Her ability to intuit more of my dream has improved the usefulness of the information from the dream. I'm pleased I brought this dream up to Mary. We shift from talking about dreams and move into questions I have on spirits. It's an area I've wanted to talk to Mary about for some time, and it ties into dreams in that I'm curious if spirits can work through a person's dreams.

I ask Mary about the makeup of a person's spirit and the boundaries that a person's spirit can work within. I ask her questions about spirit attachment and spirit releasement, two of the more unusual areas in books I've been reading. Some leading psychologists and psychiatrists have stated their opinion in these books, and I'm interested to see what Mary, who can actually see spirits, has to say on the subject. Mary talks about her feelings on the subject for the remainder of the meeting. She gives me the good with the bad and instructs me again to be very discerning around the issue of spirits. She is very straightforward and level-headed about how she deals with all these matters.

After I leave Mary's house, I again think about Allison and the discussion around the dream. It seems really important to pay attention to the information from my dreams. Was my inner voice trying to tell me the same thing as my dream but in other ways? Do dreams like these happen when you don't listen to your own intuition? I wonder.

I remember when I was in Switzerland talking to Franz Jung, son of the famous psychiatrist, Carl Jung. We talked about his father, and I asked him if they ever talked about dreams as a family since dreams were such a big part of Jung's therapy. He told me that only occasionally would he and his sisters and his dad discuss dreams, usually over breakfast.

"Allison, sweetheart, would you help me with this, please?" I ask the following Saturday morning when we're doing our chores.

Allison runs over to take my hand. She smiles up at me, delighted at the request. "I need your help with the laundry. I bought a special stool for you so you can reach the buttons for me," I report. She picks up the blue plastic stool, places it in front of the washing machine and climbs on it.

"I'm ready, Daddy," she says eyeing the row of buttons.

"Which one? Which one?"

As I watch her enthusiasm, I realize that I've spent most of my life not paying attention to my dreams. This is just another example of an inner resource that I haven't learned to use effectively. This experience has shown me just how valuable dreams can be. There is a lot of information locked up in dreams. The important thing is to develop a key to unlock them.

Lighten Up

I've found there are certain times when my mind and heart are more receptive, …when there is an openness regardless of the external situation. My hope is for just such a time when I arrive at a class being given by Carol Hansen, creator and presenter of a workshop entitled "Lighten Up." Carol is a delightful woman whom I had initially met at a health and healing seminar. She invited me to attend her class. I'm not sure exactly what it's about, but I like her optimistic spirit, and other people have recommended her class to me so I decide to give it a try. I am curious to find out the meaning of "lighten up."

Carol is author of the book, *Lighten Up Inspirations: A Motivational Workbook & Journal* and travels all over the United States presenting her workshops. Most of my exploration has been in individual sessions, so I am also interested in her class in order to experience the group dynamics of healing. Quite a few of her workshops are hosted by churches, which to be honest makes the idea of them a little more comfortable for me.

The class I attend is at a church with a large multi-use room just right for this type of workshop. All of the folding chairs have been stacked and moved to the outside walls. The banners of Jesus Christ on the cross and the ones from the Sunday service have been draped high overhead so we can move around the room more easily. When the class is underway, I'm cautious at first because the room is filled to capacity, with non-business types. It's a little uncomfortable for me, and I'm wondering if I should have signed up for this class. Rather quickly, however, I have a change of heart brought on by Carol's wonderful life story.

She begins by recounting how she lowered her blood pressure and lost over eighty pounds by learning to love herself through a process she received during a meditation. My weight has been pretty constant most of my life, so the weight issue doesn't capture my attention. I also have low blood pressure, taking after my mother's side. But I can see that Carol is developing a process, and this keeps me interested in learning her approach. She recommends her process to us as a way to heal our own issues, emphasizing that weight loss is not the goal of her class. Her first step in this process is to say to yourself, "I love you" while standing naked in front of a mirror. "It was one of the most difficult things I've ever done," she confesses to us. "It took me four hours before I could do it." The second part of her process is a daily five-minute ritual that includes applying lotion to all parts of the body while giving each body part a verbal message of gratitude and love. She says that this process will bring you to a state of unconditional love of yourself by creating energy of cooperation between the body and mind. "When your mind and body work together and love each other, then healing on all levels can take place," she says.

She teaches us many other concepts and exercises throughout the evening, such as how to change our habits and the importance of meditation. But what I receive most out of Carol Hansen's class is the concept of loving and healing myself. More than the music or the exercises, her concept of loving oneself unconditionally really hits home for me.

I have heard the phrase "unconditional love" a lot in the media. I believe that the simple exercises Carol suggests are a good start in putting this loving oneself into practice. It's like an affirmation in physical form. She suggests that every day you say positive affirmations as you go through a sequence of exercises that train your body and mind to work together to love yourself. Some of the exercises from the session don't fit my personality or my schedule so I have modified them. Whether it's meditation or prayer or movement or whatever, I adjust and modify it to my specific need in order to be successful at incorporating it into my life.

The simple process that Carol suggests leaves me less self critical. This is very good for me because I tend to be unnecessarily harsh with myself. I can drive myself harder than any boss would. Carol's workshop has helped me to start to reverse this self-analysis and self-criticism. In the past, I have been a perfectionist—trying to be the perfect businessman. I was pretty hard on myself when mistakes were made or I didn't work hard enough. Carol's class allows me to think about this side of myself and lighten up about it. I think about this class whenever I begin to get down or to be too self critical.

It would be easy for my analytical side to question just what I got from this class. I don't know if you can place a dollars and cents value on the workshop. The class is really about making a conceptual shift and the effectiveness is hard to measure.

I bought one of her audio tapes to listen to from time to time.

The repetitiveness of listening to the tape helps me at a subconscious level. Carol has also made a children's tape called *I Love Myself* with a delightful song and narrative geared to helping young children learn to appreciate and love themselves. As a parent, I find this tape very helpful.

One other interesting thing came out of the Lighten Up class. Carol has done something unique—she has combined a physical practice with a verbal affirmation. This is quite ingenious, and the combination intrigues me. I have actually used this combination for other areas of my life since then. I have even begun developing some of these "physical affirmations" with my kids.

A month ago, I visited Arcosanti in Arizona and purchased a Soleri Bell designed by Paolo Soleri. We have it hanging on our back porch. I took Carol's process of combining a physical action with a verbal affirmation and integrated the use of the Soleri Bell. My kids and I ring the bell regularly, and we say a positive affirmation for the world while we ring it. Jonathan likes to say something like "Let's bring peace to the world," while Allison may say "Let hunger go away in the world." It has become a little prescribed ritual for us, a symbol of that greater thing each of us desires for humanity. We have fun with it. When the wind blows, as it often does off the ridge near our home, the Soleri Bell rings. We say it's humanity answering us.

Piercing the Valley: A View of Balance

In an unpredictable world where the speed of change is constantly accelerating, confirmation of our feelings can bring a sense of security. Vicki and I have always taken the offensive in dealing with issues that arose from my sleep disorder. "Proactive" is the word we use for this in business. Initially, my disorder was a real hardship on Vicki, and we felt a marriage and family counselor would add to our success in getting through that period of our lives. We were introduced to an excellent counselor by the name of Lynn Bieber.

We have continued to meet with Lynn on a semi-regular basis. One particular day, the three of us gather at Lynn's office located in a small professional office building. It's a windy day, the kind of day that's just right to fly a kite. On days like this my daughter Allison likes to recite a line she wrote; "The dogs bark and the trees blow on windy days, while kids stay inside when the wind is calling them out to play."

As we enter Lynn's office, Vicki and I sit on a couch, and Lynn sits in an armchair facing us. Lynn's office is filled with a mixture of beautiful art. There are collages on the wall opposite us and decorative masks just to the left of the door. She also has a collection of Native American drums hanging neatly on the wall behind her desk.

Lynn is colorful, humorous, and has a warmth about her that allows for ease of opening up. She seems to listen with her eyes, which are intent and purposeful. Lynn is very good at creating an atmosphere of trust, and she starts off the meeting by asking Vicki a few questions. This enables Vicki to talk about her feelings.

"When Mark first became interested in the mind/body/spirit fields, I was relieved that he was motivated again," she says to Lynn. "He'd reached such a low point during his sleeping spells that it scared me. I worried he might be falling into a depression.

When he became interested in the mind/body/spirit and holistic fields, then my concern was that he might go off the deep end. This is when I became more aware that I had a strong faith in God and in Mark."

One of the reasons Lynn has been so effective is that Vicki trusts her and enjoys learning from her. This trust has enabled Vicki and me to use Lynn to improve our communication when there are conflicts arising. It also helps our confidence in her that she has raised four of her own children.

"I would imagine Mark's exploration has not always been an easy thing for you," Lynn says to Vicki.

"It has been a challenge at times," Vicki admits. "The more Mark gets into his studies of spirituality and the mind/body connection, the more I get concerned about our relationship suffering. Personally, I haven't felt as great a desire to become involved with it, but I've felt some pressure to do so because I worry about the closeness in our marriage. There are times when I'm overwhelmed by how much information Mark has absorbed, and how many people he has met. I know that there's no possible way I can achieve his level of understanding so I don't even try. I've decided the only way to deal with the 'new' Mark is to be as supportive and open as I possibly can. My nature is to watch and learn."

"Vicki, that seems like a wise approach," Lynn offers, glancing first at Vicki, then at me.

I put my hand on Vicki's shoulder because I know this is not an easy thing for her to talk about. Lynn has suggested this form of physical support in one of our earlier sessions. She has helped me to understand Vicki's needs and also the differences in the male and female way of doing things. Lynn herself is very much into sacred things and the re-introduction of the feminine into everyday life. I am captivated by a small oriental fountain inside the atrium adjacent to where we meet. The fountain creates a stream that flows through a miniature valley between two mountain peaks. It is quite beautiful.

"Mark is a wonderful husband, and father. He has become more sensitive and patient," Vicki acknowledges with a certain pride in me.

"You mean he hasn't always been this way?" Lynn asks somewhat facetiously.

Vicki laughs and says, "No. Mark can be very stubborn and inflexible like most men. But he's grown and changed in a sensitive sort of way without giving up his male strengths. His feelings seem to be expressed more easily and openly with me and with other family members," Vicki confirms as Lynn smiles in approval. "I also have learned just how consumed he can become when he's passionate about something. He gets straight after things, which is where more of his masculine qualities emerge."

Lynn says, "Sounds like Mark is using his masculine qualities to explore more feminine qualities."

My mind continues to focus on the fountain with the miniature valley as I listen to Vicki. My imagination takes over and melds with the view I have of the fountain. The water flows out of a small valley between two peaks. To me these two peaks could represent the right and left brain or the masculine and feminine. I imagine for a moment that I am climbing through this valley. I am seeking the middle way, piercing the valley as I seek to harmonize the left and the right.

"Vicki, how do you think your relationship with Mark has been affected?" Lynn asks.

Vicki admires the African violets blooming on Lynn's side table. "I feel that we have grown closer in an inner way," she answers. "We were very close before, but there's definitely a new element in our relationship that was not there previously. Trust and faith have grown stronger between us." Vicki looks at me.

"Okay," Lynn says. "Mark, let me ask you the same question. How do you feel your relationship has been affected as a result of this awakening?"

"We're more open with our feelings toward each other. I've learned to be more comfortable sharing my feelings with Vicki. I'm more *emotionally authentic* than I've been in the past. Before, I'd mask my feelings more and keep them inside. This probably impacted my body as well since I tend to hold everything in."

As I talk to Lynn and Vicki about this, I think about how emotions always seemed like a weakness to me—something that could be exploited by the competition.

"It appears your whole emotional approach has changed, which has helped Vicki's and your relationship," Lynn says. "How has it affected your business career?"

"It has changed as well, Lynn. In the past, my philosophy around business was really about how to obtain commercial or competitive supremacy. I could never turn this off. Even my duties on the Evangelism Committee at church I instinctively turned into a competition. I truly wanted to develop an outreach program that would beat the church next door. Much of this competition has changed into cooperation. Now when I think of competition, I try to replace it with cooperation."

"That's a big step," Lynn says.

"Yes, it has been a challenge but a very worthwhile one," I acknowledge leaning back on the couch. I reflect on how it has also helped Vicki's and my relationship because I no longer try to compete with her. "Cooperation" has become my buzzword whenever I feel that urge to outdo Vicki. I am more aware of the value of cooperation and the balance with this approach.

"Decisions around our relationship as a couple, as parents, and as a family, tend to be more complete and made with more consideration than before," I add.

"And how has this change of attitude affected the children?" Lynn asks Vicki.

"It's interesting," she says. "Mark and I don't notice it so much, but other people have pointed it out to us. For instance, one of the children's teachers said that she could see we were really working with the children individually and that we were allowing them to develop at their own pace, according to what's of interest and unique to each of them. She only has one of our children in her class, but during a recent parent/teacher conference when both children were present, she made the comment to me after watching them playing for awhile in her classroom."

Lynn smiles as Vicki continues, "Our intent is to try to work with our children and help them to understand their gifts. Mark's research has really enhanced this. We've delighted in discovering more about the children through some of the intuitives and systems. The kids are becoming more of who they are as individuals, and Mark and I are trying hard to let this happen in a natural way."

"Mark, is there anything you care to add to this?" asks Lynn.

"I think Vicki's hit the nail on the head. The biggest change in our parenting relationship is that we are becoming more aware of the kids' soul qualities."

"Soul qualities?" Lynn repeats, a little perplexed.

"Yes. We've begun working with the kids in such a way as to not kill their spirit or stamp out those things that make them complete. Some of these I believe are qualities of the soul. That's really where things have shifted. We haven't thrown out the way we were before. We just want the children to keep a broad perspective and not become narrow. They're so open right now."

"This seems really important, especially for you, Mark," Lynn points out.

"You're right," I acknowledge. "I guess it's because I had only a faint memory of my own childlike nature before my sleep disorder. I'd become hardened, rigid, and more closed-minded. Only a remnant of that innocent nature was still with me. Now, I've started to nurture this inner part of myself. By beginning to foster this childlike nature, I'm developing the other qualities of my soul."

"Very insightful," Lynn says.

I continue, "That's why it's so important to start our kids off in a way that doesn't close down this childlike nature. I don't want them to have to rediscover it when they're forty. I want them to have a strong inner sense about themselves."

"It's an admirable goal, Mark," Lynn says. "And, Vicki, it seems like you're becoming more comfortable with Mark's discoveries as you see their benefits to the family."

"That's true," Vicki answers and begins to talk more about the children. She likes to talk about her relationship with each child so that Lynn can comment. One of Lynn's extraordinary gifts is her ability to sense the energy in a relationship. This is quite remarkable because she can describe the energy between two people just as some of the healers can see energy in the body. Lynn spends the remainder of the session describing these relationships and giving us suggestions on ways we can improve or enhance them.

Becoming Childlike

Seeking greater awareness or higher consciousness is important but can be a humbling experience. That night, after Vicki and the kids have gone to bed, I sit down to contemplate our meeting with Lynn and reflect on the inner child. It seems to me that to respect the inner child is to welcome the grace and energy of God. Respecting the inner child and giving it life and a voice—that seems to be a big part of it. I wonder why I didn't see this before. Is it possible that I could only see things in one direction?

Many of the books I've read and people I've met talk about the child-within. At first it was hard for me to know what they were talking about. The "inner child..." what was that? The "child within..." who was that in me? These are questions that had me perplexed. I would see a PBS special on the "inner child" and not understand it at all. Once I emerged from my own wilderness of the soul, I began to realize that it was the childlike portion in me that retained oneness with the universe. It was the child in me that retained harmony with other people and nature. Somehow the grown-up part of me had forgotten these harmonies. That part of me had learned to become competitive and to take advantage of the differences between people.

My mind jumps to the analytical side of why I wasn't able to develop these childlike forces before. I had read the part of Scripture about becoming "like little children" a thousand times. Why didn't it have the effect it's having now? Why didn't the PBS programs on the inner child work for me before? If I have the child nature in me as we all do, why hadn't I felt the need to have it nurtured before? All these questions seemed to be answered by the simple fact that my life was overly influenced by materialism and the physicalness of everything. My main goal was to do well and make money. Money and achievement dominated my will. When these physical qualities alone were at work in me at a conscious level, I put off or scoffed at the notion of the childlike nature.

Hidden Asset

*Our inner self has a childlike quality to it
that is often kept hidden.*

Chapter Ten

Dealing with Change

Alternative Medicine and Crooked Neck Vertebrae

Every now and then I reflect on the chain of events that set this adventure into motion. I sit patiently in the waiting room to see Dr. Stanton, my homeopathy doctor. I have to believe my initial meeting with her set into motion the desire to explore the mind/body/spirit fields.

Following a short wait, Dr. Stanton's assistant escorts me into the examination room. I re-familiarize myself with the room filled with shelves of various vials and substances along with a number of machines sitting on the table tops. Dr. Stanton enters and greets me warmly. She adjusts the machine to start the physical analysis, and we begin what for me is always a stimulating conversation.

"Mark, bring me up to date on what's happened since I saw you last," she says as she hooks me up to the energy medicine machine.

"There's a lot that's been happening since we originally met," I say as I watch her touch my feet with the leads from the machine. "I have to tell you, my very first appointment with you really opened my eyes."

"And how is that?"

"When you suggested I begin reading books on Edgar Cayce and looking into the A.R.E. to find out more about mind/body/spirit, it really took hold for me. I branched out to learn more about other people and organizations in these fields, such as the

Anthroposophical Society, which I'm reading up on right now."

She removes the small bottle, which contains a certain mineral, from the machine and sets it to the side. "Ah yes, the Rudolf Steiner Foundation. What a wonderful man! So many contributions to humanity. Did you know he started the Waldorf Schools?" she asks, making a note of the mineral type to recommend to me after the exam.

"Yes, I found that out," I respond. I tell her about my recent trip to the Philosophical Research Society in Los Angeles. "Manly P. Hall's personal library has been preserved intact," I say. I continue by telling her that I've worked with intuitives, healers, clairvoyants, and people who interpret dreams in addition to visiting healing centers, spiritual book stores, metaphysical libraries, holistic medicine groups, and doctors with alternative practices.

"Sounds like you've been busy!" She motions for my hands, and I hold them out for her to test.

"I have indeed! Each of these contacts and organizations has helped me expand my awareness of myself as both a physical and spiritual being. It's been quite exciting."

"How about some of the areas I advised you to look into for your physical well-being? Have you investigated them as well? Like the craniosacral therapy for your nose…that sort of thing?"

"Yes, Doctor, I'm a good student, and I've followed up on all of your suggestions," I respond. "I've had three craniosacral treatments so far."

"How did you like someone manipulating the bones of your skull?" she asks me, looking over the rims of her glasses.

"It took getting used to, but it really has reduced the pressure in my upper nasal area. I believe this has helped cut down on the number of headaches I have there."

"How about the chiropractor I referred you to?"

"Yes, I saw him too. He looked at my joints and lower back to see what, if any, impact my running is having on my body. In fact, you want to hear something strange about my chiropractic appointment?"

"Sure."

"Well, you know from our first meeting that I've always had a mental block about going to see a chiropractor. I don't know if it was from a fear that they would reel me into weekly visits or that they might injure me by trying to snap something back into place."

Dr. Stanton smiles. She suggested I see a chiropractor when she examined my medical history and found out I'd injured my neck playing sports. This along with frequent neck aches that turn into headaches made her feel there might be something out of alignment. I tell her the first thing the chiropractor does is take X-rays, and then he does a physical examination. In his physical examination, as he was feeling my neck area, he asked me if I had headaches very often. I told him "yes," and he said my neck vertebrae felt out of place.

"Well," I continue, "Vicki was in the room with me. She had accompanied me to ask the chiropractor about pressure on her joints during pregnancy. I glanced over at her and rolled my eyes. I was truly thinking this guy was just trying to get another patient hooked up to a monthly service. Honestly, that's what I was really thinking," I insist as Dr. Stanton leans back in her chair and smiles.

"I go back the next week to look at the X-rays. Vicki is with me so she can confirm what I'm telling you. We sit down, and he displays the X-rays of my neck. There is one joint in the lower part of the neck vertebrae that's, in his words, 'greatly malpositioned' in relation to the rest."

Dr. Stanton's eyes get all squinty as she lets out a laugh and leans forward in her chair. I tell her that I'm not kidding. "We still have copies of that X-ray on file. That neck joint was practically sideways. I made a joke to the chiropractor and said this looks bad. He said it certainly did, but with one adjustment, it would glide back into place. Then we'd check it for a few weeks, and based on his experience, I wouldn't need continued visits."

I make a motion with my arms to show Dr. Stanton the type of adjustment the chiropractor made that day. I went back two more times for checkups. No adjustment was necessary, and it's been fine ever since. I wouldn't have believed this story if it hadn't happened to me.

Dr. Stanton says it's a great story. I tell her one last thing. The chiropractor said the joint looked as if it had been out of place for a long time. Strange how I let my prejudice against chiropractors keep me from being examined up until now. I tell her I'm usually a pretty open-minded guy, but there was something about chiropractors that kept me from going to see one. Maybe I could have fixed this problem, and my headaches, long ago.

Still amused, she tells me she'll have to file that story away to tell other patients who are skeptical of the chiropractic profession. She begins to organize the bottles of plant extracts and minerals on the machine table top as she asks, "How about your regular doctor? Have you been back to see him?"

"Yes, I had my yearly checkup, and everything was fine. My

cholesterol count was a little higher than normal for me, but everything else was excellent."

"That's good, Mark. I have something you can take for that cholesterol. It's a natural plant extract. Let's see, yes, here it is." She adds another bottle from the cabinet to the others.

I like that she approves of both a person's regular physician and alternative practitioners. I wonder if it's because she was a regular MD for so many years.

Dr. Stanton continues the examination. I've observed that some of the remedies from these alternative medical practitioners seem to come from a faculty that's almost intuitive in nature. It is more than just a textbook approach. Some of it is experience, of course. Dr. Stanton has been practicing for thirty-five years and my acupuncturist for twenty so they have seen many cases. Yet even with their experience, it seems as though the remedies are specific to me as an individual case. Whether they're prescribing herbs, some sort of diet, or a therapeutic process, the combination always seems unique to me. Somehow, many of these practitioners combine their formal training and experience with an intuitive knowledge of the individual patient. I like that!

"We're done for today," Dr. Stanton says. "You are doing well physically? Do you have any other questions?"

"I do have a question on naturopathy," I acknowledge.

"Which is?"

"Are homeopathy and naturopathy used interchangeably? It seems like I hear these two words together a lot."

"That's a good question and concerns an issue that's often confusing. As I've mentioned before, homeopathy, which I practice, is based on the principle of 'like cures like.' Homeopathic remedies stimulate a person's natural vital energy so the body can heal itself."

"Uh, huh."

"Now for naturopathy," she continues. "Naturopathy includes the whole array of healing practices such as Ayurveda, Chinese medicine, herbalism, and nutrition as well as homeopathy. The practitioner's intent is to mobilize the natural healing power of the human body through natural, non-toxic therapies. That's the link among all of the practices that fall under the general category called naturopathy. Does that answer your question?"

"Yes. I also wanted to say how appreciative I am that you took time to talk to me about holistic health and the body/mind/ spirit connection when we first met. It really was the door that opened a lot of this information for me."

"I suspect, Mark, that if it hadn't been me, it would have been someone else," she says. "The universe works this way. I've also taken notice of your intuitive development since we've met. It appears to me that you're trusting your intuition more and thereby developing confidence in this capability. I applaud you for taking the time to do this. And speaking of doors opening for you..., I have my next patient coming through that door any minute."

"See you in six months," I say.

Transcribing Beliefs

In business, much like team sports, relationship bonds are formed that can be of the most rewarding kind. The passion for building an organization and the drive to succeed, create a kind of camaraderie in most business relationships. In some cases, however, a genuine friendship develops separate and apart from the business side. In my career, I've had the blessing of numerous friendships that have begun as business relationships. This morning I have a meeting with just such a friend and partner, Kevin Lanning.

Kevin and I are now into our second decade of being business partners. He has a caring manner as well as an exceptional mind. He always scores off the chart on intelligence tests, yet he is down to earth and practical. He's been a wonderful partner and very supportive.

"Hey, Mark, how are you enjoying those books by Pierre Teilhard de Chardin?" Kevin asks me as we walk into the company lunchroom together.

"I need to be both a philosopher and a scholar to really understand them, but I'm enjoying them, at any rate," I answer. "He really was a great thinker. I like the way he was able to bridge his beliefs in terms of being both a Catholic priest and a paleontologist. It's interesting to me how someone could believe in the creation story of Adam and Eve and at the same time believe the earth is hundreds of millions of years old. I appreciate your letting me borrow the books."

"Keep them as long as you like. I have a lot of his books," Kevin says.

I admire the way Kevin has balanced his serious, philosophical nature with a friendliness that is casual and genuine.

"How's your research coming along?" he asks.

"Great! I'm taping many of the sessions. I'll have to let you read some of the transcribed notes."

"Who transcribes your tapes?" Kevin asks.

"Local transcribers. The people I work with do transcriptions mostly for doctors and attorneys."

"Your material must be a real change for them," Kevin says with a laugh.

"I'd say so. I've already had two transcribers quit on me."

"No way!"

"I'm serious," I say.

Kevin takes a seat in the lunchroom and leans back. He wants to know the whole story. I tell him the first transcriber was just fine for several months. Then she stopped returning my calls and no longer picked up the tapes. Clearly, the material on the tapes was very different from what she was used to. Instead of tapes from attorneys conducting depositions, etcetera, she was hearing tapes from lucid dreamers meeting each other in their dreams, healers working with chakras, and intuitives looking into the body. This seems to amuse Kevin.

I tell Kevin at first the transcriber didn't seem to be bothered, but I noticed, after a while, that her enthusiasm for the work wasn't there. Instead of informing me directly that she didn't want to do the job, she became more and more difficult to reach, and her timeliness in finishing the tapes trailed off dramatically.

"Finally," I tell him, "I didn't hear from her at all. I think the material on the tapes was butting up against her belief system. She made reference to this in passing on the telephone. I'm surmising that she heard things on the tapes that shook her core beliefs or maybe brought up patterns she wasn't willing to face."

"What happened with the second transcriber?" Kevin asks.

"She transcribed my tapes for a short while; then one day she called to inform me that she couldn't carry on with the work. She said that although she could see the benefit of the information, she couldn't accept the methods in which I was getting the information."

"So she liked the information but not the source of the information?" Kevin asks.

"That's right. She told me she could appreciate my being able to balance my Christian belief with this information but felt it was disruptive for her. I admired her honesty."

"Mark, I have to say, I'm really surprised about all this. Who's doing your tapes now?"

"A woman who lives in the East Bay."

"Do you think the same thing will happen again?"

"No. Not only has this woman been transcribing my tapes for many months now, but she's asked me for some of the practitioners' telephone numbers so she can call them. She's also asked me for other information that appeared on the tapes from time to time—books, places, and so on. Since I like to connect people, I've been happy to give her the information."

"I'm still amazed," Kevin says. "Who knows, maybe the information had a positive effect on the first two transcribers."

"How so?" I ask.

"By listening to the tapes, they got a better chance to examine and compare their own personal beliefs around how the world works..., their cosmology, if you will."

Kevin has hit the nail on the head. I tell him one area that really confronted my own belief system was astrology. I've read where people like Carl Jung and others supported its validity; however, it still took me a while to understand. Even now, I don't tend to follow it with any regularity, but there is clearly something to astrology that I can't put my finger on.

I tell Kevin an interesting story about how I had an astrological chart done on my children by Liz Greene, the famous astrologer in England. "The children's perspective intrigued me," I explain. "To my surprise, it provided quite a wonderful narrative outline for me, as a parent, in how to work with the kids. I was quite impressed by it. Of course, I first had it done for the kids, but when I read what it had to say, I had one done on me."

"You had a children's chart done on yourself?"

"Yeah. I thought I might use it to compare how many things my parents had done with me."

I had to admit to Kevin that when I received my copy on my own childhood astrological chart, I was amazed! Not at the information specifically but rather at how my parents had done so many of the things it proposed. This made me appreciate my parent's intuitive ability even more. And they never had an astrology reading in their life. They don't believe in it.

"Sounds a little like your own cosmology has changed," Kevin says with a grin.

"Yeah, I've used this exploration to look at my own personal beliefs," I reply. "But cosmology?" I break into a smile. "Now tell me, Kevin, does the word 'cosmology' come out of your philosophical studies or from your fascination with astronomy?" I say with a laugh as he proceeds out of the lunchroom and into the warehouse. It's the kind of thing you can say to someone who is a friend as well as a business associate.

Functional Integration

Someone once said "Health is the first wealth." My own value of health and healing is increasing. I've scheduled an appointment with a practitioner from Israel named Ofer Erez who is trained in a bodywork technique called Feldenkrais. Ofer often works and teaches classes at local fitness centers in addition to his home office.

I'm a member of a health club but have never heard of Feldenkrais before. Supposedly, many athletes use the method after a sport-related injury. As I pull into the fitness center parking lot, I realize I'm about ten minutes early. So I sit in my car and peruse a book on bodywork entitled, *The Future of the Body*. It was an unexpected gift from my brother, Thom. I roll down the windows to take advantage of the hot summer weather. At the top of the hour, I get out of my car and walk to the front door. Two women in Spandex suits and a large, powerfully built man carrying a weight-lifting belt over one shoulder enter just ahead of me. That gritty odor of sweat overlaid with cleaning solution is the first thing my senses pick up. As my eyes pan the lobby, a young man approaches from just beyond the attendant desk.

"I'm Ofer Erez. Are you Mark?" he asks as he holds out his hand.

"I am," I say, shaking his hand. He has strong hands for someone of medium build, possibly as a result of the work he performs. He leads me to a small treatment room and asks me to have a seat. As he moves about adjusting the height of the massage table, I note how his dark features contrast with the white walls of the room. He seems very serious and purposeful, although his casual dress puts me at ease.

"So Mark, why have you come to see me today?" Ofer asks.

"Actually, I'm trying to find out more about the different modalities in the holistic health field. When I asked about Feldenkrais, I was given your name by an acquaintance of mine."

"I see. You said on the telephone that you wanted to ask me some questions," he says.

"Yes, I would. Is it better to do that now, or should I ask them as you work on me?"

"It would be better now," he says, still apparently unsure of why I have come to see him.

"Can you tell me a little about Feldenkrais?" I ask, trying to get off on the right foot.

"Of course! Feldenkrais was developed in Israel by Moshe Feldenkrais. He was a scientist who had a personal trauma that drove him to explore the functioning of the body. He studied physiology and anatomy and developed the Feldenkrais Method." There is that personal trauma and healing connection again, I think to myself.

"Is the Feldenkrais Method a form of body work?"

"Yes and no," he replies. "It's usually placed in the same category as Rolfing or massage even though its design is very different."

Ofer's comment reminds me of my first encounter with Rolfing with a woman practitioner I saw in Sedona, Arizona. She defined Rolfing as the idea that the human function is improved when segments of the body are properly aligned. I remember us having a big laugh as I told her I felt like a wheel on one of those alignment machines at the gas station as she "rolfed" my face. She reasoned that an aligned body balances better against gravity, allowing it to use energy more efficiently.

"How's Feldenkrais different?" I ask, eager to find out more.

"The central theme of Feldenkrais is one's self-image," he explains. "Using Feldenkrais, I direct your body through movements that are individual to your needs. It's through what Moshe Feldenkrais termed 'Functional Integration' that I'll be working to improve your self-image and movement."

"Okay," I respond, not really comprehending what's going on here.

He seems to sense my confusion and says, "I can see I haven't been clear to you. Would you like to look at some books by Moshe Feldenkrais?" he offers, lowering his guard.

"Yes, I would," I answer, happy to have another resource.

He takes down two books from a shelf and hands them to me. It is quiet for a moment as I look them over. I feel somewhat awkward at this point as I'm not sure if Ofer means for me to look at these books now or later.

"Should I look at these now?" I finally ask.

"Please, take them with you," he says. "Bring them back the next time you come. Are you ready to experience Feldenkrais?"

"Yes," I answer, feeling more at ease, my awkwardness completely gone now.

"Good. Please lie on this table."

Ofer begins very gently but firmly moving my right leg in a circular motion. He switches to my left leg after a few minutes. The movement is very deliberate, and he takes great care in the precise handling of my limbs and torso. I lie here thinking about what he has said while he continues to work with the precision of a mechanic. He is very specific about the Feldenkrais Method and the movements he is making with my body. He shows me areas and activities where my body is getting out of alignment by the way I move. This is fascinating to me since I've never really thought about this before. Now that he has pointed this out to me, I can't help noticing some of these habits. It's like playing tennis with a poor backhand. I can see why Feldenkrais is so popular among athletes who need to have good form.

Following what seems like thirty minutes of Ofer negotiating my limbs, neck and torso, he asks me to be still for a few minutes while he leaves the room. About ten minutes later, he returns. "Do you feel any different?" he asks as I sit up and stretch.

"I really don't know what I feel yet," I respond. "It's been an unusual experience. It didn't hurt," I add reassuringly.

Ofer laughs. "That's good," he says, "It's not supposed to."

I begin to feel in my body the effects of the treatment. My lower back is less tense as I begin to move around. Ofer shows me certain body movements and a series of exercises to improve my posture without putting unnecessary strain on my back and neck. He seems to know intuitively that my back and neck are problem areas for me.

"Let's slowly walk around a bit now," Ofer suggests, "so that you can get your equilibrium back. Then, when we come back, I can show you ways to do everyday activities, like getting out of bed or getting up from a chair, that will help reduce strain and be healthier for your body."

"You mean practical things?"

"Yes," he affirms. "But first let's take a short walk outside."

I wonder if Ofer's suggestions on movement are today's road signs. If so, I know to listen more carefully to these health tips than I have in the past. Ofer is a very precise and a highly intelligent person, operating in what seems like an inexact field—the holistic health industry. I wonder how he manages this paradox.

He interrupts my thoughts by saying, "What's needed here and now in the United States is better education of how processes like Feldenkrais and other healing systems work. Along with education, there needs to be a better process of disseminating this information."

I ponder Ofer's comment, and the wisdom of it rings true to me. It is difficult to find out about some of these alternative practices. Even when I'm familiar with a particular practice, I can't always find a practitioner in my area. It took me a while to find Ofer. I wonder why it needs to be this difficult? We finish our walk, and I schedule another appointment.

As I walk to my car, I reflect on an unexpected benefit of today's session. I've gotten a unique perspective of holistic health from someone who grew up in a foreign country and has different religious beliefs. It makes me wonder just how much one's beliefs and cultural background affect one's view of healing.

I am very happy that Ofer allowed me to borrow some of his books. One title, *Healing Inner Conflict*, is appealing, particularly when I noted that Ofer was the author. The book is a collection of poetic thoughts and captures his unusual thought process on paper. In his own way, Ofer is striving to improve the education about and awareness of alternative forms of health in this country. I admire his conviction.

Speaking of Fairies...

It's easy to turn arrogant when endeavoring to bring about consciousness or greater awareness in another person. I have to catch myself from talking to Vicki as if I'm the expert about consciousness and awareness. Fortunately, Vicki is quick to set me straight when I get to the point of sounding ridiculous or condescending.

When the kids are down for the night, it's a good time for Vicki and me to sit and talk. This may all change when the new baby arrives, so we're taking advantage of the time while we can.

I flip through the pile of mail on the coffee table. I find a card from my friend Randy. He's enclosed a short letter updating me on his health. Unfortunately, there continues to be bad news on his health condition. The only positive aspect of hearing the bad news is that it keeps me motivated to seek out information on therapies that might ease his pain.

Vicki sees the card and asks, "Have you seen Randy lately?"

"No, I haven't. According to his card, he just got out of a stay in the hospital. I hope to get over to see him soon. He's not doing too well," I say sadly. "He's continuing the drug therapy along with several alternative approaches. None of them seem very effective though, because he keeps getting worse."

"That's too bad," Vicki says sympathetically.

I tell Vicki that Randy is confined to his home now and to a wheelchair so when I visit him, we stay inside, restricted to the house. No more walks down to the water. He is still the same Randy, the same person I've grown close to over the years, it's just his physical body that's withering away. I have ambivalent feelings about Randy's situation. I've recommended he see a number of healers, and he even went to see Mary Coleman. His single experience with Mary was quite beneficial for him. She made Randy a tape to help him visualize the healing process and talked to him about his own spirit. I think this conversation with Mary really helped him emotionally.

Even with these recommendations and Randy's openness to alternative medicine, his condition continues to worsen. I realize that alternative medicine, just like regular medicine, is not a panacea. For people who are gravely ill, many of these alternative approaches cannot provide cures. These different modalities might be able to lessen the pain or help the symptoms moderately, but in severe cases such as Randy's, there seems to be no dramatic change.

This makes me very sad. I wanted to find a healing method that might make a noticeable difference for him. This has not been the case. I turn on the porch light, and my mind drifts as I think about the healers I've seen. It's hard to believe more than a year has past since I drove across the Bay Bridge to meet with the Russian healer, Valentina Tolsoguzoua, for the very first time. It's been a wonderful adventure finding out about all of these processes around inner awareness and healing.

My thoughts are interrupted as Vicki mentions something about an earlier commitment I had made to rub her feet. I climb the stairs, enter the bathroom and wash my face. A final splash of cold water refreshes me, and I come out ready to try reflexology on Vicki's feet.

"Okay. I'm ready," I announce. "Are you?"

Vicki props her pillow behind her head and smiles as she lays her right foot across my lap. I'm sitting on the edge of the bed with the reflexology chart propped on the night stand in front of me.

"This isn't going to hurt, is it?" she asks hesitantly.

"Not at all," I respond reassuringly. "Reflexology is a way to balance your entire body. At least that's what the instructor told me." I hold her foot in my hand.

"Let's see, you say your lower back is bothering you. Hmm, that might be the sciatic area on this chart." I start to rub Vicki's right heel. "How does that feel?"

"Good," she says closing her eyes. "I like having my feet rubbed."

"I'm going to work my way up the outside of your foot," I inform her as I continue to rub her right foot. "Let's see, the chart says I'll be helping your appendix, then waistline and then your gallbladder."

"Oh, great! My appendix really needs help!" Vicki teases.

"I'm going to stop rubbing if you don't let me practice the techniques," I threaten.

"What is reflexology supposed to do anyway?" she asks, still with her eyes closed.

"According to what I've read and the class I took, areas of your hands and feet contain thousands of tiny nerves called reflexes which correspond to every organ and system within the body. By stimulating the appropriate reflex areas, you can relieve stress and help normalize the body."

"Is that why you started rubbing the kids' feet at night?" she asks, opening her eyes.

"Yes. Another healer showed me just the right spot to rub on the kids' feet to help them get to sleep easier. And the benefit to you, my wife, is…?" I pause to let her fill in the blank.

"I don't know, what?" she laughs.

"I get to spend more quality time with you because the kids go right to sleep, of course," I say with a little wink.

"Don't get mushy on me, big boy. I've still got the kids' lunches to fix for tomorrow," she says with a smile as she again closes her eyes.

I continue to massage Vicki's feet in the areas designated on the reflexology chart, hoping to memorize the key areas before long.

Vicki is becoming visibly more relaxed as she says, "I can see how reflexology is helpful. But what about the stuff you're coming across that isn't helpful or maybe even harmful?" I detect a nervousness in her voice.

"Yes, there's that aspect," I respond. "In fact, I would say about half of my time—maybe slightly more than half—is spent coming across information that I probably can't or won't use."

"Wow," Vicki exclaims, "I'm surprised the amount you can't use is so high! So what do you do with the information that isn't useful or helpful?"

"I place it in categories with just that type of heading. 'Don't know how to use' or 'not useful information.' It's not a judgment of right or wrong, it's just a way of looking at the information or experience," I explain.

"Now I'm curious…what areas have you come across that aren't useful?"

"One that might surprise you is psychic hotlines," I respond.

"Why? Aren't the intuitives on those 900-lines the same type of people you've been visiting?"

"To some degree, yes, but I've mainly concentrated on

intuitives who have been doing this type of work for twenty or more years. I'm really looking for their experience to help me develop my own intuition."

"You mean people like Mary and Karen?"

"Yes," I answer, "...and other people." I remind her of her own sessions with Camille in Chicago and my sessions with Sonja Choquette in Colorado and Mary Roach in Virginia.

I go on to explain that I've learned a lot about the boundaries of intuition from these people. Many of these people are superb teachers. Penney Peirce and Carol Adrienne from across the Bay are good examples. Penney spent time educating me on just how intuition works and I've found Carol Adrienne to be a wonderful researcher. Her seminars at the Learning Annex are excellent.

"Notice they're all women," Vicki observes with a grin.

"Oh, there are some men too," I remind her. "There is Scout Bartlett and I also met with an intuitive from England named Peter Bowers. I just believe men have a bigger hurdle around intuition as a consequence of our culture and institutions."

"Do you still keep in contact with Carol and Penney?"

"I do, but their travel schedules make a sustained relationship a real effort," I explain.

"So what were you going to tell me about the 900-lines?"

"Oh, that's right," I say, getting back to our original discussion. "I don't know if the environment the intuitive is working in is conducive for them to give clear readings. I actually interviewed a man who was taking incoming calls dispatched to his home from a 900 service. I wanted to see how all of this stuff was done. I observed him taking a new call maybe every ten minutes or so and between a couple of calls, he shaved and brushed his teeth."

"Amazing."

"Don't get me wrong, I do believe the man was very gifted. But he'd probably be significantly better with his intuitive faculties if his clients were in the same room and he could focus solely on them."

I can tell Vicki's caught the bug. She asks, "What other areas haven't been useful?"

I tell her that UFOs, psychokinesis, and psychic surgery are examples of areas that haven't been that useful to me. Or at least, I haven't yet seen an effective way to apply this information. I add that in some cases, I avoid them completely because I've done enough reading to know they're not useful for me. Remote viewing, or as it's known in the metaphysical community, "astral projection," is an example of an area that I've stayed away from. It's the ability to perceive things many miles away. Clearly this process has existed for eons. It's now coming out that the CIA Stargate program was all about trying to harness the process of "remote viewing." But for me, there are questions about the usefulness of this process.

"Doesn't this stuff scare you?" she asks with a little shiver.

"Sometimes," I respond thoughtfully. "The spirit beings kind of thing can be a little scary. Did I tell you I interviewed Kevin Ryerson, the guy from the Shirley MacLaine books?"

"No you didn't. Is he the one who channels spirits?" she asks.

"Yeah, that's him," I answer.

"Was he, or should I say *they*, helpful?" she smiles.

"Extremely helpful," I affirm. "But there's a unusual twist. I had a couple of sessions with him in San Rafael. One in trance and one out of trance."

"What do you mean out of trance?" she questions.

"He's a trance-medium but for the second session we just talked for an hour with me asking him questions. No spirits coming through, or any of that kind of thing. Guess what? I got more out of that session just talking to him than from when he was in trance. Strange, huh?"

"I'll say."

"I suspect somehow that Kevin's higher self and the spirits he is channeling, are intertwined in a way that makes him just as helpful out of trance as in trance. It was an unusual experience to say the least."

"Did you tape the session when he was in trance?" Vicki asks with a glint in her eye.

"Absolutely."

"I'd love to listen to what a spirit's voice sounds like coming through a person," she says.

"I'll dig it out for you," I offer.

"Have you been back to see him?"

"No, I haven't," I respond, thinking about all I've been learning.

"Hey, you stopped rubbing," Vicki admonishes, bringing me back to the task at hand.

"Oh, sorry. It's hard to practice reflexology and talk about some of these other things," I say as I reach for her left foot.

Vicki's curiosity has made me realize that with many of these processes I'm investigating, once I find out about them, record the information or experience, I move on. They might be valuable for other people, but for me it's important that I feel a process is bringing me closer to understanding myself or closer to God or helping my relationships with other people. These are criteria I always use when evaluating these sessions and processes.

"You know," Vicki says, "it's too bad there isn't an encyclopedia you can go to for information about this stuff."

"There is to some degree," I respond. "You can pick up a number of 'seekers' books and learn about most any of these processes. These books can help you define the areas that are of most interest to you and also help you to avoid ones that don't match you very well." I go on to tell her that I believe it's important to read up on these areas before going out and experiencing the processes to help a person get out of their left-brain, logical-thinking mode.

"It sounds straightforward when you talk about it, Hon, even though it's in a field that most people would think is airy-fairy," Vicki says.

"Speaking of fairies…, I saw a few of them yesterday," I tease. Vicki laughs as I continue. "But, your comment is valid. Many people are leery of these mind/body/spirit fields because they're so esoteric. But I believe if you can ground the information, and by that, I mean bring it home in a way that's useful, then you can apply the processes."

"I'm a lot less anxious now that we've discussed this," Vicki says with a sigh of relief. "It really was an area that I was worried about. You know there's so much on television now about UFOs and other things like that."

"I know what you mean, and actually I enjoy shows on UFOs from an entertainment standpoint. *The Day the Earth Stood Still* is one of my all-time favorite movies. I still get goose bumps when that huge robot comes out onto the flying saucer ramp for the first time. But I don't have a clue how I would apply the information to you and the kids. That has to be the focus of my quest. Can I integrate these processes and information into my everyday life in a safe and helpful manner—and in a way that helps me understand myself and brings me closer to God and makes me better in other relationships? That's the key!"

Hidden Asset

We narrow our approach to life when we develop inhibiting attitudes and strong prejudices.

Chapter Eleven

Expanding the Borders of Receptivity

Invisible Guidance: Grandfatherly Advice

People are often willing to develop strong beliefs around things they don't fully understand. Being of a more skeptical nature, I usually want to investigate things more fully. I have an appointment with Mary Coleman this afternoon to continue my exploration into the holistic/spiritual communities.

It's an inopportune time to be meeting with Mary because I don't feel well physically. I noticed a decline in my ability to focus first thing this morning. Anyway, I want to keep my appointment with Mary because it's something I look forward to. As we begin the session, I sit listlessly in the large armchair. I check off the question we have just discussed and scan my bullet list for the next question.

"Mark, do you feel up to being here today?" Mary asks me while I gaze at my notes. Usually, I'm firing away question after question. I glance up from my day planner without responding. "Now be honest," she adds.

"I am feeling a little under the weather today," I admit.

"I thought so. Do you want to skip today's meeting?"

"Maybe I'll cut it shorter than normal," I respond, hoping to cover at least part of my agenda. "Did I talk to you about the numerologist the last time I was here?"

"No, you didn't," Mary replies.

"Okay. Well the way it started out is I ordered a numerology chart like the one you see advertised in the *Parade* section of the Sunday paper. Have you ever ordered one?"

"Yes, but it was many years ago, now. I don't remember exactly what they send you," Mary says.

I begin to tell Mary about the numerology chart and the unique format in the way it outlines a person's personality. I'm intrigued by the use of numbers, but I'm still skeptical about the connection between numbers and a person's inner self. So I ordered a second chart from a mail-order company.

I tell Mary the information on the second chart was pretty much the same as the first. "So I decided to interview an experienced numerologist to get a better understanding of how numerology works. If the numbers connection is valid," I say, "I'm a little concerned that a person's name and birth date might reveal so much."

Mary wants to know why.

I explain by saying, "You probably think it's silly but my name and birth date are on a lot of application forms for loans and credit information, that sort of thing."

She says not to worry about institutions having this information. "But," she cautions, "it's always a good course of action not to give out your full name and date of birth to just anyone."

I make a mental note to remember that as I continue, "The numerologist did give me some good background information on numerology as a system. She told me it was developed by the famous Greek mathematician Pythagoras. According to her, it originated from something called the 'wheel of Pythagoras.'"

"Uh huh," Mary says, seeming distracted or not listening carefully.

"Of course I like math, and the system was easy for me to understand—at least the calculation part. The question I have is around the individual sections, for example, the section titled 'Heart's Desire.'" As I'm speaking, Mary pauses and turns her head slightly to the right. I start to talk again about numerology, and clearly she is distracted.

All of a sudden she interrupts me and says, "Oh, well, if this is going to persist..., I need to tell you there's a spirit behind you. I've been trying to ignore it, but it's undoubtedly not going away."

I swing around to look behind me. Nothing is there. What's she talking about? I wonder. I trust Mary and feel comfortable with her gifts, yet I'm not totally ready to believe in seeing spirits. I'm still adjusting to this metaphysics thing and haven't bought into it entirely. Maybe since I can't see the spirit, I'm not able to trust that it is really there. Or perhaps it's because I don't feel well. In any case, I'm not prepared for this unusual event. There needs to be more confirming information for me to believe a spirit is here in the room.

"I don't see anything," I state. "Are you sure you saw something?"

"Of course, and he's still here behind you," she confirms confidently.

I wait while she interacts with what appears to be a third person in the room. I am totally unprepared for what is happening.

"What does it look like?" I ask.

"The spirit is in the form of an old grandfatherly Chinese man," she continues calmly. "He's saying King, his name is King, Ken or something like that."

I'm nervous because I can't see anything. I have read about spirit presence, and we have even discussed this before, but this is my first encounter with one. "Why can't I see this thing? Is it really here?" my skeptical mind asks. But then I remember all of the things I have seen Mary do, and I have no reason to think this is not real for her. Is it my belief system that does not enable me to see this spirit? Or is it Mary's belief system that allows her to see these things?

"Is he still here?" I ask.

"Yes, he is. Keng, Sheha Keng. The old Chinese man's spirit says to go and see Sheha Keng."

What Mary is saying doesn't fit into anything I understand. At first I am absolutely quiet, not knowing what to say. A moment later I'm startled by something that comes to mind. "Mary, my acupuncturist's name is Sheila Keng. She's originally from China, and her given name is Shyan-Chyi Keng. Her first name is difficult for Americans to pronounce so she goes by 'Sheila.' Do you think there's a connection here?"

"What do you think, Mark?"

"I think I should check this out," I say, surprised at the possible coincidence. "I'll call her office today and make an appointment." I scan the room once more looking for any hint of this old Chinese man. "How is it you can see and hear this invisible person, uhm, spirit, and I can't detect a thing?"

"It requires developing your ability to discern things beyond your senses," she says matter-of-factly. "By the way, he's gone now."

I stare at Mary. I wonder if the thought of my acupuncturist would have come into my mind if Mary had not been there. Are our thoughts sometimes spirits giving us hints or communicating in this way? Ooh, it gives me the shivers just thinking about this!

"You need to enlarge the borders of your receptivity," Mary continues. "If you do this and are faithful and stay the course of development, these things will be shown to you."

This isn't the first time Mary has said this. Once I asked her about my guardian angel, and she said something very similar.

"You also need to ask!" Mary responds emphatically as if on cue. "I know that sounds simple, but you would be surprised how many people never bother to ask for what they want. Not even in prayer."

Mary is big on asking things of God in prayer. She always says what she can do, others can do if they have faith. But to me she seems to be a unique woman with an ability or faculty beyond most people's.

"Mark, an important step you must learn is to distinguish different planes of thought. Make use of and differentiate between your senses, your intuition, and the information coming in from the Holy Spirit. In a way, it's distinguishing between listening to your *lower self*, which most people are dominated by, and your *higher self*, which you often experience in meditation. Do you see?"

"Yes." I comprehend what Mary is saying but am not really aware of how to tell the difference. Distinguishing thoughts, listening to the lower or higher self—it all sounds rather difficult to me.

Mary continues, "Just as it says in the Bible, your body is a temple for the indwelling spirit of God. You need to keep your body and mind tuned to the universal consciousness in order to develop your abilities further."

I have watched Mary very closely during the various sessions we have had. She has a certain quality that I have also noticed in gifted speakers on the lecture circuit. Mary is able to impart to me a picture of the object or comprehension of a subject through some unseen method. Even though I can't see the old Chinese man's spirit-form, I am able to get a mental picture from Mary. Gifted speakers have this capability to convey to the listener that which is clear in their own mind. This is another reason that she is such a good teacher for me.

It would be easy to get infatuated with Mary's abilities. But she is always the first one to credit her gifts to God and simple truths. The "truth" is really the gemstone of her marvelous abilities, and I have gradually taught myself to look behind people's gifts to determine what's really there.

Still not feeling well, I cut our meeting short and walk to my car parked in the driveway. It's a balmy day—"good earthquake weather" is how I often describe it. I reflect on how Mary is so honest and forthright with the information coming from the spiritual realm. There isn't any judgment or criticism; just communication of the information as she receives it. Although I do not have the gifts that Mary possesses, I can learn from her receptivity. If I can be more receptive to these different planes, I can increase the clarity of the information.

Meridians of Health

Later in the week I visit my acupuncturist, Sheila Keng, at her office in a large medical complex. As I walk by the various doctors' offices I'm curious about how accepting they are of acupuncture and traditional Chinese medicine. In the waiting room I thumb through the office copy of *Alternative Medicine*. I wonder if I would have come to see Sheila today if not for the session with Mary and the incident with the old Chinese spirit. I haven't yet gotten into the routine of coming to see Sheila when I'm sick. I don't know if it's because of lack of familiarity with acupuncture and Chinese medicine in general, or because I'm so conditioned to the ways of Western medicine. In the past I would have simply asked my doctor for an antibiotic to get me back on my feet. I'm not sure I've been completely fair with my regular doctor in the past by asking him to "just fix me up and get me feeling well enough to go back to work."

I met Sheila Keng at a lecture she gave on the uses of acupuncture. I have since found acupuncture to be a positive method for increasing my energy level. Sheila is from China and now practices the medicine from her native country in the Bay Area. She is tall and has a very slim figure. Her facial features are long and thin.

Sheila explains acupuncture as a way of balancing out the flow of chi, the vital life energy, throughout the body. A model of the human body, marked with specific points along the body's meridians, stands on a table in the corner of the waiting room. "Meridians are circulatory channels within the body which can be stimulated by inserting thin needles into these specific points," Sheila told me during my first visit to her months ago. She said that each meridian is linked to an internal organ. No wonder it takes years to master how to do this, I thought.

I walk by shelves containing glass jars filled with loose herbs on my way to the treatment room. While I wait there, I examine the large charts on the wall describing the points on the meridians in detail.

"What, no kids today, Mark?" Sheila asks as she enters the room.

I normally bring one of my kids along with me. I enjoy having them learn about health. I bring them to my regular physician when I have my blood drawn or my blood pressure taken for the same reason. "No, not today," I declare, knowing that the kids are going to miss out. Sheila once let my son take out some of the needles after the treatment. We both had a real laugh when he said next time he wanted to put the needles in!

"So, how can I help you today?" she asks.

"I haven't been feeling that well," I reply, describing my symptoms.

She asks me a few questions, then says, "Let's see what's going on."

Sheila's presence and voice have a calming effect on me. I lie down on the table as she begins to measure my pulse and perform a series of diagnostics on me. She records my answers on a chart she has attached to a clipboard.

"Mark, most of your energy is low, particularly your liver meridian. No wonder you've been feeling so fatigued and unpleasant."

Sheila opens a new package of long thin needles. She has told me that the needles are never reused. Painlessly, she inserts the especially fine needles just under my skin in carefully selected points along my arms and legs, and I find myself relaxing as the process proceeds.

"Sheila, did I mention I plan to see an acupressure practitioner?"

"No you didn't," she says as she continues to insert the needles ever so delicately. "Is this part of your research?"

"Yes, I want to investigate how they stimulate energy points with the use of manual pressure. I've read where they rub and knead areas along the energy pathway instead of using needles."

As the treatment begins to take effect, Sheila says, "When we're done in here, I'll prescribe herbs that along with the treatment should increase your energy in a couple of days." She leaves the room, turning the heat lamp on.

Sheila is also an herbalist and practices traditional Chinese herbal medicine. It seems so natural for her. She has told me that the majority of people in China use herbs over pharmaceutical drugs. I'm sure it's an economic imperative as well as the traditional form of health care. Sheila let me take home a book on her counter called *Chinese Herbal Medicine*. It was a little complicated for a layman, but it made me appreciate the comprehensive training that Sheila has gone through to become a certified herbalist.

About 25 minutes later, Sheila returns and begins to take the needles out. "I'd like to see you again next week," she states.

"All right," I say, feeling slightly disoriented from lying down. "I guess that old Chinese spirit was right," I mumble under my breath as I proceed from the table to a chair.

"What was that?" she asks.

"Do you believe in people being able to see spirits?" I ask tentatively, not knowing how she will respond to this.

"What do you mean?"

"I mean, do you think some people have the ability to see spirits?"

"Yes. When I was a little girl in China, I was taken to an old man in our village who could do this."

"Really?"

"I think it is a rare gift, but there are healers in China—very few—who can. They use the spirits to help them see into the body. Very rare, very rare," she emphasizes.

As I put on my shoes and socks, I wonder if my encounter with the old Chinese spirit is similar to what Sheila is describing. There is a connection here between this spirit, whom I still cannot verify was there, leading me to the healing process, in this case, acupuncture. I am glad the message and influence was there from another realm; however, I am not yet convinced there is a cause and effect relationship here.

When I leave, I notice a *Book of Mormon* on the table in her office. I know from past conversations Sheila has converted to the Mormon religion. I wonder how she is able to balance the belief in chi, the life force, and her religious beliefs. I also wonder how she handles her childhood experiences with these healers who use spirits, along with her religious doctrine. I make a note to talk to her about this the next time I see her.

Healthy Skepticism

People will go to amazing lengths to convince themselves something is real. Accordingly, I've set *usefulness* and *effectiveness* as important goals to determine if the various phenomena I'm coming across are valid. It's actually just an extension of the way I am in business. My marketing background often has me on the lookout for the way products and services in the various fields are packaged, promoted, and delivered.

One day on my way home from work, I notice a sign on a local Holiday Inn announcing upcoming events. According to the marquee there is a psychic show this weekend. I jot down a note to attend and place it in my weekly planner.

When the weekend arrives, I park in front of the hotel and enter the conference suites side of the building. There is a cover charge at the door and an offer of ten minutes' worth of services for $10. I'll be interested to see what value you get for a dollar a minute. I enter through the double doors to find about fifty people sitting at large folding tables. In the front of each table are chairs facing the readers. About half of the chairs are filled with customers here for a reading. Each practitioner has a sign-up list next to them.

I wander around for about ten minutes before sitting down in front of a blonde woman. Her name tag says Barbara. "How are you, Barbara?" I ask.

"Great! Are you ready for your ten-minute reading?"

"I am," I reply, handing her a ticket that I had paid for earlier. The tickets are good for one ten-minute reading or one ten-minute healing session and if you buy four, you get one free. I bought four. Barbara does not know that I've interviewed dozens of intuitives and psychics from all over the country. What has me interested today is more the process than individual questions. I'm curious to see what type of information I can get at a local hotel filled with a room full of psychics. This isn't my first exposure to this type of promotion, and I've had both good and not so good experiences in the past.

"Are you planning on seeing a healer with one of those tickets?" Barbara asks noticing the other tickets in my hand.

"I don't know yet. I would like to visit the NLP practitioner over in the corner before I leave."

"Neuro-Linguistic Programming is okay. I tried it for a while but now I just do psychic readings. So, let's begin. Please say your full name three times."

"Mark Bryant, Mark Bryant, Mark Bryant."

"There... good. I've got your spirit in my mind," Barbara says with her eyes closed. "I see you like to have fun. Are you involved in computers at all?"

"No. I mean I have a computer at home and at the office, but I'm not really into them. In fact, I'm not really into technical stuff," I tell her.

"Yes, I can see that. Are you married?"

"Yes, and I have two children."

"They're lovely, I can see their little spirits. Girl/boy?"

"One of each."

Barbara gives some information on the kids but most of it is general and nothing really jumps out at me. I've had these type of readings before, where there doesn't seem to be anything concrete to work with.

"Are you into ecology or something like that?" she asks. "Something to do with the color green?"

"I'm not sure," I say as I'm starting to think this lady is grasping for straws. Maybe there is something green around but I'm not sure what she's reaching for here.

"Can I ask a couple of questions?" I ask Barbara as she momentarily opens her eyes to look around the large hall.

"Yes, but let me just tell you some things that I'm getting from my guides first. I see that you and your wife have lost a relative recently, and there is a lot of grief around this. I suggest you let go of this grief. What's your wife's name?"

"Vicki," I answer, not really sure what this woman is talking about. Both our parents are alive and the last relative that's died on either side of our family was more than ten years ago. I glance at my watch.

"I think Vicki may be going through some things too. Has she ever gone to a hypnotherapist?" she asks.

"Not to my knowledge," I say, short and to the point. I'm kind of upset that I've nearly run out of time, and I haven't gotten anything. If I turn over her flyer and it says she's a hypnotherapist, I'm going to get up and leave.

"We're almost out of time, would you like to go another ten minutes?" Barbara asks.

"Can I ask some questions this time?"

"Sure."

I tell her okay and hand her another ticket. I'm starting to think this ten-minutes-per-ticket deal is not too helpful. Maybe it's the setting or the person, I don't know. But I'm here to learn, and I can add this to my research. Barbara starts the small egg timer type clock and we begin the second session. I'm really conscious of time now.

"Can you look and give me feedback on how I'm aligning spiritually with my professional career?" I ask.

"I can tell you're not happy where you're at. There is something about your boss being too harsh. His energy is too hard on your body."

I don't have the heart to tell her I don't have a boss. I own my own company so, unless she's talking about how hard I am on myself or one of my partners, I'm not sure where she's going with this. About now, I'm wondering if I should have gone with the second ticket.

"I can also see that you want to make a change of residence and live in the tropics somewhere, maybe Hawaii," Barbara says while closing her eyes again.

"Okay," I say. I begin to look around the hall now. I have a really strong intuitive sense that Barbara would like to go and live in Hawaii. It almost seems as if she is reading herself and her own desires, not mine. What she doesn't apparently realize is that I lived in Hawaii a number of times when I was growing up and enjoyed the time there, but I've never been back even when I've had the opportunity. It's sort of like "been there, done that." If I had the chance to visit Hawaii vs. someplace new, I'd always choose somewhere I haven't been before. I like discovering new things.

Barbara talks to me about other areas of my life for the remaining time. She does hit on a couple of areas I can apply. But by and large, most of the information she's talking about, I just can't use. Somehow I feel a little cheated. I don't know if it's the money or the lack of useful information or the way I felt rushed. Given that I chose her strictly because there was an open chair has taught me something. There needs to be a more credible way of determining a practitioner's ability. It might come down to experience and years in the business. If it follows other fields, a person will usually get out of a certain type of business after a few years if they're not successful. Without satisfied customers, practitioners can't get repeat business. Years of experience might be helpful, but clearly this is not an exact science.

Energy Management

Without knowing quite when it happened, I have forgotten my own anxieties around health, probably because I enjoy sharing the information I'm uncovering with my family and other people. One therapy I've been curious about is qigong, the Chinese healing practice that I've heard about from Dr. Stanton. She says it's excellent for balancing one's energy and improving the immune system.

I've made an appointment with a qigong master, Dr. Wu. He was brought up in China and trained in qigong there. He came to the United States to get his Ph.D. in psychology from UCLA and currently gives lectures at universities in the Bay Area. He has offices in Berkeley and San Francisco.

I arrive at his home office in Berkeley, just down from the University of California. It's a bright clear day, and as I come across the interchange, I can make out Angel Island in the middle of the bay. The university is on semester break so the streets are empty, and it's easy to find a place to park. I ascend the stairs and enter a small waiting area. Beyond this small lounge area is a room full of bookcases, a desk, and a long waist-high table. After introductions, I sit down across the desk from Dr. Wu. It's hard for me to tell how old he is, but judging by his degrees and experience, he must be at least fifty. He looks in great shape and is wearing loose-fitting, casual clothes. He has a pleasant demeanor and smiles a lot. He says he would like to answer my questions before beginning the treatment because it would give him a little background about me and what I'm looking for.

"Dr. Wu, so far I'm trying to learn more about what I'm calling energy management. It appears to me that different healers and intuitives are using energy to do what they do," I begin.

Dr. Wu lets out a pleasing laugh. "It's a good term, energy management," he says, while adjusting his black-rimmed glasses. "I don't believe most people look at it this way. Our belief in China is that all energy is the same whether it is used for healing or for psychic use. It is all qi (*chi*) energy."

"If it is all the same, then it must be the practitioners who're different," I surmise.

"Yes," Dr. Wu agrees. He goes on to explain that there are three primary types of healing systems used worldwide. There is the Swedish massage method, which works with the cardiovascular system. There is the psychic energy system, which works more with emotions of the head and heart. Then there is the meridian system, which is what he does. Each system is using and manipulating energy in a different way.

Dr. Wu is very knowledgeable. I ask him why there are different methods. He says much of it has to do with beliefs and culture and that most of the healing systems were spread through religion. He says in China, the meridian system is a natural form of medicine accepted by millions of Chinese. While in Europe, many Europeans accept the Swedish massage method as a form of releasing energy blocks. He believes both methods are less accepted in the United States, partly due to people's belief system and partly due to the medical technology available.

I'm impressed with Dr. Wu's explanation. I've never thought about healing techniques being spread by religion. It's an interesting premise and sounds logical. I glance around the room and notice quite a few books on Tao and Buddhism on the shelves.

"Chinese medicine is based on the theory that illness results from the improper flow of qi—the body's vital force—through the body. Proper qi flow depends on the balance of two opposing forces, yin and yang. These forces manifest in our bodies as qualities, including cold and heat, heavy and light."

"Okay," I say, recalling all the jokes I've heard about the yin/yang principle. But Dr. Wu is quite serious about this. He brings up the Ayurveda system that's become popular recently and says this is a healing system also based on balance. He says the system is from India, is thousands of years old, and is known as the "science of life." It's based on the concept of prana or life force. According to Dr. Wu, prana must be in balance within a body to ensure health. He says balance in the Ayurvedic system is determined by the equilibrium of three of the bodily qualities called doshas. Doshas determine not only the physical body types but the emotional and mental constitutions as well. He tells me that if I need a further explanation, a good book on the Ayurvedic system is *Quantum Healing* by Dr. Deepak Chopra.

"Okay," I respond. "Speaking of life force, I've been told that you have the capability to perceive this life force energy in the body."

"Yes, that's true," he confirms.

"Would you say this is a gift, or is it through training that you've come by this capability?" I inquire.

"In China, there are a few who have the gift from birth. Many times these individuals are sought out in their teens because it is believed that if the gift is not developed by the time they're twenty, it will go away. The most powerful qi masters are those who have the gift *and* formal training," he informs me.

According to Dr. Wu, everyone has the use of psychic energy at a certain level. This would seem to follow other paradigms, as well. Music is an example. Clearly there are people who are more musically gifted from birth. Mozart was a genius in music at a very young age. When in Europe, I had a chance to visit the home of his youth in Salzburg, Austria. His compositions even at the age of five or six were quite remarkable. He was undoubtedly going to be a much better composer of music, if developed correctly, than somebody who did not have that natural gift. This seems to support the idea of discovering your children's gifts and working with them while they're still young. I wonder if Dr. Wu can discern whether children have the gift of healing just by looking at them.

"But many healers are fake!" he declares unexpectedly.

I shift in my seat, a little uncomfortable with such a direct statement. It's obvious that Dr. Wu is not one to mince words.

"What do you mean?" I ask.

"Most healers don't have the ability to heal."

"Why do you say that?"

"In China, they have developed machines that can measure the qi force. When many of the healers are put through this machine, it registers that they have very little healing power. The real qigong masters can increase the machine's magnitude a thousand times a normal person's qi power."

"Are there machines like this in the United States?" I ask.

"Yes," he states. "I helped design one of the first here in America at UCLA. But the better ones are still in China."

Dr. Wu is very matter of fact. I look around his office. It is sparsely decorated with just the bare essentials for his work, although he does have a beautiful oriental painting on the wall and a small sculpture in the corner.

"When I go to healers, they sense the energy in my body in a variety of different ways. How do you explain this?" I ask.

"All healers use different psychic energy to determine what's wrong with a person. They use vision, touch, smell, even hearing to sense where the energy is not right. For example, I can tell where the energy is wrong by the curvature of a limb or the contour of a muscle. This is all training."

"How can you tell when a healer is a fraud?" I inquire.

"Without a way to measure their qi, it is difficult," he admits. "A qi master will get very tired after a healing. This is one sign."

His comment makes me wonder about the abilities of the healers I've seen so far. I wonder what their healing measurement would be on such a machine. I know that some of the healers I've interviewed have been tested at different universities using similar equipment, but how about the rest? If they haven't been tested, how would you really be sure of a healer's abilities? I look around the room to see if any such testing equipment is in sight.

"You mentioned psychic energy," I continue with my questions. "Do you believe in the capability of psychics to use energy to convert information?"

"Yes, though the use of psychic energy is the most undeveloped while the use of the meridian system is the most developed," Dr. Wu responds.

"What do you mean exactly?"

"Psychics have developed their own way of doing things because most of them learned through trial and error," he says. "Those who have done it all their life can be very good, yet each uses a unique approach. Because of this, the use and study of psychic energy is more individual and undeveloped than the use of energy in the meridian system."

"How then would you account for intuition?" I probe.

"Ah, I see what you're after," Dr. Wu says with a smile. "Human beings have become very logical thinkers. This logical thinking puts too much demand on their system, and intuition becomes weak. We need both. A qi master is logical *and* intuitive. Qigong invigorates more of the brain so that intuition and the logical mind can be used. It can work the other way for some, where intuition suppresses the logical. Enough questions for now. Would you like a healing session?"

"Yes, very much." I respond, at the same time thinking how I would like to ask Dr. Wu a lot more questions. He is a wealth of information.

"Please get up on the table," he directs me.

I climb up on the table and lie on my back. I stare up at the ceiling as Dr. Wu explains what he is going to do. Closing my eyes slowly, I hear Dr. Wu making some sort of swishing sound. He proceeds to place herbs enclosed in a bag on my stomach and explains the process to me as he does this. He then begins to massage my limbs lightly. Occasionally during the session, there is an extreme amount of heat coming off his hands. I can feel the heat even when he is not touching me. I feel a little woozy, which is similar to the feeling I've experienced with a number of other healers.

After a half an hour of this, he asks me to rest on the table for fifteen minutes. Lying there quietly, I think about what Dr. Wu has said. He soon returns, helps me sit up and we talk for a few minutes longer. Dr. Wu is a very amiable and modest man, so it is difficult for me to assess his abilities with qi energy. It would almost take this machine he was talking about, or another qi master, to ascertain the specific level of his abilities.

As I get up to leave Dr. Wu's home, he suggests that I do three exercises daily to improve the overall energy flow in my body. To my surprise, for the next twenty minutes he works with me, positioning my legs and arms in the proper way to maximize the effect of the exercises. He is so patient that I don't feel rushed. In fact, I have already paid him so all of this extra time spent on teaching these movements is freely given on his part. I've not met anyone quite like him before, and I know I'm not able to appreciate fully his exceptional talents.

In our conversation Dr. Wu called the use of clairvoyance a natural gift. He refers to his own abilities as that of a gift *and* years of training. He says that just because an ordinary person doesn't have the gift doesn't mean they can't develop healing abilities through training, and he feels a lot of this formal training can be acquired in China.

After leaving Dr. Wu's office, I check my phone messages. My eyes begin to sting with tears as I listen to a message about my friend, Randy, left by a mutual friend of ours. Randy has died today. I don't go to my next appointment, but instead drive to the creek near Randy's house. Taking a long walk along the creek, I gather my thoughts and remember our friendship.

It was one of the few times in my life I have cried, ...and I cried hard. It was as if I released years of tears that had been stored up inside of me. I had always been proud of the fact that I never cried. But no more. I now realize that in a way, I was out of balance by never wanting to cry or show emotions at losing someone. I loved Randy a great deal. I loved his openness and caring nature, and I will miss him.

In Proverbs, it says that a friend can sometimes be closer than a brother. I'll miss Randy like a brother. Saying a prayer of thankfulness for Randy and the years of friendship we had together, I keep my mind focused on good thoughts for him. I have come to believe that a good thought for someone never dies.

———◉———

Hidden Asset

When we raise our awareness, our energy becomes a force we can work with.

Chapter Twelve

Discovering the Intrinsic Value of Spirit

Spiritual Kindergarten

On layover at the Sky Harbor airport in Phoenix, I head for Gate 20 with my boarding pass to New York tucked inside my pocket. Outside, the Arizona sky is crystal blue. Karen Kenney, the gifted intuitive I've talked with by telephone, has agreed to meet me at my boarding gate. I'm eager to see what she looks like in person. I am surprised by the number of people in the boarding area when I arrive. "Excuse me," a woman's voice says. "Are you Mark?"

"Yes, I am," I reply, putting down my overnight case to shake her hand. "It's great to finally meet you in person, Karen. I'd have recognized that voice anywhere."

Karen smiles and helps me with some of my carry-on luggage. "There's a less crowded spot two gates over," she suggests. "How much time do you have?"

"My flight leaves at 12:30," I answer, noticing her casual, colorful style. She is taller than I imagined, I observe as I follow her. The youthfulness I have noticed in her voice during our phone sessions is also reflected in her walk, and she seems just as warm in person as she has been on the phone.

"Good then, this way," she says, leading the way.

"I really appreciate your meeting me here like this."

"Glad to," she says as we locate two lounge chairs in a remote part of the terminal. "What would you like to discuss today?"

"I was pondering that on the flight here. I'd really like to delve into this body/spirit thing. At times during our sessions, it seems like you're talking about my body, and other times it seems like you're speaking of my spirit," I say, surprised by how comfortable I am now talking about this. It's definitely not the type of language I'd use in a business setting.

"Most of our conversation is basically giving you information about who you are spiritually —what your talents and abilities are," she responds.

"Are you talking about the essence inside of me?" I ask.

"Let me place it into a context you're familiar with, Mark. You've told me you're a Christian."

"That's right," I respond.

"So what's your belief system around pre-birth and the afterlife? In your mind, is there an essence there?" she asks me.

"Yes. I believe I'm a spirit with God before birth and again a spirit with God in heaven following death. I've always believed this even when I attended churches that didn't talk about existence before birth. It's just something that's always resonated with me. Vicki and I often tell our kids that they looked down on us from heaven before they came into the world."

"In short, then, you believe that when you're not in a body, you're a spirit."

"Yes," I answer, realizing I've always believed this but never spent a lot time thinking about it. It was never that important to me to think of myself as a spirit within a body. I laugh and wonder what my spirit looks like to a clairvoyant. Is it round or large or small or what? I make a note to ask Karen what my spirit actually resembles.

"When you're a spirit," she continues, "there's no past, present, or future. It's all the same thing. But in a body, you're dealing with time and space. So the body presents a different set of circumstances. Most people consider themselves to be just one thing—a body. The problem is that there isn't just one of you, there are at least two of you. There is a spirit and a body, ...and the body is extremely different. But people have forgotten."

"Forgotten what?" I ask, noticing a group of airline pilots walk past us.

"Forgotten that they are a spirit," she answers.

"Okay. Well, then how do you start to remember that you're a spirit within a body?" I ask as I realize that a lot of my search has been about waking up to the fact that I have a spirit side too. My sleeping disorder was a wake-up call to my spiritual side, and I answered it. Now I'm finding out about those areas that I either had forgotten, as Karen says, or that I had suppressed in order to concentrate on my physical side. For that reason, I am eager to find out more about my spirit side.

"It's really pretty simple," Karen says. "You take care of the body, and you take care of the spirit. You've taken good care of your body so you've got a body that's fairly neutral. It's like a window that's rather clear. This is important because your spirit has to work through your body so you need your perceptions to be clear. The first step is to take care of your body."

"Uh-huh." I utter and think back to my sessions with Joy Lasseter, the nutritionist. She said the same thing but used different language.

"What you eat, how you think, what you take in, whether it's food or exercise, all those things are affecting your perception at the physical level," she continues.

"In other words, if I fill my body with things that are bad for it, then my perception will be less clear."

"Absolutely!" she says. "That's why you might notice psychics can't work as well when they're taking prescription drugs. It's hard for their perceptions to be clear when the drugs are in their body."

"Okay, so let's say I'm taking care of my body, and I'm remaining clear. What prevents me from forgetting about my spirit then?"

"Basically, what's good for spirit is communication," she replies. "A spirit doesn't really need a lot, but it definitely needs communication. Communication helps the spirit create time and space."

I bend down to make sure my tape recorder is still recording. "What sort of communication?" I ask.

"'Hello, I see you! I see what you're creating.' Recognition, …that's the best kind of communication."

Karen makes it sound so simple, and I realize I haven't done a very good job of communicating with my spirit or giving it recognition. If it weren't for my wake-up call, I still would be disavowing my spirit side.

Karen continues, "Most people don't even recognize the spirit of a child. The child's spirit doesn't get enough communi-cation. Therefore it starts to think it doesn't exist, and it goes dormant. To wake it up is sometimes painful for that person."

Karen continues to talk about the spiritual aspect of a person for a while. She makes it sound so simple and obvious, but for a person like myself, most of this information is new. Karen mentions more than once that waking up to your spirit can be painful if not done in an orderly manner. It reminds me of the hardship my sleep disorder caused my family and business colleagues.

"In a way it can be called 'spiritual kindergarten,'" Karen says. "If you can teach a person to start having their spirit in their body, in their life, in their work, they can take on other creative things. One problem very often is that teachers and spiritual counselors want to open a person up too quickly to things of the spirit. It's important to do it gradually so they can learn by taking baby steps. You have to do this in a non-threatening manner to start with."

"Speaking of baby steps, do you know we're expecting?"

"Yes," she says with a smile.

"I'm curious. Is it too early to start to communicate with a baby's spirit when they're still in the womb?"

"Not at all," she quickly responds.

"When I get back from my trip, I'll have Vicki give you a call, and you two can talk about the baby's spirit."

"Yes, have her do that. The key, again, is a slow and careful manner in starting out," she reiterates.

"Got it."

"And you have a plane to catch," she says checking her watch. "I think I heard the first announcement for Gate 20 to New York."

"You've given me great information, Karen," I say gratefully while gathering up my things.

"I have to be about my Father's business and teaching people about spirit is that business," she says, hugging me. "It was good to finally meet you in person."

"Same here."

"By the way, why are you going to New York?" she inquires.

"It's just a layover on my way to Europe. I'm going to visit a hospital where they practice a holistic form of medicine called anthroposophic medicine. The hospital was founded in the early part of this century by a woman doctor named Ita Wegman. I'm very interested in talking with the nurses and doctors and finding out as much as I can first hand."

"It sounds exciting. Blue-green algae will help the jet lag," she suggests as I walk towards my flight.

The ticket agent takes my boarding pass, and I begin the walk down the long ramp toward the plane. I like that last phrase Karen used about being about her Father's business. This is a phrase Jesus used. Karen has great reverence for God, and it comes through often in our talks.

Once the plane reaches cruising altitude, my thoughts are silent for a while. Then a picture begins to form in my mind. Words come to me that are a combination of everything I've been experiencing. First, I think about how intuition is helping me to have a better, and sometimes different, understanding of the things I am experiencing. I think about my experiences with the healers, both the mental and physical types. As I relate these to the airport conversation with Karen, I realize all at once that there's been a healing of my own spirit. The healing of my spirit—that recognition of spirit in my life—is what this has been about. Recognition of my spirit side has enabled me to integrate a richer inner life with my outer life.

Synchronized Valentines

There are days when everything seems to be inspired, when every idea, every action seems to go right. Sport psychologists have labeled it the "C" zone, while professional athletes just call it the "zone." I've found there is a physical sensation that accompanies the zone. It's almost a feeling of invincibility, that nothing can go wrong. A few days before Valentine's Day, I find myself in the zone. It's a good time to buy Vicki's card and gift and take advantage of the zone.

I stand among racks of cards, calendars, and notebooks looking for a card that has humor, romance, and a heartfelt message. Finding just the perfect card for Vicki is not an easy task. I hope I can find just the right one.

"May I help you, sir?" a cheerful clerk asks.

Realizing she is talking to me, I respond, "I'm just looking, thanks." This is quite a private matter, choosing something that will express the exact feelings I have for my wife, my love, the mother of my children. Not too mushy, not too corny. It has to be just right. Just as the cards start to look all alike—red, pink, roses fringed with white doilies—one jumps out at me. It has a beautiful photo on the front. On the inside the message is perfect. I know Vicki will like it. I wonder what she will pick out for me. That is what's special about Valentine's Day: we get to be reminded of how much we love and are loved in return.

That night I stay up late to write a special message to Vicki in the valentine. I write from my heart. I acknowledge how much she means to me. At five the next morning, I leave the card and gifts next to her bed-stand to surprise her when she wakes. As I slip out of the house, I find a card and gift addressed to me next to my day planner. I tuck the card away to read during a break in my day.

The client is late for my first meeting, and I take out my valentine card from Vicki as I wait. It feels warm in my hand, and I know she will open hers before the kids are up. I open it carefully. At first glance it is beautiful. There is a familiar quality about it, and then I laugh because I realize all at once that Vicki and I have given each other the exact same card!

This sort of coincidence seems to be happening to me with more and more regularity. My heart feels good all day after I open that card. I know if I had to size it up, I would say that our inner sense is at work and was very strong around the choosing of this card. Somehow, going to two different stores in two different towns, we chose the same card. My logical side jumps in to rationalize this incident. It seems highly unlikely from a probability standpoint that this would occur. "Cancel, cancel," I say to myself. It's a short phrase I've learned to say to clear my thoughts. I use it for negative thoughts or when I over analyze a situation. I would just rather enjoy the spontaneity of it all.

Parental Guidance: A Father's View

Thunderstorms continue to bombard the West Coast. Farmers are beginning to worry the rains could severely damage the crop this season. It's the kind of day to stay inside and keep dry.

Randy's passing makes me want to spend more quality time with those that I love. I decide to visit my parents on this rainy Saturday afternoon. They've been married for over 40 years.

When I arrive, Dad tells me that Mom is out shopping. Dad is a tough cookie. He had a career in the military and is a "get after it" kind of guy. He has that strong disposition that I admire in people who were raised during the Depression years. Having grown up on a farm, he still has that "down home" hospitable manner, despite his years as a technical adviser in the Air Force.

One of the things I love about my father is his integrity. I have never seen him act without integrity in anything, which says a lot about him as a father and a role model. Once he told me that his way of contributing to the world was to be the best dad he could be for us four kids. I never forgot that.

He settles into the light-colored recliner that it seems like he's had forever. No one else sits in this chair but him. The kids always say, "That's Grandpa's chair."

Raising his hands over his head to stretch and adjusting the chair backward ever so slightly, Dad asks, "How is Vicki feeling?"

"She's good," I reply. "I don't know if she likes gaining weight and all, but her pregnancy checkups have shown that everything is fine with the baby."

"That's good. Are you enjoying your research?" he asks.

"Yes I am, Dad," I say, caught off guard momentarily by his interest.

"Are you sure you haven't overspent on this research?"

I have to laugh to myself because Dad is really into the stock market and the valuation of things. There is a *Value Line* binder just to the side of his reading chair.

"Under normal circumstances, I probably have," I admit, "and there are probably a couple of reasons for this."

"Such as?" he questions.

"Well, for one thing, these body/mind/spirit fields are filled with very creative types who are fantastic at what I'd call product development."

"Product development?" he quizzes.

"Yeah, many of these people would be in the R&D department if they were in business. They're highly creative," I say, leaning back on the couch. "The problem is many of the processes are not that well organized, maybe because it takes a different set of skills. So consequently, I spent quite a bit of money just tracking down many of these processes and the practitioners. This all cost time and money that under any other circumstances, I'm not sure I would have spent."

"No efficiencies built in, huh?" Dad deduces.

"Exactly! As an example, it took me quite a bit of time to find a Feldenkrais practitioner in my area. And I went to a number of clairvoyants specializing in looking at your aura before I could find ones that I felt really had the true gift."

Dad doesn't say anything but just looks at me. I think the word "aura" has thrown him a little.

"The way the current system works, you could spend a ton of money on just trying to find the right person for you in these fields," I add. "I hope a better system develops in the future for people."

Dad offers me a couple of ideas on cost effective ways to gather data. I tell him it's not just about gathering information. It's important for me to also experience these processes.

"For where I'm at in life, Dad, there is value for me in growing spiritually. There's the old saying, 'You learn in the first twenty years of life, you earn in the second twenty years, and you give time and service in the third twenty years of your life.' I'm at the threshold of giving."

"Are you equating giving and growing spiritually?" Dad asks.

"It's probably more realistic to say giving is a by-product of being more spiritual," I reply.

He doesn't respond to this at first. He stretches his left arm up and rolls his shoulder as if to work out a kink in his neck and shoulder. Finally, he asks, "So what are some of the benefits of this growth?" I feel like a child justifying a "B" on a report card. I know Dad is wise and is looking out for my best interests, but somehow I still feel a little tense in talking to him about this.

"Better yet, walk me through some examples in your research to help me understand the benefits relative to cost," he requests.

"Okay. Let's take examples on each end of the application continuum, Dad. First, take meditation or what some call silent prayer. I never meditated when I was younger. I knew about meditation and had close friends who talked about their meditative experiences, but I never had the desire to try it. But as I researched more, I realized that meditation can help the average person."

"Okay, you learned meditation," he speaks up. "Is it worth it?"

"In short, yes," I respond. "Meditation is inexpensive to learn and maintain, and it has the benefits of improving my overall health."

He seems content for the moment. "Weren't there hidden costs that you had to factor into this?" he asks.

"About the only hidden cost in meditating is lost opportunity. You know in business, an opportunity cost is where you give up one thing to do another. So the question is, am I better off spending this time in the morning in meditation, or should I take this time to work on business? I'm like most people; I'm going to work eight to ten hours a day. Therefore, spending some quality time in the morning for health reasons isn't a sacrifice of time at all. In fact, it is a relief to start the busy workday this way."

"Am I speaking to the same son who didn't take a vacation for years?" he says laughing.

"Yes, and I've learned my lesson. Actually, I take a vacation every morning during my meditative state," I reply, and we both have a big laugh over this. I love to hear my dad laugh. A father's laugh is one of those sounds from childhood that stays with you your entire life.

The telephone rings, and Dad lets it ring without moving immediately to answer it. Finally, he gets up , still chuckling about my daily vacation comment. It's my older sister Sharry on the phone. While Dad is speaking with her, a feeling of missing her comes over me. She lives out of the area, as does my younger sister Lynda. I have been able to share my travels and discoveries with my brother but not much with my sisters.

My sister Lynda and I are much alike in both appearance and competitiveness. We often passed as twins when we were young. She is a pharmaceutical economist and is in the business of health. She is highly educated and deals with sophisticated health procedures. I wish there were a way for me to have more sit-down discussions with her about the holistic healing communities.

I can hear my dad ask Sharry about her job. She is a kindergarten teacher and the salt of the earth. She has the most nurturing spirit, and it is only now that I can see she has always had balance in her life. Quite honestly, I never put much value on balance and wholeness until now. I am sure she notices the biggest change in me. I would have to say that of all the kids in our family, I was probably the least balanced, and my sister Sharry was the most balanced. Maybe there is a predisposition for some people to develop more balance in their lives. Somehow they preserve the wholeness.

Dad gets off the phone and returns shortly. "Okay, where were we before I answered the telephone?" he asks.

"Meditation," I respond.

"That's right. So if meditation is a process where you found good results, what's an example of a low-results process—something in your research that doesn't get a high rating?"

I can see the conversation with Sharry has softened my dad up a bit. I can sense he is moving more into his teaching role—wanting to get me to really understand what it is I'm learning.

"First of all, Dad, my evaluation system is unique to me. Someone else might rate meditation low in usefulness. Five years ago I definitely rated meditation low."

Dad settles back into his chair, stretching out his legs and clasping his hands behind his head. I tell him how I wasn't into developing my inner life back then; how all of us are different, and need to find what works best for each of us and at the appropriate time.

My dad seems more comfortable with the discussion now. I tell him about Vicki's Uncle Lew and how he's begun to follow Deepak Chopra's meditative practices from the book, *Ageless Body, Timeless Mind*. Lew does this every day, and he's eighty years old. Did this help him get to eighty? No, but he was doing other things similar in his life to help him. Lew has told me that he's done some visualization all his life. He started practicing visualization techniques when he was shot down over Germany during World War II and became a prisoner of war. He's says it was the men who could muster an inner strength that were able to survive the hostile environment. I take my hat off to Vicki's uncle for modifying his visualization process and accepting an entirely new way of doing things at his age. He's always trying to find new ways to strengthen his body, mind, and spirit.

"Do you have that Deepak Chopra book?" Dad asks, sounding a lot more interested.

"Yes."

"Pass it along to me. I'd like to read it."

"Sure."

Dad gets up and offers me something to eat. I express my thanks, but tell him Vicki and the kids and I are going out to dinner later. I invite him and Mom to go with us. He says they will go next time. I follow him into the kitchen so we can keep up our conversation.

"You asked about a low results process. *Extended* fasting is one example of a low-results process for me," I say, maneuvering my way onto one of the counter stools. It's funny that the subject of fasting comes up just as we move into the kitchen. For me, fasting for long periods has a high cost—wear and tear on my body. In my research I found people who fast for ten-day intervals or longer. It's hard to believe people in the Bible went on forty-day fasts. It's just not practical for me in business, because it's generally advised to take naps, get out in the sunlight and walk a lot. I've tried lengthy fasts before, and they're just too hard on my system. I can't seem to go very long without protein.

"Still, I do believe in the benefits of fasting, and it is an inexpensive method for keeping you healthy," I say to my father. "I've read enough to realize that fasting allows the body to rid itself of toxins. So I've created a system of fasting that's effective for me. Just like Vicki's uncle made meditation suitable for him using Deepak's approach."

"Sounds interesting. What did you create for yourself?" he asks.

"Well, I worked it backwards. I looked at the people who were fasting ten to fifteen days once a year, and then again three or four days once a quarter. Then I talked to a zoo keeper at the local zoo and casually asked her what they did for the animals. I figured even though we have a spirit from God within us, we have a physical body more like that of an animal."

"Innovative approach, son. I don't know if I would have looked at it this way," he acknowledges.

"She told me they feed many of the animals six days a week and on the seventh day give them only water. This helps regulate their systems and keeps them healthy. In essence, the animals were fasting once a week. I asked her why this was the process they used. She said they were trying to simulate the wild, where the animal might not be able to find food. So guess what I started?"

"A snack bar for zoo animals on the seventh day!" Dad proclaims with a laugh.

"Very funny, Dad."

"It fits your entrepreneurial nature," he teases.

"I've started to fast one day a week. I figured this would

give me the bodily benefits of fasting on a schedule that I could maintain. So fasting one day a week is beneficial for me with minimal cost or drain on my body."

"I liked the way you figured out how to make fasting work for you," Dad says. "But don't you get a headache from the lack of protein?"

"I take a powdered supplement that my homeopathic doctor gave me on the days that I fast. It provides the nutrients and minerals as well as helping to cleanse my body."

"Sounds good," he admits. "I like the system you've set up for yourself, son. Are you sure I can't interest you in something to eat?" Dad asks, opening the refrigerator.

"No, thanks."

From here our conversation drifts to sports and how some of the local teams are doing. We have always shared a bond in relation to the challenge of sports. The "challenge factor" is also an important element in my research because it keeps me motivated to continue seeking answers.

As I get up to leave I tell him thanks for the idea of a snack bar for animals, and we both laugh. I give my dad a hug around his shoulder as he continues to slice a tomato. I never hugged him like this in years past, but now it's more important for me to show my affection in this way. He seems to enjoy it.

Hidden Asset

*To achieve wholeness, we must be willing
to recognize our spirit.*

Chapter Thirteen

Exploring the Wilderness of the Soul

Tears from the Soul: Love Transcended

I find it interesting that a person can be unaware of something, even as it's taking place under their very nose—often, over long periods of time. In my case, misplaced pride and the desire to be above showing emotion was the culprit. Fortunately, a wide variety of experiences during my exploration, including Randy's death, have begun to chip away at this haughtiness. I've become more open to situations that stir up my emotions. Even still, I'm not really sure why I have decided to experience a soul retrieval session with John Turberville.

I am clearly skeptical around the subject of soul retrieval, an age-old Shamanic technique. Maybe I'm nervous because the process sounds so medieval and less psychological or systematic. I don't know for sure. To think that my soul might be fragmented and that practitioners could actually retrieve parts of it seems to be something superstitious, maybe out of a 1920's movie— reminding me of unfriendly tribesmen not wanting to have their pictures taken because their soul would be lost.

But something has led me to John. It's more than just a referral. It's more than just wanting to find out about soul retrieval. But what is it? Although I am skeptical, and there is a sense of mistrust, I follow my inner guidance and end up here. As in my first session with Mary Coleman, I truly feel that I am being led by a power stronger than myself. Is this just an example of listening to my inner self? In any case, I make a mental note to pay more attention to this feeling of being led.

I know I was not nervous when I had sessions with Native American medicine men. In fact, their sessions were quite revealing to me, not only about myself but about their native cultures and the ways of their people. One shaman, who is the son of a Cherokee Chief in Oklahoma, presented to me a travel-diary written by his great-great-grandmother during the infamous "trail of tears." The information in the diary gave me insight into how their spiritual leaders worked hand in hand with the tribal leaders to help the people through this difficult period.

If it's not fear of shamans, then there must be something else about this particular encounter that has me unsettled. I walk up the short flight of concrete steps to the small porch and knock on the old wooden door. It is quiet. No sign of life about. No dog. No approaching footsteps. As I check the street number in my day planner, the door swings open.

"You must be Mark Bryant. I'm John Turberville. Come on in," says the large, amiable man. He gestures towards the front room. "Have a seat. I'll be right with you."

I choose the green corduroy chair and unlace my shoes while candles flicker in the center of the fireplace. Otherwise it seems like a normal place—children's toys and shoes here and there. The familiar smell of chicken roasting sneaks into the room. I glance through the window at the neighbors' front porch and wonder if they're even aware of what takes place in here.

"Okay, let's begin," John says when he reappears. We talk briefly first and discover that we have more in common than each of us would have believed. John has recently become a father, and I have a baby on the way. This creates a bond and trust between us.

"I'm ready," I say, not knowing what to expect. "What are we going to do?"

"I'm going to do a soul retrieval—retrieve parts of your soul that have been taken, lost, or given away," he explains. He then lies down, adjusting a blindfold over his eyes after turning on a drumming tape. Several minutes go by. "I see a swan up ahead," he says as though he is traveling. "There are three houses up on my right—one green, one pink, and one brown," he relays to me. There are long moments of silence between his observations. I remain still and silent, feeling somewhat skeptical about what's going on here.

"Mark, someone has part of your soul on the other side," John says suddenly.

I realize I have been in a semi-conscious state. Hearing my name, startles me into a conscious state again. Other side? The other side of what? What's he talking about now—the other side? Then I recall "the other side" is a term metaphysicians use for people who have departed, have passed on. The other side, the departed, is not an area I am interested in researching because I can't see an application for it. I will sit through this since I'm already here, I tell myself, but I would not have chosen this.

"Are you willing to ask for this piece back?" John murmurs in a deeper voice.

"Of course," I reply, feeling really skeptical now.

"Now I'm going over to the other side. I'll act as a guide for you," he says slowly. "I'll go and communicate with this departed spirit that has a piece of your soul."

Uneasy silence follows. "Mark, I've found the spirit who has the piece. He's willing to give it back to you. He says he only took it because he loved you so much that he wanted a piece of you when he left his physical body. Mark, he wants you to know how much he loved you, and he is now freely returning something that's made him happy. He took this piece of you when you were only four," John continues.

I feel my body tighten as sorrow begins to overcome me. I am not sure why or where this is coming from, but the inescapable feeling is clearly sorrow. I hold it back and am puzzled because I don't really believe in this soul retrieval thing.

"Charles wants you to have this back and thanks you for letting him keep it for all these years."

Charles? Charles who? I'm wondering. He must be making this name up. It hasn't hit me just yet. It's as if John is talking about someone foreign to me. Yet my body seems to be reacting to something, and I'm getting very emotional. I sit there immobilized, my thought process temporarily frozen while at the same time my emotions are erupting. I wonder why. Then it dawns on me. Could he be talking about my Uncle Charles? No. It's been too long. But soon, it is clear the feelings of sorrow I have concern my Uncle Charles. I don't know how or why the feelings have come up like this. It's strange. I haven't thought of my uncle in many years. It was so difficult for my mom when her brother Charles died. It hurt me deep inside to see her so sad. Those earliest memories of my mom crying over her brother's death remain imperishable in my mind.

The memory and essence of Uncle Charles floods my heart somehow, and I feel him near to me. It's a little hair-raising, almost terrifying. My fear gradually dissolves as I feel a love for my uncle and the grief of losing him. It was so long ago, and I was so young when he died. He was just a young man, cut down in his prime by an organ disease before transplants were available. What was it about him that made my love so strong? Sorrow wrestles with my heart and finally wins.

"It's time to go now, Mark, but Charles wants you to know he'll always love you." John says a few other things that my mind doesn't seem to hear. Then there is a silence that feels endless. My eyes are closed, but I can hear John moving about. After a while he begins to speak again, using guided imagery to bring me back to a conscious state.

Once our session is completed, I thank John and we sit at his kitchen table and talk for fifteen minutes. He offers me lunch, and I cordially decline, informing him of a business appointment I have. Although a complete stranger, he seems to be offering his friendship in addition to his services. I'm less hesitant about someone like John than in the past. At the beginning of this quest, I didn't know how to bridge the gulf between myself and people in these spiritual communities: John a healer and metaphysician, and me a Christian. Gradually, over many months of determined effort and experiences, I have overcome this gulf. Possibly the greatest reward for me is that today, with casual words, John and I seem to be able to reach across this invisible divide.

I walk quietly to my car wondering what all this has meant. I don't believe in contact with the dead and have not pursued it, but I can't deny what just happened. Maybe it was just an isolated incident. What am I to learn from this? Is it just about sorrow and grief, or is there something more?

One thing is for sure: it was real. The emotions were real, and the presence of "something" was there near me. Was this a spirit? Was this what a spirit presence feels like? I wonder, was this what Mary was seeing when the old Chinese man came into our session? This clearly is affecting my belief system, stretching my comprehension and my own sense of reality. It seems to lie well beyond the realm of believability.

After leaving John's home, I stop the car at a red light and practice a grounding technique Maria Strauss has taught me. She told me to use it whenever I felt a little spacey (which to her clairvoyance meant my spirit was partly out of my body). I get a better grip on myself and take stock of the situation by questioning what it is I'm learning here. Do I really believe that someone took part of my soul? No, I don't. Do I believe there was some presence there greater than I understand? Yes, I do. Could I sense some energy in the room apart from my own and John's that seemed to be my uncle's? Yes. Did it evoke the memories of my uncle and my own emotions around his loss? Absolutely. Do I understand fully what happened? NO! What am I learning here? It will take me a while to integrate this.

Moving forward with the green traffic light, it finally strikes me that this session has really been about love. For the first time in my life, I can really say I feel love to be eternal. I've always felt that love is the greatest of all emotions and often wondered about love transcending the physical body. However, this was my first personal experience with love transcending. It's not an experience I will soon forget.

In the quiet confines of my car, I thank God for this session with John Turberville. To feel my uncle's love again gives me a warm feeling inside. I try to place this unusual experience within the context of my belief system. I think about the Gospel story in the Bible where a man in hell asks to have his brother on earth warned about transgressions to try to save him from the same fiery fate. It makes me wonder if my uncle is in heaven or hell. I don't know. But what I do know is that it is a place where my Uncle Charles can still love.

Just as I'm about to turn onto the freeway entrance, I realize all at once I have left my day planner. My day planner is like my wallet—I can't do without it. As I return to John's house to retrieve it, I realize that forgetting my day planner reveals how shaken I am by this singular experience.

Early the following morning, I sit in the lobby of a local computer company. As I review my notes for a business meeting, I just can't seem to get the session with John out of my head. My memory of that curious experience is vivid.

As I admire the beautiful watercolor on the wall across the lobby, a fleeting thought occurs to me. Underlying my exploration is a change in me that stems from understanding differences between people's beliefs. I sit here reflecting on how differences in beliefs have often been the cause of misunderstandings and difficulties in my life. It seems to me that on a global level, differences in beliefs are responsible for many conflicts and wars. Suddenly, I am better able to see the underlying unity—in this case, love. This concept hits me from out of the blue.

I watch other business people come in and out of the lobby and think about the session with John. Was this the true nature of love? Even now, my emotions well up within me as I reflect on love; the love of God, the love of oneself or the "God within," and the love one has for other people. It's becoming ever more clear to me that this is the common denominator. It seems that whether it's my church, or a healing institution, or a group of intuitives working together, love is the underlying mission for all of them.

George Washington "Wannabes"

The idea of "triangulation," or determining a certain point from two totally different aspects, has always intrigued me. As the exploration winds down there have been numerous triangulating points along the way. The ones that stand out most readily encompass my family.

One evening in the kitchen, excitement carries over to the dinner table.

"And the lizard was this big," Allison demonstrates, knocking over her glass of milk in her exuberance.

Jonathan jumps up before the white stream dribbles down on to his chair. "Ooh, there's milk in my mashed potatoes," he bursts out.

"It was an accident. It was an accident," Allison says defensively.

Vicki grabs a towel. "I'll get you a new plate, Jonathan. These things happen."

"Yeah, remember last summer on vacation when Jonathan spilled his orange juice in that restaurant," Allison pipes up.

"Where was that?" I ask, trying to recall what we did last summer.

"It was that little place where we had breakfast in Arizona," Vicki responds as we continue with our meal.

"Oh. That reminds me, Vicki, where are we going for vacation this year?" I ask.

"I don't know yet," she replies. "Do you have any ideas?"

"You seem to be able to pick the good spots. I almost hate to interfere," I concede.

Included in our longer-range plans is to possibly move to another state. We feel a change someday might be good for the family. Vicki has planned vacations during the past few years with this in mind. She has chosen areas for family vacations where we might consider living. So far, she had been successful in choosing places we all seemed to enjoy. We spent a week in Victoria, British Columbia three years ago and ten days in Colorado the year before that. Oregon was a lovely place to unwind two years ago, and last year was the Arizona trip.

"So what do you think?" I ask Vicki later that evening as I unfold a map of the United States on the kitchen table.

"Well, to be quite honest, I've been thinking about New Mexico this year," she says, pointing to the state on the map. We go on to discuss vacation dates and possible travel arrangements. The travel topic makes me realize just how much Vicki uses her intuition in family matters. As Vicki talks about places to visit in New Mexico, I am reminded of a similar conversation with an intuitive, Roberta Herzog, who lives in Pennsylvania. What is unique about Roberta is that she reads the Akashic Records to get her information. She explained to me that the Akashic is an etheric field believed to contain all pieces of information about a person, including their past lives.

Past lives conflict with my Christian beliefs. It's not an easy concept to reconcile. The past life philosophy, better known as reincarnation, follows an Eastern tradition and is quite foreign to me. I know it says in the Bible, "it is appointed for men to die once and after that come judgment," so I haven't been able to reconcile the two different beliefs. Nevertheless, I have to say that many of the issues Roberta brings up from supposedly past lives are, in fact, the very same issues I am facing today. I can't explain it. Is this just coincidence?

According to Roberta, the way it works is certain emotions and issues carry over from past lifetimes. I've actually used this past-life process to take inventory of some of these issues. For all I know, Roberta could have made up the lives. But she couldn't have made up the emotions and issues, which have been very accurate.

When I first met with Roberta and found out about her process, I was secretly hoping to have been someone famous in a past life. Maybe I was a famous head-of-state or explorer—yes, a George Washington or Christopher Columbus. But that was not to be the case. In fact, according to Roberta, I was not anyone famous at all. Roberta explained to me that many people are so impressed by an individual that they believe they were that famous personality in a past life. Roberta told me that I must understand this.

One of the most fascinating twists with Roberta came to light from a simple question. I had mentioned that Vicki and I were eventually thinking about moving out of California and casually asked her where she sensed would be a good place for us to live.

I remember her reply clearly. "Out of California," Roberta

said after thinking for a moment. "First of all, I notice that California is a positive place for both of you. For you, Mark, the South of France would be strongly positive but not so much so for Vicki. Also for you, Washington and Oregon are good places. British Colombia and Colorado are strongly positive for both of you and many areas in Arizona are good as well. Hawaii is very good for Vicki and for you. Santa Fe, New Mexico is another strong location for you, Mark, and less so for Vicki."

I find it fascinating that Roberta can articulate the same places that Vicki felt to be the right locations for us. Also curious is the fact that I've invested or started businesses in California, Oregon, Washington, and Arizona. Could this be coincidental or something more? Maybe it's just that I'm becoming more accepting of alternative approaches that exceed the boundaries of my understanding.

Inner Landscapes and the Language Barrier

Often, things that are exciting or mysterious can also be deceptive. Even with a mind that's been trained to look for cause and effect, I'm sometimes drawn into situations where I lose my impartiality. For this reason, I've contracted Alexis McKenna, a professor at a local university with a background in psychology and communications to consult with me. She provides an objective view for me and she is very straight forward. I like that. We've scheduled our meeting on a day when a strong weather system is sweeping through California. I turn the collar up on my overcoat as I run in the rain from my car to the building. There is a cozy quality to the small coffee house where we meet to talk. It is bustling with business this morning.

Alexis is wearing striking colors, just as she was the first time I met her. Her outfit enhances her dark hair and blue eyes, making her a noticeable tall, slim figure in the cafe. She certainly takes care of herself, I observe as she stands at the coffee counter. Alexis helps herself to French roast coffee before joining me at my table in the far corner.

"Mark, how's the process of understanding all of these holistic and spiritual communities coming?"

"Good," I reply.

"How are you organizing the information?" she asks while I review my data for our morning meeting. "I'm curious because it seems like it'd be a such a large task."

I think to myself that it *has* been a struggle to try to organize. There is intuitive information, healing information, spirit information. Alexis is right when she says it's a large task.

"I've begun to organize the information by breaking it down into categories," I say, knowing she'll appreciate this from an organizational standpoint. "I appreciate your working with me. I guess if we weren't working together on this, I'd keep most of this in my head or in little notes on my day planner."

"It's the same thing I'm doing for my doctoral students," she says. "I enjoy hearing what you've learned and giving you my evaluation. What are the categories you've decided on?" she asks, taking out a notepad.

"I've recently created a matrix for these categories. Hold on, I think I might even have a copy of it with me," I mention as I search through my papers. "Here it is. Your questions in our previous meeting prompted me to create this matrix."

Organizational Matrix
of Spiritual & Holistic Communities

Holistic Health Practitioner	Physical/tool-user/information
Intuitive Counselor	Spiritual/non-tool user/ information (psychic energy)
Psychiatrist	Mental/Non-tool-user/information
Pastor/Priest	Spiritual/non-tool user/information
Healer	Physical/tool-user/healing energy
Personality Profile	Mental/system-user/information
Medical Doctor	Physical/Tool-user/energy
Acupuncurist	Physical/tool-user/energy

She reviews the matrix while I explain it to her. "I've tried to keep this simple so I can apply it more easily. As you can see, I've used three levels of classification. First, I classify the practitioner as either spiritual, mental, or physical. I'm able to make more sense out of their healing systems by placing them in one of these categories. You can see, for example, that I've classified a medical doctor under physical, a priest under spiritual, and a psychiatrist under mental."

"That's straightforward," she says.

"The second level of classification is tool-user/non-tool user. I find, for example, some intuitives use a tool or a system to help them focus their psychic energy. Other people use no tools or system, but rely on their own abilities entirely."

Alexis reviews the matrix. She seems to be enjoying my descriptions. This is probably the most analytical I've been with the information I'm uncovering, yet I need to ground this information so I can work with it. It is beneficial for me to talk to Alexis about this because it helps clarify the information for me as well. I hope she isn't finding this information too compartmentalized. Many practitioners don't want to be put into categories like this, yet it's the only way I can begin to organize these fields to understand what's going on here.

Discussing the matrix reminds me of one of the kid's teachers who has been recently diagnosed with cancer. Unfortunately, the cancer was discovered very late and had already progressed to the most advanced stage. She was immediately placed on chemotherapy to try to save her life. All I could do was recommend the qigong master who works with energy to try to keep her from getting too weak after she had completed the chemotherapy. The matrix helped me think about what information I had that might help.

"I'm beginning to get a clearer understanding of your method," Alexis says, apparently finding the matrix an interesting way to look at these fields.

"The third and final level of classification is energy versus information. I've noticed most practitioners use either energy or information to assist other people. I realize that many people believe information is a form of energy. But for purposes of this category system, I'm defining energy in its purest form. My acupuncturist is an example of someone who uses energy in her work, and you're someone who uses information in your practice."

"So according to your matrix here, an intuitive counselor is classified as someone who's spiritual, who's a non-tool-user, and who uses information."

"Yeah."

"Interesting that a priest or minister fits into exactly those same categories," Alexis says.

"That is interesting," I confess, not having noticed this before. "Do you care for more coffee?" I ask, needing to stretch my legs.

"Please," she says. When I go to the counter for refills, I notice a group of women sitting together at a large table created by pushing several smaller ones together. A man sits alone nearby, busy at his laptop.

"I've never seen this place so busy," I say when I return.

"Me either. Thanks. Did you know it was bought by two women?" Alexis asks me.

"No."

"Yes, and they offer it to be used by professionals after the dinner hour and as a place to give personal growth workshops. They also have musicians come in once in a while. I'm thinking about offering a Guided Imagery and Music training here next month."

"Would this be similar to the sessions I had with you where you used classical music?" I ask.

"Yes, although I'll have to change the format to accommodate a group of people. Still, the basic idea is to use classical music as a catalyst for imagery. You may recall, this process was developed by Helen Bonny in the early 1970s."

"Remind me to tell Vicki that she might like to work with you on this. She really enjoys music, and I believe this is a transformative process that would match her nicely."

"I'll do that," Alexis says.

"By the way, I still have the renditions I did as part of our session. The one I titled 'Serenity' is still my favorite," I tell her. I had always associated guided imagery with reducing stress before Alexis introduced me to Guided Imagery and Music (GIM).

Alexis and I spend the next thirty minutes talking about various practices and systems. She talks about Don Campbell, another pioneer in the field of music, health, and education. She says he likes to say "music is the bridge to the soul." I go on to tell Alexis about my recent interviews, after which she says, "I believe there are some exercises we can do together that will clarify your learning."

"I'm open to trying them," I say.

"One process I have in mind is called 'mind mapping'—it might be worth doing at our next meeting," Alexis continues. "It could help you get the bigger picture about what's going on with your research. There's a good book on this called *Mindmapping* by Joyce Wycoff, if you want more information on it."

"Yes, I'd like to get some of this material down on paper so that it doesn't seem so chaotic."

"Curious you should mention chaotic, Mark. My concept is that the inner world is not chaotic. Just unknown and unfamiliar. Our society tends to view the internal world as chaotic since it's unfamiliar and doesn't operate according to linear logic and cause-and-effect. This is why initially everything in your research seemed strange to you," she says, writing something on her notepad.

I nod in agreement.

"But what you soon found out is that there are maps available for traversing the inner realms," she explains. "These maps are readily available, but they often are in a 'foreign language.' If you're going to use the maps, then you need to learn the foreign language. All of the systems you're learning about, such as the chakra system, the aura fields, feng shui, and so forth, have their own language. This language usually has a different 'logic' structure—a different system of organization, syntax, and grammar."

I have to laugh a bit at Alexis' comment about grammar and syntax, because English was my least favorite subject. And Alexis' comment on language systems is also quite appropriate. Initially, my secondary research or "library work" included reading the glossary in each book, in order to understand the terms being used in these fields.

"So what you're saying is I'm learning new languages…in a way?"

"Yes. As you have traveled the roads and highways of this inner landscape, you've encountered multiple languages and symbol systems which you slowly began to understand. Each one has given you new information, concepts, ideas, and understandings—about yourself, your world, and others who are important to you. Ultimately, you'll reach a point where you need to take all the information and integrate it in a meaningful way. That's kind of it, in a nutshell," she concludes.

As Alexis finishes her coffee and begins to gather up her things, I realize she has summed up some of the differences with her theory on language. We say our good-byes, and I leave the cafe. One thing is clear from our conversation. There are no *short cuts* to greater awareness—in any language.

———◉———

Hidden Asset

*The internal world is not chaotic,
just unknown and unfamiliar*

Chapter Fourteen

Recognizing and Honoring Diversity

Communicating with Spirit

The birth of a child very often marks a turning point in a person's life. In my case, the upcoming birth of our next child will bring my research to a culmination. I'll always be grateful that I had this time and the support of those close to me to look into these various fields. In a peculiar sort of way, I'm really just trading one adventure for another. Parenthood has all of the fears, anxieties, and joys that I've discovered exist in the fields I've been researching.

After meeting with Karen Kenney at the airport in Arizona, I've scheduled an appointment for Vicki with her to talk about some issues Vicki has around her upcoming delivery. Vicki is eager for the session, and I ask her to let me talk to Karen when they finish.

While Vicki is talking to Karen on the kitchen telephone, I use my office line to talk with the principal of a company called INC. This clever acronym stands for International Nutritional Consultants. The partners in the firm are endeavoring to bring nutritional education and analysis to the public via the World Wide Web. Nutrition continues to be a part of my ongoing research. I speak with one of the founders, and we agree to meet for breakfast the following week. After hanging up the telephone, I check the clock, and notice it's getting near the end of Vicki's call to Karen. I quietly go back into the kitchen and nonchalantly eavesdrop on their conversation.

"I do get tired," I hear Vicki say. "But then I sit for a while, and I feel better," she says while sitting on her favorite stool in the kitchen. "That sounds good. I like this idea," Vicki laughs while the conversation continues. "Thank you, I feel so much better already." I glance at my watch to calculate what time it is in Arizona. I still have a few minutes left to talk to Karen before she has to go. Vicki hands the telephone to me.

"Hi, Karen. How are you?" I ask.

"Great! I just had a really good session with Vicki. I know she's going to get a lot out of it," Karen says to me enthusiastically.

"I'm glad to hear that. Karen, I think you're very good for Vicki because of the way you explain things. You're more practical and down-to-earth than many people in the spiritual field. I think this matches Vicki very well right now."

"You're right about Vicki, Mark, and I do believe we work well together. Now, I have a few suggestions for you around the baby. Vicki and I spent most of the time talking about how she could work with the spirit of the baby, and in doing so, have the baby help with the delivery. It's very important that you support her during the labor and remind her of our conversation when things get tough. That's one important job for you," Karen emphasizes, reminding me a little of our Lamaze teacher.

"Thanks, Boss! I'm writing it down as we speak," I say.

"You can also help Vicki with the physical part of the labor. There are some areas on her feet and legs that are definitely going to feel the strain from the labor. If you can remember to rub these areas in addition to all the Lamaze techniques, then she will have a much easier time of it," she explains. Karen begins to talk about some of the changes in the female body during labor. Some of her comments are very graphic and although I've been in the delivery room for both my first two children's births, it's still a little awkward for me to talk to Karen in this degree of detail. After talking about the physical aspects, Karen again mentions the importance of the baby's spirit.

"Vicki and I have talked about what she needs to do, and I believe she'll be fine. However, in the midst of the pain of delivery, it's hard for a woman to focus. It's important that you talk to her and remind her to work with the baby by communicating with the baby's spirit."

Karen proceeds to give me necessary details of the most sensitive areas for me to rub, telling me how hard, for what length of time, and in what order so that Vicki will get the maximum relief during the delivery.

"Is that it?" I ask, making a diagram of the areas she's speaking about.

"That's it for you, but remember these are critical things for you to do during the delivery. Also, I'd suggest practicing this rubbing technique now in the weeks remaining before the baby comes. Vicki will enjoy having her feet rubbed anyway," Karen says with that lovely laugh of hers coming over the line. "And you'll be really setting this up and conditioning her for the delivery. While you're doing this, remind her to talk with the baby's spirit. It's very important for them to work together, mother and child, on this delivery. Okay?"

"Got it!"

Following the session, I spend a few minutes talking with Vicki in the living room. "How did it go with Karen?" I ask her.

"It went very well. Karen and I connected really well on the baby and the upcoming delivery," Vicki says enthusiastically.

"Connected how?"

"We connected with the baby's spirit and actually talked to the baby about the delivery. It was like Karen was translating for me. She was communicating to me what the baby wanted. She was teaching me how to talk directly with the baby's spirit. I really enjoyed that part of our conversation," Vicki replies tenderly.

"That must have been special, feeling the baby's energy and thoughts before the baby arrives," I say, feeling envious as I place my hand on her stomach. But even as this feeling comes over me, I'm delighted that Vicki is opening up to a greater awareness. She never would have had this conversation with Karen with the births of our first two kids. Her belief system would not have allowed it. I know my own beliefs would not have; this was well beyond the realm of our sensibility. As I caress her, I think how much we both have expanded our awareness and understanding.

"Yes, it was a special feeling," she confirms, touching my hand. "I'll always remember that conversation because it felt so right to me. I really do want to work with the baby during this delivery."

"I know you do, sweetheart, and I'll be there to remind you to do it just as Karen suggested."

After our conversation, I leave for the office. Through Vicki, I have gotten firsthand experience of working with the spirit. This is what Karen had talked to me about at the airport in Arizona. What an exciting way to apply her information about recognizing the spirit and communicating with the spirit of the person! I feel the thrill of this rare experience rush through my body. From listening to Vicki talk, we can expect a wonderful soul in this next child.

A few weeks later, we are blessed with a second daughter, a happy, healthy 8 pound, 22 inch baby girl. Our thanks are to God for this tiny precious spirit; children are surely a gift from God. We named her Kristen. Vicki and I followed many of Karen's suggestions, and the delivery went very well. I forgot to do some of the things Karen told me now and then, but Vicki let me know about it right away.

Kristen has a striking resemblance to our first daughter Allison. Our two older kids can't wait to hold their baby sister, especially Allison. We have to help Allison hold the baby because she is still young herself, but I can already see them bonding. Karen had told Vicki during their phone session that Kristen would learn a lot from Allison in this lifetime. It's sure starting off in a fine way.

I grin as I remember the baby poll. I will have to send Scout Bartlett a card declaring he was accurate on his prediction that the baby would be a girl. A lot of the intuitives talked about the baby's energy and how she would be a wonderful child. Of course we won't know if they're right about this until Kristen is quite a bit older.

It does make me think however that children are always an uncertain proposition. It's beyond my understanding as to why some children turn out to have an extremely difficult life, while others do not. If the parents are consistent in child-rearing, is one child more receptive than another? People I've met in the spiritual/holistic communities believe ultimately every person is responsible for their own conduct. Even so, I hope Vicki and I can set a good example for our children.

Developing a Broader Vision

Going back to my childhood home always gives me a comfortable feeling. One quiet Sunday afternoon a few weeks after Kristin's arrival, I stop in to see my parents while Vicki and the kids visit her aunt and uncle. My father is working in the yard when I arrive, which gives me the opportunity to spend time alone with my mother. She has been an elementary schoolteacher for many years. Before that she was a beauty college instructor while we were in school. She has always been a teacher at heart. That seems to be her purpose in life—to teach.

My mother has a youthful appearance with very beautiful skin. Having been born in Georgia and with such a lovely face, she can rightfully lay claim to the expression "Georgia peach." She is highly intuitive and also young at heart. Her energy, which I am beginning to have a deeper sense of, is like a teenager's. Sensing a person's energy is easiest for me with those I am closest to.

After I fill her in on the latest activities regarding her grandchildren, she asks me about my adventure. "Mark, I'm inquisitive. What's the main thing you've learned from all of this research you've done?" I've intentionally kept my mother less informed about some of the areas I've been exploring. She's a worrier, and I didn't want her worrying about me needlessly.

"I've learned to be a more balanced person, Mom!" I respond.

Mom gives me a puzzled stare. I know the reason, I think to myself… she's thinking I'm already a balanced person. My mother is focused on the external signs. I go to church, I work hard, I am a good dad, a good son. Those are the things she sees, as do others.

Nevertheless, over time as my physical assets increased, my spiritual side diminished. I was gaining power and wealth at the expense of my spiritual life. I was going spiritually bankrupt.

"The irony in me starting businesses is that the increase in my material holdings brought greater spiritual unrest," I explain.

"Spiritual unrest?" she questions.

"I slowly began to realize that I'd been seeing things entirely from a physical or material standpoint. This was the very thing that was barring me from understanding more of the spiritual principles."

"What do you mean exactly?" she asks. I can see my mother is starting to think I'm being too hard on myself.

"Don't worry, Mom," I reassure her. "You see, my exploration is about renewing my soul through spirit, that essential part of me that's beneath the surface."

"Do you mean that part of you that's from God?"

"That's right. You taught us kids that all of us have a spark of God within. It's that part of us that's described in the Book of Genesis: 'God breathed life into us.' Whether you want to call this soul or life or breath or whatever, it's that part of us that's within."

I wonder if "spirit" being defined as the "breath of God" is why breathing seems like such an important part of the mind/body fields. Whether it's meditation, yoga, qigong, or biofeedback, each of these systems seems to rely heavily on maintaining proper breathing techniques.

"Mom, all I can say is that I have a greater connection to God than I had before."

"It sounds a little like faith to me," she says.

"I guess that's part of it. I've had to learn to exercise patience in the pursuit of faith. It doesn't come all at once. It's like my soul turning towards faith so my spirit can connect with the kingdom of God," I tell her.

"Somewhat like an education of the soul," she says.

"Hey, I like that, 'education of the soul.' It sounds good coming from an educator," I reply and smile.

My mother continues to ask about the various people I've been seeing on my journey. She is as curious as Vicki when it comes to some of the unusual experiences. We move from the living room to the kitchen as she cleans up some papers on the counter. She asks me if this research is something I plan to start a business around. Other people have asked the same question. I wonder if I am so stereotyped as a business developer that everything I look into has to be about starting a company.

I tell her I'm not sure what sort of company you could do around this. But I do feel the information and experiences will help me be a better business owner. In a way, I'd lost touch with my soul. I was so caught up in making money and accumulating material things that I lost sight of that other part of myself—my inner self.

She tells me there's nothing wrong with making money. "In the Bible, remember Abraham was a very rich man, and he was still called the 'friend of God,'" she says with authority. I smile as I admire that teacher aspect in my mother.

"That's it precisely, Mom. Abraham was able to bridge these two parts—the physical and spiritual. It's one of the reasons he's such a great example in the Bible. Abraham was a wealthy person but didn't forget his inner nature—that part of himself that walked with God."

"Young man!" she says emphatically. "You were in church the week you were born, and you've gone to church all your life."

"Yes, church is an essential part of my life and always will be," I say. "But in the past I've lived in a compartmentalized way. I went to church on Sunday but lived in the material world Monday through Saturday. I always seemed to be living a divided life."

My comment to my mother makes me think in the past I've somehow put my friends into categories. Let's see, ...I have my Christian friends, my business friends, and it would be easy now to create buckets for my holistic/spiritual friends. Somehow I need to eliminate the walls between these groups and get rid of the buckets. I don't know if there needs to be a division anymore.

I can tell my mother is not convinced of what I'm saying. I think she may still see me as the adolescent son. It's probably hard for any mother to think of her son or daughter as anything but perfect. She begins to prepare lunch for us. She likes to fix me something to eat when I visit. Maybe it's that southern hospitality coming through.

"I've met people of all races and creeds and interviewed many people from different religious walks," I continue. "I've met Native Americans who have helped me have a greater respect for the Earth. Tibetan Buddhists have improved my meditation process, which has helped me slow my furious pace. The key is I wasn't looking at their religions but at the tools that they used to improve their lives. I've adopted the tools that can improve my life. This hasn't changed my religious belief; it's just increased my understanding."

"You're not thinking about changing religions after all of

this, are you?" she asks, checking the pizza in the oven.

"No, it's not like that," I laugh. "I was born an American in a Christian society. There must have been some reason for this— some plan from God. But even more to the point, my exploring isn't about changing my religion. It's about enlarging my understanding by the use of tools and resources available from many belief systems."

"Can you give me an example?" she asks, somewhat less skeptically.

"Take yoga. Now I don't practice it myself, but Vicki does. Yoga is a series of physical postures, breathing exercises, and meditation practices developed in India. It's been practiced since before Buddha's time. Yet on any weekend, you can travel and find yoga being taught or practiced at many Christian centers across the United States. You see what's happening here?"

"Sort of," she replies.

"Americans see that yoga can benefit one's health and well being. Its association with Buddha has no detrimental effect on one's belief system. A Christian who practices yoga doesn't become a Buddhist. He or she just enlarges their understanding and well being by taking a practice made popular by Buddhists and using it to live a healthier life."

Mom goes out to the garage to get something from the freezer. When she returns I take up where I left off. I'm on a roll. "Reiki is another practice that is everywhere. Vicki told me that Reiki classes are now offered through our local parks and community programs. And this very ancient practice was revitalized and brought to the West by the Japanese."

She smiles as if she's agreeing. I know my mom is a good

listener, but I wonder how much of this discussion is impacting her own belief system. I decide to move away from the religious overtones we've been discussing.

"By the way, I have you and Dad to thank for the way I've done this exploration."

"Why do you say that?"

"When we were young, you two had a plan to see the world and give your children a better chance to explore many cultures," I remind her. "You've often told us that you didn't want your children to grow up with prejudice against a culture or creed. You wanted us to have the broadest view of things."

"Yes?"

"I've taken this same approach in balancing my physical, mental and spiritual sides. You and Dad were great examples for me. I've taken the belief you've instilled in me to guard against prejudice in any form and applied it to my exploration of the various holistic/spiritual communities."

"I think your dad might be interested in hearing you say this," she says as she pulls the pizza out of the oven.

"Good idea. I'll call Dad in from the cornfields," I say with a laugh.

Mom puts her hand on my shoulder as I walk past her. There is nothing that feels quite as good as connecting with your parents.

Growing Apart and Becoming Close

In every partnership, marriage and business alike, there are periods when circumstances test the faith and trust that govern a relationship. My adventure has been just such a test for my wife and business partners. Consequently, I'm always on the lookout for threads in our relationship that might be unraveling.

As I flip through the pile of mail on my desk at the office one of my partners, Kevin Lanning, stops in to chat. "Hey Kevin, how's that killer serve of yours?" I ask him.

"I'm playing every day now, and I just bought a new graphite racquet," he responds smiling. "Would you like to schedule a match sometime soon?" he says as he picks up a book off my desk.

"Not a chance. I'd have to hit the ball around for about a quarter of a century to survive out there on the courts against you," I reply.

"I know of a good tennis coach out your way," he teases.

"Thanks, Kevin," I remark dryly. "I'll keep that in mind if I ever decide to get serious about the game."

"Okay then, just trying to help," he says, setting the book back on the corner of my desk. "What's this book *The New Bottom Line* about?"

"It's a good book. Take it, you'll enjoy it."

"I like the title," Kevin says.

"Yeah, good choice. The subtitle is even better—*Bringing Heart & Soul to Business*. The book is complete with controversy and inspiration. It looks at the question of whether business and spirituality mix."

"Do they?"

"Read it and tell me what you think," I say. "I've tried to ask myself this question all during my exploration. I have an entire shelf in my library devoted to these type of books. Most of them seek to answer the question, 'Can business and spirituality go together without conflict?'"

"It looks like a good collection of thinkers—Tom Peters, Ken Blanchard, Thomas Moore, …I think I will borrow it," Kevin says as he picks up the photos I have displayed on the edge of my desk. "Your kids are getting big! How's the new one doing?"

"Kristen's doing fine," I reply.

"And how's Vicki?"

"Good. I made a commitment to her to wind things down with the research once the baby was born. I'm pretty much wrapping things up as we speak."

"Great!" He says, setting the photos back on the corner of my desk. "It will be nice to see your mug around here more often. You're fortunate, you know, to have a wife like her, supporting your exploration."

"I agree. And a couple of very supportive partners," I add quickly with a big smile. For an indefinite moment I am caught up thinking about Kevin's comment about Vicki's support. I think about how much Vicki has been through and the degree to which she has seen me change. Kevin's right; she has, of course, been a great partner for me. There's been an emotional shift going on for me, and Vicki has always been there to talk about the experiences and how I'm feeling. Part of this trek has really been about bringing Vicki and me closer together.

"You know, Kevin, recently I came across a figure that might startle you."

"What was it?"

"There were over a million divorces in the U.S. last year."

"Really? Wow! Although I don't know why I should be surprised," he remarks.

"Time has a way of wearing on a relationship, and intimacy

can disappear," I say. "I never want to take my marriage for granted. One of my personal goals of this journey has been to become more intimate with Vicki."

"Are you talking about the racy kind?" he teases.

"You and your naughty thoughts. No. I'm talking about a more intimate bond for us that's based on a deeper understanding of each other."

"You two always seemed to have a close relationship to me," he observes.

Kevin's comment makes me wonder if Vicki's and my relationship has really changed on the outside. I know that she and I have learned so much about each other during this time. But maybe this is not as apparent to other people.

"Don't you think Vicki might be just a little fearful about you two growing apart because you've gotten so much into all this spiritual stuff?" Kevin asks. I am immediately struck by Kevin's question. I wonder if Kevin's intuition is kicking in. I can feel my own insecurities surfacing about my relationship with Vicki.

"That's a good question," I say while trying to not to show my concern. "Vicki and I had a lot of dialogue about this off and on, but we haven't talked about it recently. Now that you raise the issue, though, I'm going to bring this up with her the next chance I get."

Kevin has asked an insightful question. And one thing I admire about Kevin is his unusual ability to hone in on the most important issue at hand in any given situation. We can be in a meeting with ten people involved and Kevin may only say one thing the entire meeting, but often it's the most important.

After Kevin leaves my office, I think about what a good friend he has been in addition to being my partner. Even more than my other partners, Kevin has been accepting about the fields I've explored. He has been open to assisting me with intuitive exercises and listening to me try to make sense of everything that is happening. His insight is important to me, and I make a note to talk with Vicki about his and my conversation today. Insight from a true friend is a valuable gift indeed.

Awakening at Different Rates

There are moments now and then when I question whether I've done the right thing for my family. Was it the right time in my life to look inward? Vicki, to her credit, has stood by me each step of the way, frequently acting as a sounding board for the information I'm sifting through.

"Will you be helping out in Jonathan's classroom tomor– row?" Vicki asks one evening after the kids have gone to bed.

"Yes," I answer enthusiastically. "I signed up for every other Friday till the end of the year."

"I'm going to the nature museum tomorrow with Allison's preschool," she informs me as she closes the blinds in the living room. "Come sit and talk with me for a while."

As I join her on the sofa, I reflect how content she seems even though our third child has brought on additional financial burdens and responsibilities.

"I've pretty much wrapped up the research," I say as we get comfortable on the sofa.

"I was wondering when you were going to bring that up," Vicki replies. "We can definitely use the money you've been spending on the research for other things we need around the house."

Changing the subject I say, "I had a talk with Kevin this morning and something he brought up has made me curious."

"Oh, and what's that?" she asks.

"It made me wonder if you are concerned we may be drifting apart because of my involvement in these spiritual and healing fields," I state.

She grabs a cushion and hugs it to her before she responds. "You know, Mark, you're not the man I married," she answers carefully. "I have to be honest and tell you that the sleep disorder really scared me. And now all this time you've spent looking into these different fields makes me wonder if you'll still be happy with me and who I am."

My heart immediately feels a tremendous tug. To lose my relationship with Vicki would mean the very end for me. I don't know if I could stand the emotional loss. I don't even want to think about it.

"You see," she continues, "I'm awakening but not as quickly as you are. I'm opening up but at a different pace from you. You do everything so quickly!"

"Now don't get testy!" I say in nervous jest.

"No, really, Mark, I'm serious. I'm sure you've heard this from your business colleagues: You think fast, you talk fast, why ... you even walk fast. The kids find it tough keeping up with you when you're walking."

"What does this have to do with awakening?"

"Mark, your personality and your background has allowed you to open up faster."

"What makes you say that?" I ask, surprised by what's she's saying.

"Part of it is that you have a higher sense of urgency around things that are important to you. That's just who you are. Who else do you know would put all this time and energy into researching spiritual and holistic influences?"

"Well...."

"Well what!" she retorts, before I can answer. "There are very few! They'd do it gradually, more like what's happening to me," she says. "Your tendency is to do it quickly. There's nothing wrong with fast or slow. It just worries me that the faster you go and the slower I go, the bigger the gap will grow between us."

Again, my emotions flare up around the thought that Vicki and I could be growing apart. I am really glad now that Kevin and I had that conversation in my office. His intuition was clearly picking up on the gap Vicki is talking about. I hadn't taken this "gap" concept into consideration before, and it's good she's pointing it out to me now. It's hard to accept the possibility, but her idea is sensible.

Vicki continues, "Another thing you probably haven't noticed is you've been better situated to make some of these changes."

"How's that?"

"You had a stronger foundation than most people to start with. You've gone to church all your life. The Bible is your favorite book. It's not an image thing for you. You enjoy being in church. You like to go to cathedrals and holy places. Do you know I had one of the moms who helps in the class ask me if you were a pastor? She heard Jonathan's teacher reading his paper about you enjoying visiting missions and monasteries." Vicki sounds rather sarcastic.

"I hope I don't seem too eccentric," I say, smiling.

"No. My point is you're already strong in your religious beliefs, and your increasing awareness has only served to strengthen and expand those beliefs. The difference is I'm new to some of my religious beliefs, and they're not as strong as yours. I need to proceed more cautiously in my own awakening to make sure I'm on firm ground. Mark, do you see the difference here?" Vicki asks with emotion in her voice.

I stare at her without replying. My thoughts are on Vicki's feelings and how I have really overlooked the issue. She is absolutely right in her evaluation of the situation. Finally, I ask "Vicki, what is it I can do to help?"

"I don't want you to feel bad over any of this, Mark. I just need to be truthful with you, sweetheart," Vicki says.

"I appreciate that."

"You've been great at including me in all of your discoveries even when the material was unusual. You've taken the time to explain what you're doing and how you're doing it so that I feel secure about things you're looking into," she says. "You've given me the names of people you genuinely felt could help me with my own awareness or give me suggestions around my inner health. I really do know you're doing these things for me and the kids as well as for yourself," she adds, gently putting her hand on my arm.

I feel less insecure about our relationship now that we're talking about it. I appreciate Vicki being open and honest with me.

"Mark, I've enjoyed many of these people, but I'm also independent like you. I need to be able to grow and increase my own awareness in a way that matches me. My background and the way I like to proceed on things are different from yours. I might want to investigate art or the way things are placed in our house instead of spiritual areas."

"Oh, …you mean Feng Shui, the Chinese art of placement!" I say, teasing her.

"Stop! You know what I mean. All I'm asking is for you to understand this difference in us and to somehow close the gap that might arise."

Vicki has let me know her feelings. Her nature is kind and gentle. It's one of the many qualities I like about her. She has discussed an issue that she could have delivered in a much more hard-ball way. I feel compassion and love for her well up inside me as I think how considerate she is of my feelings.

"Vicki, I love you more than any other person in the world. I need you to balance out my life and our relationship in marriage," I say, taking hold of her hand. "You're highly perceptive, and you're right about this whole issue. I've been so caught up with the exploring and the experiences and principles I've learned, I forgot the root of all my research."

"And what's that, Mark?"

"It's relationships, Vicki, and ours is closest to my heart."

-----◄●►-----

Hidden Asset

People's paths are different: it's crucial to recognize and respect these differences in a close relationship—such as marriage.

Chapter Fifteen

Getting to the Heart of the Matter

Conveying Emotional Authenticity

It's impossible to start out on an adventure and say with surety, "This particular thing or that specific thing will happen." There's always the possibility of the unexpected happening. One unexpected but pleasant outcome of my exploration is, I feel closer to my parents than I have in years. Somehow this adventure has helped me to see them in a different light. I'll forever think of my parents a little differently than before. It's a similar feeling I have for other people around me. It's as though the exploration opened my eyes to look at the world in a different way.

A dividing of the way had evolved over the years between my parents and me. I realize now that my developing a higher perspective has enabled me to reconnect with them. An intuitive once told me that my parents are highly evolved souls who are here as husband and wife to further develop the souls of their children. She of course was using her gift to look at them at a soul level. It evoked a picture in my mind of me being this very young soul my whole life, and my parents watching over me as very old souls. It's hard for me to believe this because, ...come on, they're my mom and dad and just regular folks.

The beeper startles me, and I notice that it is my parents' number. They have not called my pager number before that I can recall.

"Excuse me, people," I interrupt the meeting. "I've got an important call to return. Go ahead without me."

My mother answers when I call. "Mark, he was feeling dizzy, and he couldn't keep anything down," my mother says.

"Are you okay, Mom?" I ask hearing the anxiety in her voice.

"Yes. Sorry to page you at work, but I felt this was an emergency. He was weak and passed out for a while. So he called me at work, and I rushed home and drove him to the hospital. I'm home now getting some of his things."

"Is it Dad?" I ask trying to clarify things.

"Yes, it's your father. He's in emergency in El Camino Hospital right now."

"Do the doctors know what's wrong with him?"

"They're not sure. They're running tests."

"Mom, I'm leaving right now. I'll meet you back at the hospital." A lump rises in my chest. My dad has never had an emergency before. As I drive to the hospital, I pray to God for my father's safety. I try to intuit what's going on with him, but I can't get anything. My emotions are running high, and I can't seem to focus. I see my mom sitting near the nurse's station when I enter the emergency room. She clutches a rumpled tissue and her red sweater as she waits for me.

"Oh, Mark, I'm so glad you're here," she says, rushing over to me. "The doctor said he thought it might be a stroke. I'm so worried about him."

"He's going to be okay, Mom," I reassure her, trying to hide my own apprehension. A strong smell of disinfectant in my nostrils makes me even more unsettled. "Where is Dad now?"

"There are several doctors running tests. Someone comes

out about every fifteen minutes. He's been gone for awhile having blood tests, diagnostic and other tests. I think it could be really serious."

While this period of waiting is going on, I try to display some confidence in the situation. "He's going to be fine, Mom," I say, taking her hand. "You know how strong Dad is; he's like an ox."

She nods. "I know," she says, making a decent effort to keep a strong front. "I know, I've just never seen him like this before."

"How are you holding out, Mom?" I ask, still holding her hand.

"I'm doing fine, I'm just worried, that's all."

Her fear is apparent even though she tries to conceal it from me. "Well, if you need anything, Mom, you let me know."

"Yes, son, I will. Thanks."

"How long has it been since you talked to the doctor?" I ask.

"There's one of them now," she points toward the double doors that are swinging shut behind a tall, bearded man in white. As he approaches, I straighten my tie and introduce myself.

"I'm Fred Bryant's son, Mark. Have you been able to determine the problem? My mother says you think it might be a stroke."

"We're doing everything we can to determine what's causing the pain in your father's chest and abdomen," the doctor says. "We're running a series of tests to isolate the condition. It could be a stroke, but it could also could be something else altogether. We're covering all bases to be sure. You can go in and see him for a few minutes while we take another blood sample."

I'm feeling extremely thankful for medical doctors right now. Their experience and training are critical in situations like these. And the hospital staff is so accommodating, it makes me appreciate health care from an entirely different perspective.

Mom leads me to the room halfway down the hall. A man sits up slightly on the gurney. His skin, a waxed paper hue to it, is white like the tightly tucked sheet he lies upon. He glances away from the door slightly so that he is spared the shocked expression on my face. We have the wrong room, I at first assume. Who is this pale man in my dad's place? My heart goes out to him. I silently pray for strength.

"Dad, how are you feeling?" I ask him, touching his arm. "Mom told me what happened. The doctors are doing everything they can. Is there anything you need?"

"Son, it's good to see you, but you don't need to hang around here. I've just got indigestion or a stomach ache or something. It's nothing serious," he calmly says to me.

But I notice an unfamiliar grimace on his face, one of apprehension and wavering uncertainty. "I'm here for you, Dad. We're all here," I say.

A new doctor comes in and motions us into the hall. "You get some rest, Dad, we'll be back as soon as we can."

"I'm glad you're here," he says as I leave. "Take care of your mother."

My brother, Thom, arrives, and the three of us stand quietly together as the doctor reports to us. "He's experiencing internal bleeding, but we can't tell where it's coming from. We'll just keep testing," the doctor tells us.

"Doctor, do you have any idea at all?" Thom asks, seeking to narrow down the possibilities.

"It could be any number of things. His symptoms are quite severe. We don't know what the cause is yet, but there's a team of physicians working on it. We're running as many diagnostic tests as we need to until we narrow it down. In the meantime, we're keeping a close watch over him. We'll keep you informed."

"Thank you, Doctor."

"We need to think about what our next step should be," Thom suggests. "It seems pretty serious. I hope Dad can pull through this."

"What do you propose we do, Thom?" I ask him.

"It seems we have enough doctors here so another opinion is redundant. I suppose we just have to wait it out. At some point we'll need to let Lynda and Sharry know what's going on. We'll need to keep an eye on Mom, too. She's having a tough time with this," Thom observes.

"You're right." When Mom returns from the rest room, I excuse myself. I know I need to go and be by myself for a few minutes. My father's physical self is being taken care of; everything is being examined and looked at in this regard. But what's going on with him emotionally? The doctors cannot examine this. What does his soul need right now? I find an inconspicuous place in the lobby and sit down and shut my eyes.

I begin to relax and empty my mind of all the fear and clutter. I try to disengage myself from the busy hospital environment. I rehearse in my mind all that I have learned from the intuitives. I am highly motivated now to use their techniques. I affirm to myself that physically my dad is going to be fine. My emotions start to return to normal as the adrenaline rush subsides. I start to feel for my father's emotional state, wondering how he is handling all of this.

"How can I help him? What does he need from me now? How's he feeling?" I ask my inner self. I know I can sense it if I listen.

"Tell him that you love him, let him know that you love him. That's the most important thing you can do right now," my inner voice gently speaks out.

"Is there anything else?" I ask myself silently.

My eyes are closed, and I focus my thoughts squarely on my dad. I repeat over and over in my mind, "What does Dad need right now?" It is difficult to concentrate because of the hospital noise. "Well, I notice a fear about him. I have never seen him afraid before, or at least, I don't remember," my inner self says to me.

This feels right to me. "He's facing fears within himself about mortality. He's feeling that if this isn't the end, then something like this might eventually bring on death. He's also feeling embarrassed to be seen this way. He's concerned that his sons won't respect him any longer because we're seeing him in this situation. Just tell him how much you love him," my inner voice continues.

"Tell him that it's okay that you see his vulnerable side. Let him know that you don't think any less of him, that, in fact, you respect him more than ever. Be affectionate even if it feels uncomfortable. This is what he needs right now," my intuition is revealing.

You know, all this makes sense, I think to myself. Just let him know that I respect him even though I see that he is not in complete control of the situation, the way I normally would see him. I don't believe I have ever seen Dad not in total control.

"He might hardly be aware of this consciously," my inner voice continues. "It's more of a feeling he has of being uncomfortable now that the roles are reversed with Thom and you temporarily. You're the stronger ones at the moment. He needs your support now rather than the other way around."

My conscious mind thinks about what my intuition is saying. "Yeah, it felt like that when I had seen him kind of helpless. It must be difficult for him emotionally as well as physically," I think to myself.

My intuition about my father's situation is much clearer than I had at first realized. I can sense that he is going to be fine. The best thing I can do for him now is to comfort him, reassure him, that kind of thing. He might be uneasy with this, but he will relent after a while because his spirit needs this and will allow my love to come in.

My mother's essence gradually comes into my meditative state. I notice that she is more concerned than she is letting on. She is having a very difficult time with this. "Comfort her too," my inner guidance says. "Reassure her that your dad will be fine, that he will pull through this."

I could see Mom was upset, but she seemed to be doing okay under the circumstances. She is a worrier, but she doesn't always show it. I intuit that she doesn't want me to know how afraid she really is. She doesn't want me to worry about her when my father is the one who is so ill.

"Just stand by her," I hear from my intuitive voice. "Don't leave her alone for too long. Your reassurance will give her hope and help to diminish the fear that's beginning to numb her."

As thoughts of my mother subside, I wonder if the inner peace I feel will last only as long as I remain in this meditative state. Gradually, my inner thoughts drift to my older brother. "It might be helpful for you to realize that your brother is managing all of this a little differently from the way you are. Understand that his needs regarding validation and comfort aren't the same as yours. He's very spiritual, but the two of you show it in different ways. It's important for you to accept these differences. You are you, and Thom is Thom," my intuitive voice says softly.

It's easy for me to assume that Thom should be managing the situation in the same way. However, he and I do manage things differently, and I need to keep this in focus so as not to judge him.

I am suddenly brought out of my meditative state by my mother coming to sit down next to me.

"Oh, Mark, it's not looking good," she says. "One of the doctors just came out again and said his symptoms don't match up with any one thing." She dabs her eyes beneath her glasses.

"Mom, don't worry. Dad's a strong guy, and he knows we love him, and I believe that's working in his favor. This time next week he'll be at home recuperating, and we'll know what all this is about. I know in my heart that he'll survive this." As I talk to Mom, I know the information is coming from my intuitive side. I really feel this way deep down.

The doctor comes over to us and says, "You can go in and see him again for a few minutes."

Dad is half asleep when we enter the room, and tubes dangle from him. "Dad, I know you're going to get better, I just feel it. You're going to be fine. I love you, Dad—more than you know. You're the greatest. You've always been there for me. I just wanted you to know that," I tell him while I stroke his white hair. "You're my dad, but you're also a good friend to me, a trusted friend who has always guided me wisely. You know it's okay if you just relax through all this now. We love you."

We don't say anything else for a while. In the silence I think about what has taken place and what I've learned. I listened to my intuition and integrated my emotional and spiritual sides to nurture my father. This incident with Dad has strengthened my emotional authenticity and my faith in my own intuition.

As the weeks pass, my dad does get better. The violent reaction he had was brought on by a rupture of his spleen. Although severe and painful, it was not life-threatening because the doctors were very thorough in their diagnosis and treatment. Surgery repaired the damage, and Dad recovered fully.

As I reflect on this incident, it feels as though my decisions are now coming from who I really am—that genuine person inside me. In the past, there was a tendency to act solely on who I thought I was based on my training and societal influences. I've become more balanced with a greater integrity around emotions and what I'm really feeling inside. I have an emotional authenticity that was not there before. I feel really good that I have been able to be honest with my father. I feel a real love and appreciation for him.

Finding Common Ground

There are times when you can read something and it remains etched in your mind for years to come. My business partner and long-time friend, Dan Lawson, wrote something very eloquent just before attending his twenty-year class reunion. He wrote, "We've all chosen a variety of paths to follow over the years—and I for one have no compelling desire to compare individual accomplishments with one another as we're each a product of all we've experienced over the years." This simple sentence has stuck with me and has helped me to be less judgmental of other people's paths.

Although I can no longer devote the resources to exploring the holistic/spiritual fields that I once did, I continue to run into people I have met along the way. I walk into the French bakery. I glance around for an empty table, enjoying the sweet aroma of croissants and scones. At 7 AM it is already busy. As I wait patiently for Megan David to arrive, I feel a sense of gratitude for some of the things that she has done for me. She comes from the holistic/spiritual community and with her open ways, has helped me tremendously. She is an unusual individual even within the community because she is a healer and intuitive as well as a professional environmental engineer.

I met her fairly early on at a lecture on healing given by Barbara Brennan, who wrote the book *Hands of Light*. Megan is slender and tall, very attractive, and has the most unmistakable aqua blue eyes. She seems like a great mother to her two children, and we enjoy sharing stories about the kids, as all parents do. One evening when we socialized as couples with her, Vicki and Megan enjoyed making light of some of my experiences. They took the now famous "Women are from Venus" approach, and the men took the typical "Mars" approach during the evening.

Megan is on a quest of her own, and we enjoy comparing notes from time to time. Her quest is different from mine with a different focus, but she's quite a researcher in her own right. She is much more active as a participant in the healing community, whereas I tend to be more of an observer. Recently she told me that when she does an energetic healing session, it feels like she's helping the person recharge their energetic battery. "I just give them a little boost, but ultimately a person heals themselves," she explained. She also said that her experiences as a healer have changed her belief system dramatically, perhaps in a similar way that my exploration has affected me. "There are probably as many ways to reach the same place of understanding as there are people," Megan expressed to me.

"Happy birthday, Mark," she says, handing me a gift when she arrives.

"Thanks, and this is for you for your half birthday," I announce, giving her a gift.

"I didn't expect anything," she says, surprised.

"It's also an appreciation gift," I respond.

"Appreciation?"

"I've wanted to get you something ever since I officially ended the research. Unofficially, I still enjoy the holistic and metaphysical fields even though I find I have less time now that I'm back at the office full time. The appreciation is for the referrals you've given me."

"Well, thank you," Megan says.

"And besides, how could I forget a birthday that falls exactly six months opposite my birthday? You know, ever since you shared the idea of half birthdays with me, Vicki and the kids really have a fun time with them."

"That's great, Mark. I know my kids enjoy it a lot too. Can I open this now?" she asks, shaking the package.

"Sure, and I'll open mine."

We begin to unwrap the gifts. There is a smile on Megan's face as she unwraps a rose colored Bible.

"I remember you saying you wanted to read the Bible more," I tell her.

"Thank you, it's lovely," she says, noticing her name

inscribed on the cover. "I'll look forward to reading this."

"Just what I need," I say when the *Metaphysical Bible Dictionary* appears from under the wrapping. "This will help me to understand how metaphysicians like yourself interpret the Bible. I always enjoy different perspectives on the Bible."

"I thought this dictionary might be helpful when you have a conflict between your Christian beliefs and the broader spiritual/physical belief system in metaphysics," she says.

"Thank you for being so thoughtful," I respond.

"Do you think you can remain open to these universal principles while still finding strength in your religion?" she questions.

"I believe I can, Megan. I'm more convinced than ever that there are similar philosophies in understanding our universe and our existence. The church offers an organized way of developing this. That's why it's important to me to have my children attend church, to read Bible stories before bed, and recite the Lord's Prayer, all of the things we do around our religion."

Megan asks me if I think there will ever be common ground for the church and the metaphysical and healing community. I tell her I don't believe the two are mutually exclusive. I add it's my belief that more and more churches will include broader applications as part of their ministry. Somewhere along the line many churches have gotten away from the gifts of the Spirit. But now people are getting reacquainted with these gifts. Churches will follow suit if there's a genuine demand made by the congregations and a need in the community. I tell Megan that last week there was a Reiki healing workshop at the Christian Conference Center near my home. Next week there's a body/mind/soul workshop for Catholic women. To me this is an indication that things are already changing.

Megan responds by noting that she meets more skeptics than believers, while at the same time she is noticing that more and more people are opening up to alternative health practices.

"It seems that sometimes people will give energetic healing a try when other more traditional methods have not given them the results they desire. Many people are simply afraid of what I do, so I attempt to educate them about the process if they are interested. If not, I change the subject as I realize that hands on healing may not be for everyone. It's not my place to try and convince people that energetic healing has the immense value that it does."

One of the things I like about Megan is she's committed to a healing process that will help better people's lives. This matches her nature of a very caring person.

"So, Mark, how do you respond to the skeptic who says there are still charlatans in our ranks?" Megan asks, putting me on the spot. I take a sip of coffee before responding.

"In my time on this odyssey, I've seen the fake and the extraordinary. I believe there are those in the community who are genuine and truly have remarkable gifts. Then there are those who are just trying to make a quick buck. Let's hope there are more of the former."

"How about the skeptics who say we're all frauds?" Megan asks.

"I can only speak to my own experience. I believe there are gifted practitioners who possess amazing gifts. I think it would be wrong to say that these are fraudulent. I'll continue to use these people's services as long as I can apply their gifts in my life."

We continue to talk about religion and metaphysics for thirty minutes and then part ways. I end our conversation by telling Megan that exploration into areas of inner awareness, personal growth, and health will always be a priority for me, adding, "Otherwise, I could easily fall back asleep, figuratively speaking."

Mentors and Enlightenment

There are no guarantees that a person's life will turn out as planned. Frequently, the consequence of *not* taking a risk here or a chance there, can make life equally uncertain. As I look back over the last few years, I'm glad I took the time to explore realms and dimensions of reality that previously, I had discounted.

Now a break from this exploration seems in order. Vicki agrees and has planned a romantic weekend for us in Cabo San Lucas. Kristen, our baby girl is old enough for us to leave with my folks for the weekend. The other kids are going to stay with Vicki's sister and aunt. When I stop at the post office to pick up my mail before we leave, I spot a familiar face. She sees me and smiles back. It is Alexis McKenna, the woman who helped give me a psychological perspective of my journey. She and I live in the same town, but this is the first time I have run into her since my quest ended.

"How are you, Alexis?" I ask her.

"Oh, I'm fine," she says. "I came by the post office to mail some things to my grad students. How's life post-quest?" she asks with a warm smile.

"Do we ever stop questing?" I reply with a laugh.

"No, we never do."

"At any rate, it's back at the office full time but with a new view of things," I respond. "I want to thank you again for the help you gave me."

"It's all about mentors, Mark. We're like coaches and mentors in the different areas of your life," she explains. "My background is psychology and Dr. Stanton is alternative medicine, while Mary Coleman's is metaphysics. Your pastor meets the needs coming from your deep-rooted religious feelings. Each of these people, and other people like us, educate you in a unique way and are really mentors for you."

I laugh to myself as Alexis talks about this because she has, of course, moved into her role of mentoring me right here beside the post office boxes. What a natural teaching gift she has!

"It sounds like you're a real advocate for mentoring." I say smiling at her.

"I am. It's why I enjoy working with my graduate students so much."

"The mentors really did have a special role in your exploration," Alexis continues. "Through the help of these mentors, you were able to learn new languages. The new concepts and ideas that you learned opened up a whole new world to you."

"It was all very exciting for me," I respond. "At times, I might have been uncertain of where things were heading, even a little disorganized. But there was always something new and fascinating just around the bend that I could apply in my life."

"Mark, the opportunity is there to create something new if we remember to use all the information and are willing to hang out in uncertainty until the new order appears. And that's what you were willing to do."

"Again, with the help of people like you," I remind her.

"I just facilitated the process through some timely questions and exercises. The only advantage I had was that I understood the process of 'order out of disorder.' I've been through the process enough times myself to know how to read the signs and follow the road maps, even though I didn't really know where your journey would lead you. I was simply willing to engage in the process with you," she says.

"I'll call you my 'making-sense-out-of-chaos' mentor!" I declare. Alexis smiles in amusement. "I'm not always able to stay with your psychological concepts, but I know you have it all straight in your head," I say.

"My sense is you're good at integration," she says. "You've done the same process in business. A mentor helps you first translate and then integrate the information into a meaningful whole that works for you. That's the bottom line, as you businessmen like to say."

"Hey, what time is it?" I ask, suddenly remembering an appointment.

Alexis glances at her watch and says, "One fifty. Why?"

"I have to be at Jonathan's school at two o'clock to do a little enlightening and educational mentoring," I say with a laugh.

Alexis smiles and says, "It's as we've discussed many times, what good is enlightenment if it doesn't help you live a richer life?"

Hidden Asset

Our authentic selves appear when the outer image aligns with our inner nature

Afterword

An Inspiring Frontier

I had promised Vicki that after I met my exploration goals and wound down the research, I would take her on a vacation— just her and me—to a beach somewhere. We ended up down here on the west coast of Mexico. We are really enjoying ourselves. No kids or work—just sand, sea, and sun. I've brought a pen and pad out to the lounge chairs as we sit near the surf.

"What are you writing?" Vicki asks as she applies sunscreen on my back.

"Oh, just some inner thoughts on what the adventure was really about for me."

"Can I see?"

"When we get home, you can. I want you to just have fun. Remember this is a 'thank you' for all your support."

"Sounds fair. But before I forget, I did hear about your friend Mary Coleman the other day."

My ears perk up. "Really," I say, shielding my eyes from the sun. I haven't talked to Mary in a while so I am intrigued to hear what Vicki has to say.

"Yes, and of all places, it was at another hairdresser's."

"No kidding," I say, thinking of the interesting topics that seem to be discussed at women's hair salons. "What is it you heard about Mary?"

"I have a new hair stylist I've been seeing for a few months. Her name is Sherri. She told me she was thinking about opening her own hair salon, but she kept going back and forth on the idea for various reasons. She seemed kind of stressed by the need to make a decision so I suggested she ask Mary about it. I knew Mary could give her a different perspective on the situation."

"Seems like good advice to me. Did Sherri go and see Mary?"

"Yes, Sherri had a session with Mary, and apparently what Mary said was helpful because Sherri seemed calmer around this issue. But the intriguing part of the story is that during this session, Mary asked Sherri if she had ever lost a baby. It was one of those unexpected questions Mary likes to ask."

"Oh, one of *those* questions," I reiterate, reclining back.

"Sherri was nervous and admitted she had miscarried a year ago. It must have been difficult for her to talk about it, but you know how comforting Mary can be."

"Yes I do."

"So then Mary says that she can see Sherri is pregnant again. This *really* surprised Sherri, of course, because she hadn't told anyone. Only her husband knew, and they wanted to keep it a secret until she got past the time when she could miscarry."

"Now the good part!" Vicki continues enthusiastically. "Mary tells Sherri she knows she's pregnant because she can see the baby's spirit, and it's the same spirit. 'The same spirit?' Sherri inquires. 'The same spirit that you miscarried last year,' Mary proclaims."

"Wow," I utter under my breath.

"Sherri immediately begins to cry in front of Mary. Apparently, Sherri was anxious during the previous pregnancy because she was concerned whether she could take on the responsibility of another child. She felt guilty when she had the miscarriage. She has felt responsible ever since and carried that guilt around. Can you imagine how much joy she felt when she heard that the spirit of the baby lost last year was the same one with her in this pregnancy? I cried when Sherri told me the story," Vicki confesses.

"That Mary! What a wonderful use of her gifts."

"Mary also told her that this baby would make everything whole and complete for her. Having this baby with a supportive husband would help her to heal what she didn't have in her first marriage."

"That must have made Sherri feel a lot better," I say.

"And there's one more thing," Vicki adds excitedly. "Sherri told me that Mary said the spirit had a lot of feminine energy and likely will be a girl. Sherri already has two boys and was hoping for a baby girl. Isn't that wonderful? What Mary said really helped Sherri come to terms with the grief she was feeling around the miscarriage. Isn't that a beautiful story?"

"Yes, it certainly is!" I reply putting my arm around her.

Vicki gazes at me and says. "At times we can't make sense about what life gives us, but intuition can help us see the spirit in it all."

"Bravo, Vicki!" I say, pulling my hat down over my eyes. The sun is disappearing behind the famous natural arch of Cabo San Lucas, also known as Land's End. There's a slight breeze coming in off the Sea of Cortez. I think about Vicki's comment and about the spirit in all of us. I think how much of the exploration was about awakening to a higher level of consciousness. I smile at her under my hat and she catches my smirk.

"What is it?" she says laughingly.

"All I have to do now is stay awake!"

— *The End* —

Book Reference List

Ageless Body, Timeless Mind by Deepak Chopra, M.D. (Harmony Books, 1993)

Allergies, Fatigue and Your Immune Response by Joy Lasseter, Ph.D. (Body Mind Connection Publishing, 1997)

Anatomy of the Spirit: The Seven Stages of Power and Healing by Caroline Myss and C. Norman Shealy (Three Rivers Press, 1997)

The Aquarian Conspiracy: Personal and Social Transformation in the 1980's by Marilyn Ferguson (J. P. Tarcher, Inc., 1987)

The Artist's Way: A Spiritual Path to Higher Creativity by Julia Cameron and Mark Bryan (J. P. Tarcher, Inc., 1992)

Chinese Herbal Medicine by Daniel Reid (Shambala Productions, 1992)

The Divine Millieu, by Pierre Teilard de Chardin (Harper Collins Publishers, 1989)

Drawing from the Right Side of the Brain: A Course in Enhancing Creativity and Artistic Confidence by Betty Edwards (J. P. Tarcher, Inc. 1989)

Eat More, Weigh Less by Dr. Dean Ornish (Harper Collins, 1994)

The Enneagram: Understanding Yourself and Others in Your Life by Helen Palmer (Harper San Francisco, 1991)

The Four Fold Way: Walking the Paths of Warrior, Teacher, Healer and Visionary by Angeles Arrien (Harper San Francisco, 1993)

The Future of the Body: Explorations into the Further Evolution of the Human Species by Michael Murphy (J. P. Tarcher, Inc., 1993)

Hands of Light: A Guide to Healing Through the Human Energy Field by Barbara Brennan (Bantam Doubleday Dell Publishers, 1993)

Healing the Inner Conflict by Ofer Erez (Self Published, Walnut Creek, CA, 1994)

I Love Myself: A Lighten Up Message for Kids, audio tape by Carol Hansen and Marianne Ort (Open Heart Productions, 1998)

Intuition by R. Buckminster Fuller (Impact Publishers, 1998)

Intuition at Work by Roger Frantz and Alex N. Pattakos (New Leaders Press, 1996)

The Intuitive Way: A Guide to Living from Inner Wisdom by Penney Peirce (Beyond Words Publishing, 1997)

Leadership and the New Science: Learning about Organization from an Orderly Universe by Margaret J. Wheatley (Berrett-Koeller Publishers, 1992)

Lighten Up Inspirations: A Motivational Workbook and Journal by Carol Hansen (Open Heart Press, 1998)

Lighten Up! audio tape by Carol Hansen (Open Heart Productions, 1996)

Lucid Dreaming by Stephen LaBerge, Ph.D. (Ballantine Books, 1990)

Metaphysical Bible Dictionary by Charles Fillmore (Unity School of Christianity, 1995)

Mindmapping: Your Personal Guide to Exploring Creativity and Problem Solving by Joyce Wycoff (Berkeley Publishing, 1991)

The Mozart Effect: Tapping the Power of Music to Heal the Body, Strengthen the Mind and Unlock the Creative Spirit by Don Campbell (Avon Books, 1997)

The New Bottom Line by John Renesch and Bill Defoore (New Leaders Press, 1996)

The Omega Seed: An Eschatological Hypothesis by Paolo Soleri (Double Day, 1981)

Passages by Gail Sheehy (Bantam Books, 1984)

Quantum Healing: Exploring the Frontiers of Mind Body Medicine by Deepak Chopra, M.D. (Bantam Books, 1990)

Tam's Charge by Jill Raiguel (Self Published, Los Angeles, CA, 1996)

Practical Vegetarianism for Today's Lifestyles by Joy Lasseter, Ph.D. (Body Mind Connection Publishing, 1997)

The Psychic Pathway: A Workbook for Reawakening the Voice of Your Soul by Sonia Choquette (Crown Publishers, Inc., 1995)

Rudolf Steiner and Holistic Medicine by Francis X. King (Nicholas-Hays, Inc., 1986)

Secret Teachings of All the Ages by Manly P. Hall (Philosophic Research Society, Los Angeles, CA, 1988)

Seer Out of Season: The Life of Edgar Cayce by Harmon Hartzell Bro, Ph.D. (Penguin Group, 1990)

The Soul of a Business: Managing for Profit and the Common Good by Tom Chappell (Bantam Books, 1994)

Soul Retrieval: Mending the Fragmented Self by Sandra Ingerman (Harper San Francisco, 1991)

The Way of the Peaceful Warrior by Dan Millman (H.J. Kramer, Starseed Press, 1985)

About the Author

Mark Bryant is a highly respected entrepreneur and business consultant who has launched million dollar corporations in construction and transportation and has pioneered new forms of distribution throughout the western United States. Recognized as an expert in developing and writing business plans for start-up ventures, he has facilitated strategic planning sessions for many companies and associations.

Mark has a degree in marketing with a concentration in research and promotional strategies. His postgraduate studies are in the areas of business management, communication technology, organizational development, psychology and world religions. He is an astute observer of human behavior and a talented communicator who integrates psychology, spirituality and philosophy with professional experience in business development and management.

In 1993 he was struck with a persistent undiagnosed health condition. Unable to find answers within the traditional Western medical field, he took time away from his businesses to research the fields of holistic health and spirituality. From 1994-96 he traveled across the United States and Europe searching for answers. Using his research and organizational skills, he extensively documented his experiences and developed a model that enabled him to assimilate and synthesize the many disparate pieces within these varied fields. *Hidden Assets* is the culmination of his research and the story of his two year adventure.

Mark lives in the San Francisco Bay Area with his wife and three children.